SERVING DIVERSE STUDENTS
IN CANADIAN HIGHER EDUCATION

Serving Diverse Students in Canadian Higher Education

Edited by

C. CARNEY STRANGE
AND DONNA HARDY COX

McGill-Queen's University Press
Montreal & Kingston • London • Chicago

© McGill-Queen's University Press 2016

ISBN 978-0-7735-4750-6 (cloth)
ISBN 978-0-7735-4751-3 (paper)
ISBN 978-0-7735-9942-0 (ePDF)
ISBN 978-0-7735-9943-7 (ePUB)

Legal deposit second quarter 2016
Bibliothèque nationale du Québec

Printed in Canada on acid-free paper that is 100% ancient forest free
(100% post-consumer recycled), processed chlorine free

McGill-Queen's University Press gratefully acknowledges the Canadian
Association of College and University Student Services for its support of
this publication.

McGill-Queen's University Press acknowledges the support of the Canada
Council for the Arts for our publishing program. We also acknowledge the
financial support of the Government of Canada through the Canada Book
Fund for our publishing activities.

Library and Archives Canada Cataloguing in Publication

Serving diverse students in Canadian higher education / edited by
C. Carney Strange and Donna Hardy Cox.

Includes bibliographical references and index.
Issued in print and electronic formats.
ISBN 978-0-7735-4750-6 (cloth). – ISBN 978-0-7735-4751-3 (paper). –
ISBN 978-0-7735-9942-0 (ePDF). – ISBN 978-0-7735-9943-7 (ePUB)

1. Minority college students – Services for – Canada. 2. Minorities –
Education (Higher) – Canada. I. Strange, Charles Carney, author, editor
II. Cox, Donna Gail Hardy, 1961–, author, editor

LC3734.2.S47 2016   378.1'97089   C2016-901811-3
                                        C2016-901812-1

This book was typeset by Interscript in 10.5/13 Sabon.

To forty years of students
whom I have had the privilege of
accompanying on their learning journeys:
who were like all other students;
who were like only some other students;
and who were like no other students.
Your many and varied gifts and expressions of
who you are made all the difference.

CCS

To the past:
In memory of Eric and Hettie,
who celebrated differences and taught us acceptance.
To the present:
Students and colleagues who collaborate in
building supportive learning environments for all.
To the future:
Mark, who is beginning his own post-secondary journey,
and Joel, who enlightens us from his own
diverse teenage world.

DHC

Contents

Tables and Figures

Preface

Like many modern institutions of higher learning, the post-secondary system of Canada historically served the socially privileged and powerful. Among its traditional constituents were mostly white males of European descent whose means placed them not only among the elite but also gained them access to opportunities not ordinarily afforded society's less fortunate. For the past fifty years, though, the history of such systems has changed dramatically. Realizing the power of learning to open once closed doors, previously disenfranchised sectors of society began pursuing new opportunities and, with their successes, forever altered the demographic profile of a once exclusive and homogeneous base.

Such change has not been without struggle, though. With the influx of large groups of student veterans in Canada's colleges and universities following the Second World War, seeds of the "new traditional" student body were sown. The revolutionary growth of the 1960s further diversified campuses at a time when movements of justice and human rights dictated that the status quo in higher education would no longer suffice. Through pioneering efforts of returning mature students, racialized students, and students who were the first in their families to access such opportunities, the demographic of many Canadian post-secondary institutions began to reflect an increasingly diverse texture. Questions of justice further fuelled the mix as individuals of other cultural and social identities demanded their opportunity as well. The result has been a rapidly evolving student enrolment shift, reflecting more and more the new normative pattern of an increasingly diverse society.

Understanding the nature of these new groups on campus has been equally challenging to a faculty and staff accustomed to serving a more traditional constituent. Furthermore, research on these new groups has only begun to emerge in the literature on Canadian higher education, guided too much perhaps by the work already being done in the United States on such topics, but nonetheless finding a voice of its own as new Canadian scholars have taken up the effort. This is the case, in particular, regarding the research in student affairs and student services in Canadian post-secondary education. Primarily a field of applied practice, student services has long struggled to generate an evidence-based framework of principles, theories, and programmatic outcomes of its own, relying perhaps too much on anecdotal exchanges and interactions instead. However, student services has witnessed its own revolution of sorts in the past several decades, with the advent of an emerging sense of professional identity that has found a home in burgeoning organizations such as the Canadian Association of College and University Student Services (CACUSS), whose membership includes academic and student services staff in virtually all of Canada's colleges and universities. Association proponents share in common a commitment to students and their learning, both within and beyond the classroom, fueled by an ethic of equity in opportunity, especially on behalf of those whose backgrounds have limited their access and success in the system.

It is this narrative that forms the context of the present volume. In these pages are overviews of various student groups that reflect the new traditional enrolment profile on many campuses today. Within each overview (authored primarily by current practitioners) is a survey of ideas, research, and issues that illuminate the status of so identified students and suggest practices responsive to each groups' needs. In concert with its companion volume – *Achieving Student Success: Effective Student Services in Canadian Higher Education* (Hardy Cox and Strange 2010), focusing on the design of student services themselves – the work of these authors here adds insight to the groups of students being served, thus extending the base of ideas to advance the field.

Although much of what is reported here represents the beginnings of many institutions' efforts to support diverse groups in Canadian higher education, the authors at the very least are intent on opening the discussion about how best to proceed in shaping a system that incorporates diverse voices in its policies and practices. Rather than definitive, this volume is meant to be provocative of current assumptions and approaches while leading to steps that will improve the prospects for success of diverse students on campus. The limits of current research and theory development are acknowledged and hopefully serve as incentive for others to take up the mantle of discovery in advancing the agenda. These are nothing more and nothing less than snapshots of the problems and their solutions. Their currency depends further on those engaged in this work being willing to challenge, correct, and ultimately improve claims and observations that are meant to encourage a more diverse view.

Three sections are featured in this volume. In section I, chapter 1 focuses on the changing enrolment pattern in Canadian post-secondary education, as it has evolved into a system of diverse students with unique needs and interests. Chapter 2 focuses on the theoretical underpinnings addressing the learning, growth, and development of diverse students in Canadian higher education and examines ways of conceptualizing services to foster their success.

Section II provides an overview of the characteristics, challenges, and practices encountered in meeting the needs of diverse student populations in Canadian post-secondary education. Each chapter gives attention respectively to one of eight student groups featured here, identifying significant issues (both evolutionary and emergent) that shape the experiences of these students and benchmarking services and protocols that support them. Accordingly, chapter 3 highlights Aboriginal and Native students; chapter 4, Black students of African and Caribbean descent; chapter 5, Francophone students; chapter 6, gay, lesbian, bisexual, transgender, queer, and questioning students; chapter 7, international students; chapter 8, students with disabilities; chapter 9, returning mature and adult learners; and chapter 10, first-generation students. Chapter 11 addresses the dynamics and facilitation of inter-group relationships, a critical tool as campuses continue to accommodate these non-traditional students. While not all-inclusive, such groups represent a significant portion of non-traditional applicants seeking access to the post-secondary experience in Canada. Lessons learned from attention to their diverse characteristics can serve to inform the basic dynamics of responsiveness to all student groups, a point of focus for the final section of this volume.

Section III distills in chapter 12 understandings and conclusions from the preceding chapters to frame both strategic and procedural directions for the design of services dedicated to the support of diverse students in Canadian institutions. It concludes with an affirmation of the importance of student services leadership in effecting changes that will better serve institutions in their desire to accommodate a more diverse student population.

The student services role in Canadian higher education has come of age in a system that is rapidly changing as diverse prospective students explore new opportunities. As widespread interest in rankings of Canadian colleges and universities continues to grow, students' expectations of institutions and their services have increased. Consequently, institutions are being asked whether they have the resources to address this multiplicity of needs and whether they can succeed in attracting students based on their respective resources. This book provides insights into this view of the Canadian postsecondary landscape and considers ways to best respond to student diversity and thus optimize students' learning. It is informed by current Canadian experiences with and understandings of how best to shape policies and programs to support diverse students' postsecondary success.

C. Carney Strange
Donna Hardy Cox
January 2016 .

Section One

1

Student Diversity in Canadian Higher Education

DONNA HARDY COX AND C. CARNEY STRANGE

Once institutions that catered primarily to the elite and privileged of society, Canada's universities and colleges today reflect an increasingly diverse array of student groups, whose participation in post-secondary learning is challenging educators to respond more creatively to the differences they represent. Such groups span a variety of demographics and identities, some historically disadvantaged and others emerging as marginalized groups on campus seeking a stronger voice in matters that affect them. Among these are Aboriginal, Black, international, adult, gay, lesbian, bisexual, transgender, queer, and questioning, those with disabilities, Francophone, and first-generation students, to name a few. Such groups continue to face significant barriers and challenges in their pursuit of the benefits of Canadian post-secondary learning, beginning with their initial decision to participate. As the data in Table 1.1 suggest, the crucial first step to enroll in a college or university is influenced differentially by the very characteristics of the individuals attempting it, and unevenly so from one region of Canada to another. For example, Aboriginal youth are twice as likely to enroll in a college rather than a university program in the Province of Ontario, but the opposite is true in Atlantic Canada; similarly, a first-generation immigrant is much more likely to enroll in university in Western Canada than in the Province of Quebec, and so forth. All of this suggests that the mix of demographics and educational opportunities varies from one region of Canada to another to affect different outcomes in the initial steps

Table 1.1 Post-secondary participation rates by select demographic and region of Canada

	Region			
Demographic	Ontario	Atlantic Canada	Quebec	Western Canada
All	36.4[a]	24.6	40.0	26.1
	45.4[b]	51.1	30.3	42.8
Income below 50K	39.3	29.2	41.3	26.5
	35.2	36.1	19.7	36.4
Aboriginal	38.7	19.5	35.3	20.9
	17.8	40.7	25.6	22.4
1st gen immigrant	30.1	12.6	44.5	24.1
	58.4	82.6	29.1	63.4
French minority	43.0	26.3	n/a	21.0
	39.5	48.4	n/a	50.0
Disability	46.2	26.4	41.6	28.5
	22.1	37.9	16.5	27.4
Single-parent family	41.1	24.4	41.9	24.8
	36.4	39.7	24.9	34.3
Rural	44.6	30.4	40.0	28.7
	28.6	42.5	40.0	33.1
Father w/ no PSE	43.5	30.1	38.5	27.5
	25.7	30.1	16.7	28.6

[a] College
[b] University

of the post-secondary experience. Extrapolating these differences over a longer period of time makes it clear how they lead to patterned differences in these groups' participation from one province to another or one type of institution to another. While one group might gain over time, another one might lag farther behind.

Beyond the actuarial patterns, though, much of this variation is due to differing cumulative legacies of limited academic preparation across these demographics. For example, among Aboriginal youth between the ages of twenty and twenty-four years old, 40 per cent have not completed high school in comparison to 13 per cent of their non-Aboriginal peers (Statistics Canada 2008a); and another example is found among first-generation youth (whose parents who have not attended PSE), where only 53 per cent participate in post-secondary education, compared to 81 per cent of those whose parents have a university education. It appears that the level of parental education, rather than income, is the primary driver in such cases (Statistics Canada 2011a). On the other hand, some immigrant groups (e.g., Asian) are even more likely than Canadian-born youth to participate in post-secondary education, a probable artifact of higher parental education being favored in immigrant selection policies and practices. Nonetheless, much like their French-speaking Canadian-born counterparts, these immigrant and international groups also face significant challenges of adjustment to new languages and different cultural norms. Similarly the other sub-groups highlighted here also share the experience of being "special populations" (Smith and Gottheil 2011) on campus, that encounter extraordinary physical, social, psychological, and instrumental hurdles to their success as they pursue post-secondary education. Often outside the normative profile, such students are at further risk for retention and ultimate achievement of their educational goals, especially in the absence of affirmative programs that anticipate and support their needs.

CHANGING PROFILE OF CANADIAN STUDENTS

The *Trends in Higher Education* enrolment report (AUCC 2011) observed that Canadian universities have experienced tremendous growth, especially since 1980. At the undergraduate level, enrolments expanded by 81 per cent to reach a total of 994,000 students by 2010. Overall, post-secondary enrolments have more than doubled in the last thirty years to the current level of approximately two million students, mostly in response to increasing demands for a more highly skilled and educated labour force entering an economy shifting toward the service sector. A significant portion of these enrolment gains have come in the form of diverse student groups whose participation in post-secondary learning has been either historically limited (e.g., Aboriginal students) or whose current circumstances have placed additional burdens on their success (e.g., students with disabilities, first-generation students). These increases have also partially mirrored broader shifts in the population at large. For example, in the 2011 National Household Survey (NHS) (Statistics Canada 2011b), 19.1 per cent (6.3 million) of Canadians identified as visible minorities, doubling their numbers since 1996 when they represented only 11.2 per cent of the population. During that time there also has been a significant influx of immigrants from non-European countries, especially South Asians, Chinese, and Blacks. In this same survey

(NHS) more than 200 ethnic origins were reported by respondents, with thirteen of them surpassing the one million mark. Almost 1.4 million reported a First Nations ancestry, about one-half million Métis, and 72,600 Inuit. By these measures alone, it is clear that Canada is becoming a much more diverse nation.

Another report (Hango and De Broucker 2007) also warns of an impending major demographic shift when, by 2030, the population over age sixty-five will double, while the working age (twenty-five to sixty-four years) will increase by only 8 per cent. This shift will result in further economic, social, and labour market demands, and "universities will need to both expand access to higher education for untapped segments of the population and international students, and increase the quality of education students receive" (AUCC 2011, 5). Similar reports are available from organizations overseeing other sectors of the post-secondary system (e.g., Association of Canadian Community Colleges). All point to the critical role of advanced education opportunities in securing a future in particular for those groups historically disenfranchised or underrepresented in the system.

All of these population and participation portraits suggest that the composition of Canadian post-secondary enrolments is changing and remains varied from one region of the country to another. An illustration of such regional impact on post-secondary enrolment is contained in The Higher Education Quality Council of Ontario report (Zhao 2012), based on data from the 2007 Survey of Labour and Income Dynamics (SLID). In it are highlighted a number of demographic factors that influence post-secondary attendance rates among underrepresented Canadian populations in the Province of Ontario, as one case in point. Relatively low participation rates were found among: males; those from families with income in the first and second quartiles; those whose parents have no post-secondary education; Aboriginals; those with a disability; and those from single-parent families. Among those surveyed between ages eighteen to twenty-one, 69 per cent indicated having enrolled in some form of post-secondary education (See Table 1.2 and Table 1.3), with 76 per cent of females reported having done so, in comparison to 62 per cent of males. Participation rates for those in the first (lowest) family income quartile was 49 per cent, versus 84 per cent in the fourth (highest) quartile. Enrolment rates for Aboriginal students were 58 per cent, for immigrants 75 per cent, for Francophones 83 per cent, for those with a disability 59 per cent, from single-parent

Table 1.2 Participation rates by select demographic in Ontario colleges and universities (2007)

Demographic	College	University	Total PSE
All	27.0	42.2	69.2
Female	23.3	52.4	75.7
Male	31.1	31.3	62.4
1st quartile income	18.5	30.4	49.0
4th quartile income	24.8	59.0	83.7
Aboriginal	21.4	36.3	57.7
Immigrant	15.7	58.9	74.7
French & other speaking	29.3	53.4	82.6
Disability	29.1	30.2	59.3
Single-parent family	16.4	46.1	62.5
Rural	42.1	25.0	67.2
First generation	30.9	34.4	65.3
Father w/ no PSE	33.8	31.8	57.8
Father w/ BA degree	19.6	72.9	92.6

Table 1.3 Ontario college, university, and combined enrolment by demographic (2007)

Demographic	College	University	Total PSE
Female	44.2	64.0	56.2
Male	55.8	36.0	43.8
1st quartile income	15.1	15.9	15.6
4th quartile income	22.6	34.5	29.8
Aboriginal	3.9	4.2	4.1
Immigrant	7.5	17.9	13.8
French & other speaking	25.6	30.0	28.2
Disability	22.4	14.9	17.8
Single-parent family	9.7	17.4	14.4
Rural	16.4	6.3	10.2
First generation	65.3	46.7	53.9
Father w/ no PSE	50.0	30.1	38.0
Father w/ BA degree	18.1	43.1	33.3

families 67 per cent, and being first generation 65 per cent. Among those whose father had completed a university degree, the participation rate was 97 per cent, in comparison to 58 per cent for those with less than a high school education. Again, most of these demographic effects were explained by level of parent education, indicating that where a parent had completed a university degree, chances of post-secondary participation were much greater, regardless of income or ethnic identification. Like the data reported above, post-secondary participation rates in Ontario (with the largest Aboriginal population in Canada) is a function of the mix of demographics and opportunities. Similar differential patterns specific to other provinces have been observed where the data are available.

Assuming that these differential rates of participation will continue to fluctuate unevenly, the future of Canadian post-secondary education bodes even greater complexity in terms of the range of services that will be required to respond adequately to its evolving profile. In light of such trends Kirby (2009) forewarned, "If participation in the system is to grow further and make the necessary shift from mass to universal participation, policy makers must devote specific attention to increasing the educational participation and attainment levels of disadvantaged and under-represented groups" (3). However, achieving such a goal is deceptively simple, as one of the immediate challenges is accounting accurately for the presence of these groups on campus. While some of the above special populations are visible as minorities on campus (e.g., Black students) or identification is available through the application process (e.g., Francophone), others are dependent on self-identification (e.g., LGBTQQ and disability) or the selective reporting of various student service offices that interact with them (e.g., international students). Even within a given province, depending upon staff resources and varied reporting mandates, the data on these sub-groups of students are often disparate and unsystematic. Regardless, these are all student populations that would benefit from a more intentional approach among post-secondary educators and student services staff to understand their needs and to accommodate them more effectively.

It is this new awareness of these different student populations that has caught the attention in particular of student services personnel, since it often becomes their charge primarily to create programs and practices (e.g., orientation, residences, career services, advising) that accommodate these underserved students and effect their transition into and success within the academy. However, to date there are surprisingly few resources available in the Canadian higher education literature that address these specific student groups on campus. Thus the risk of less-than-effective strategies and misapplied approaches is quite high, especially when it is assumed that such groups bring with them the same backgrounds and supports that have long served the traditional enrolment base of most Canadian post-secondary institutions. The present volume seeks to remedy some of these shortcomings by focusing attention on understanding and accommodating a selection of these student sub-groups. In doing so it is the intention of the authors to advance conversation about these students in ways that will guide readers to better assess their needs on campus and develop more effective policies and practices. The goal is to effect a parity of opportunity, if not achievement, so that regardless of background all students can reach a point of success in their post-secondary aspirations.

DEVELOPMENT OF DIVERSITY SERVICES

The presumed homogeneity of students in the past has given way to current celebrations of unique student groups and individuals, as evidenced by the revision and creation of new policies and services (Farr, 2005). The growing presence of an identifiably diverse student population in Canadian post-secondary education has become more readily apparent, especially in recent years as different learners and their expectations and entitlements have challenged institutions to broaden their offerings. Much of the impetus for such development though has come from four sources of influence on campus: a) the rise of student advocacy groups; b) provision of student services translators; c) renewed interest in student data collection and analysis; and d) the confluence of student consumerism and institutional mission.

Grassroots student advocacy groups have long served as agents of change in Canadian post-secondary education. Whether through efforts of a pioneering individual or organized cluster of affected groups, the allocation of physical and human resources to meeting students' needs has often resulted from such student involvement on campus. Student unions have also provided a vital support through various clubs and society structures. Typically, initiatives to educate a campus and lobby for policy, services, and supports are launched by student organizations or community interest groups beyond the institution. As leadership evolves, movements are often further accelerated largely by external factors such as human rights legislation and political pressures. On this basis, for example, Aboriginal students, students with disabilities, and international students all have modeled paths toward more responsive services in Canada's higher education system. New student populations bring with them motives for change as they seek to better fit the institution to student needs. A case in point has been the shift toward a predominance of female students on campus, which has led to new institutional policies on sexual harassment and equity, the creation of women's centres and childcare services, and the development of women's studies curricula and co-ed residences.

A second influence on the evolution of Canadian campus diversity services has been the appointment by some senior student services officers of "translators" to coordinate responses to any emerging diversity needs. Such an assignment could range from a student researching further on the issue to adding specific duties to a job description, chairing an advisory committee, or creating a new position for full-time service. These individuals often became the voice of the diversity group and worked to translate and transmit diverse perspectives to the university community. For example Queen's University, through a similar approach, became one of the first post-secondary institutions in Canada to allocate a full-time position to addressing LGBTQQ concerns on campus. Such efforts have been bolstered further by the adoption of relevant legislation. In particular, the Canadian Charter of Rights and Freedoms has had a significant influence on the provision of diversity services in post-secondary education. As institutions began to recognize morally and practically the importance of serving individual students, campus advocates pursued an equity/human rights agenda to bring about significant changes. Subsequent social justice, economic, and cultural agendas have included the recruiting and supporting of various marginalized groups and have led to the development of networks of students and associations of diversity service professionals, for example, in the name of the Canadian Association of Disability Service Providers in Post-Secondary Education (CADSPPE) and the National Aboriginal Student Services Association (NASSA).

Critical to the mix of campus diversity efforts has been the importance of data gathering, a third source of influence on challenging the responsiveness of Canadian post-secondary institutions. An illustration of this point is found among students who formed the National Educational Association of Disabled Students (NEADS), the first such organization to convene students with disabilities nationally in order to advocate for related research. Subsequently, the first comprehensive survey on disability and post-secondary education was completed in 1989 by NEADS, illuminating both the extent and the nature of student disabilities, in particular the range of "hidden" or less visible disabilities among students. The data revealed, for example, that most of Ontario's post-secondary institutions had populations with disabilities of between 200 and 1,200 full-time students. Of those reporting, 36 per cent had learning disabilities, or attention deficit disorder, 30 per cent mobility impairments, and just below 30 per cent identified sensory disabilities such as limited vision or hearing conditions. Persons with mental health conditions accounted for only 5 per cent of the survey respondents (Ontario Human Rights Commission 2003). The potential for social stigma attached to such questions however suggests that this figure may be in fact an underestimation of that population. Another illustration of this effect is apparent in the case of Aboriginal students, whose participation rate in post-secondary education is approximately half that of the Canadian general population. Despite being the fastest growing youth population in Canada, one in three Aboriginal Canadians point to finances, or their need to work, as reasons for not completing post-secondary schooling. Such information is vital and has been used by student services translators to communicate to and educate their respective campuses about emerging diversity needs. Being able to answer questions like "How many students?" and "What do they require?" lies at the heart of the data gathering function, and the need for such data presses beyond the institution to encourage organizations like Statistics Canada to systematically gather information on diversity variables such as disabilities and visible minority membership. Regular benchmark data provide a powerful position for students and other campus groups to advocate for diversity service development. For example, research such as the "Best Practices in Increasing Aboriginal Post-secondary Enrolment Rates" (Malatest 2002) has provided useful information on how to best be prepared for the increased participation of this cohort in the coming years. Similarly, data suggesting the rise of global demand for post-secondary education and the potential financial benefits to be realized from enrolment of international students have led to an increased emphasis on their recruitment at a time when institutional resources are diminished.

A final step in the current evolution of campus diversity services has been the formal linking of the diversity mandate to institutional mission, in response to expectations of new diverse consumers. This fourth source of change is unmistakable as staff and resources are becoming aligned to ensure that evolving services meet emerging needs. For example, one can read that the University of Toronto "is dedicated to fostering an academic community in which the learning and scholarship of every member may flourish, with vigilant protection for individual human rights, and a resolute commitment to the principles of equal opportunity, equity and justice." Furthermore, it pursues its objectives through commitment to, among other principles, the "promotion of equity and justice within the University and recognition of the diversity of the University community" (University of Toronto 1992a). Such statements speak volumes to those within and without, and underscore the importance and strength of a commitment to building a diverse institution. Even more explicitly, through a strategic planning process, the University of British Columbia has formalized its intent to offer an exceptional learning environment, based on its commitment to Aboriginal engagement, international engagement, and intercultural understanding. Accordingly it states: "The University engages Aboriginal people in mutually supportive and productive relationships, and works to integrate understandings of Indigenous cultures and histories into its curriculum and operations ... creates rich opportunities for international engagement for students, faculty, staff, and alumni, and collaborates and communicates globally ... and ... engages in reflection and action to build intercultural aptitudes, create a strong sense of inclusion, and enrich our intellectual and social life" (University of British Columbia 2012). The message seems clear that UBC is an institution that values, and indeed depends upon, the contributions a diverse campus environment can bring to the betterment of all. Finally, as yet another example, the University of Saskatchewan communicates the value it places upon "the diversity of our University community: the people, their points of view, and the contributions they make to the realization of our mission" (University of Saskatchewan 1993). All such statements convey a critical institutional commitment that signals a distinct appreciation for the involvement of diverse groups, the basis for a critical milieu that promotes the success of diverse students. The recent legacy of these trends and influences is brought to focus in the analyses, issues, and programmatic strategies described by the present authors who, as Canadian post-secondary student services professionals, offer their observations and experiences from serving these student groups.

2

Theories of Diverse Student Success

C. CARNEY STRANGE

INTRODUCTION

Achieving student success entails articulating the goals that define this concept, as well as the pathways that lead to its attainment. This involves an examination of an emerging body of knowledge that addresses various aspects of diverse student development during the post-secondary years. As we consider in the chapters to follow implications of the diversity of students now being served in the Canadian system of higher education, it is imperative to have an understanding of some of the theories that inform the journeys of these students and consider what they mean for the design of educational policy and practice.

The present chapter first outlines key theories that have informed the learning, growth, and development of post-secondary students over the past several decades; second, it provides an overview of select new theories and concepts in recent literature that have begun to inform policies and practices in response to the needs of an increasingly diverse student population on campus. Admittedly, sources for these analyses are rooted, almost exclusively, in the literature on US students. However, to the extent that these may chart processes purportedly more universal than particular in nature, their application to the Canadian context nonetheless should be considered critically. While the developmental patterns articulated in these theories might not vary fundamentally, particular cultural, customary, and sociological factors could certainly influence the rate and sequence of students' development over time, especially as they relate to differences between Canadian and US cultures, for example, in their respective emphases on collectivist vs individualist values. The point of emphasis here is that there is a considerable literature evolving in the field that continues to inform the role of post-secondary learning in the overall growth and development of students.

UNDERSTANDING STUDENT DEVELOPMENT

The literature on student learning and development during the post-secondary years can be understood in terms of three overlapping so-called "waves" or generations of theories. Over the past five decades these waves have mapped out the dynamics and steps students encounter as they mature during the post-secondary years. The delimitation of these waves or generations of theories is arguable, but meant to distinguish a general sequence of ideas about student development that emphasizes an evolving understanding over time, from universal to differential to intersectional. Each subsequent insight emerges from the previous one(s), articulating an ever more complex view of the topic.

The first wave of ideas is rooted in models and conceptual frameworks generated mostly between 1960 and 1980. Several comprehensive volumes (Knefelkamp, Widick, and Parker 1978; Parker 1978) first introduced many in the field to the principal theories of this first wave, exploring their potential to shape student services and the design of the post-secondary experience, within and beyond the classroom. For example, rooted in the earlier insights of Erikson (1950) and others, Chickering (1969) first identified seven psychosocial tasks or "vectors of development" associated with the transition from late adolescence to young adulthood. He averred that education was most meaningful and powerful in its effect when connected more directly to the resolution of these tasks. For example, the study of the discipline of psychology achieves even greater and immediate relevance when an individual is encountering questions of personal identity and interpersonal relationships. Also included in this line of theory development is the work of James Marcia (1966), a Canadian scholar whose model of identity statuses (e.g., diffusion, foreclosure, moratorium, and achievement) illuminated the dynamic between crisis and commitment among adolescents as they addressed issues of occupation and ideology and, by implication, the potential for formal education in mediating this process.

Another category of ideas during this first wave of theory building addressed how students constructed meaning in the midst of their experiences. Accordingly, Perry (1970) (in the domain of intellectual and ethical development) and Kohlberg (1969) (in the domain of moral reasoning) each identified a hierarchical sequence of cognitive structures that students were thought to progress through as they advanced from simplistic to more complex forms of reasoning about issues of truth and fairness. Approaching experiences through the lens of dualistic and pre-conventional reasoning for example comes with expectations of certainty and self-serving motives. In contrast, relativism and principled reasoning brings an appreciation for ambiguous contexts and compelling evidence, as well as a commitment to underlying universal values. Following the groundwork of previous scholars (e.g., Erik Erikson, Jean Piaget), each of these theories presumed initially to address a "universal" experience among post-secondary students, independent of any personal identifiers. Collectively such theories constituted the state of the art in knowledge about post-secondary students for at least a decade and more.

Spurred on perhaps by a caution that "the excitement of the initial discoveries has worn thin, over generalizations have led to misapplication, and what once seemed like a perfect match [that is, between student affairs and student development theory] now is something that clearly demands solid rethinking and hard work" (Moore 1990, 84), a second wave of theory building ensued in the early 1980s and continued through most of the 1990s. These new areas of "evolving" theory began with challenges to the relevance of the first wave's work, inasmuch as it purportedly failed to account for the experiences of students whose identities varied from the dominant culture and context. Thus, researchers such as Carol Gilligan began to explore how the experiences of women, different from men, shaped their responses to various moral dilemmas. Culminating in her signature contribution, *In a Different Voice* (1982), Gilligan deconstructed some of the long-held tenets of Western psychology and drew attention to the differential emphases on autonomy and relationships as metrics of human maturation. Her insight was that women are often socialized to function through relationships with others, whereas men are drawn more toward independent and autonomous situations. Thus, while traditional models of growth and development tended to focus on achieving personal independence as the ultimate goal, emerging models such as Gilligan's underscored the importance of interdependence and relationships in the mix of maturity.

Similarly, extending a gender-based critique to cognitive developmental theories as well, Baxter-Magolda (1992) challenged assumptions implicit in these first-wave models that young adults, regardless of gender, followed a single progression of cognitive structures; in contrast she concluded that men and women in fact approach "self authorship" (her term for advanced functioning) along characteristically different paths, noting some stage nuances aligned with gender, between *receiving* or *mastering* knowledge, *interpersonal* or *impersonal* knowing, and patterns that are *interindividual* or *individual* in nature. Also by then, in response to increasing enrolments among adult or mature learners, others (Levinson 1978; Levinson and Levinson 1996), underscored the significance of age differences, extending notions of learning and development to encompass the entire human lifespan and clarifying the dynamics of stability and transition as individuals proceeded through life-structure-building and life-structure-changing eras from childhood to late adulthood. Like the earlier, groundbreaking work of Bernice Neugarten (1968), a lifespan approach sensitized educators to the patterns of age-related phases (e.g., Midlife) as they prodded and oriented individuals at predictable intervals to affirm or alter various aspects of their lives through formal education. This notion, in turn, was complemented by the work of Schlossberg (1995) who further articulated the dynamics of life transitions with implications for the role of formal education in the process.

Other dimensions of identity also came to the forefront of educators' thinking during this second wave of theory building, for example, through the insights of Cross (1995) (in the domain of racial identity), Cass (1979) and D'Augelli (1994) (in reference to sexual orientation), and Phinney (1990) (in terms of ethnic identity), to name a few. Each of these theories purported to have highlighted what was presumed unique about the experiences of various campus subgroups as personal identifiers situated them in a context deserving of a unique response. This second wave of theories, many of which are summarized and critiqued in Evans, Forney, and Guido-DiBrito (1998), Evans, Forney, Guido, Patton, and Renn (2010), and Cox and Strange (2010), thus created a new breadth and depth of perspective on diverse students for the first time and spurred a new generation of researchers who in turn began to articulate a more finely tuned understanding of their learning, growth, and development during the post-secondary years.

Perhaps the overall import of these second-wave contributions has been a heightened awareness of various identifiers in examining the student development experience and constructing theories that attempt to explain it. Rather than uniformity, a principal conclusion extending from these insights has been the *variability* of students' experiences and the need to consider, and accommodate accordingly, how student services are designed and implemented. Consequently, services that responded to individual group differences (e.g., transition programs for Aboriginal students) began to take root in the portfolio of many campus offerings, creating the need for advancement in understanding the nuances of identity development. This question has become the focus of yet another wave of theory building in the field, one that extends the emphasis on interpersonal group differences to the dynamics of intrapersonal development.

THIRD-WAVE THEORIES

A third wave of theory building is currently underway in the literature on student development, focusing primarily on the role of intrapersonal identities and driven by the principal insight that identity is a highly complex and interactive process involving the subtle and situational interplay of the many aspects of human development. Unlike second-wave theories that articulated identifiers as exclusive and independent features of select groups of students (e.g., Blacks, gays, and women), theories representative of this third wave have begun to explore the complexity of identity development and expression as a dynamic of simultaneous influences and contextual factors, resulting in evolving compositions of identity that are as much fluid and situational as they are fixed. In doing so, such theories have not only advanced an understanding of the whole and complex nature of students' lives, but more importantly have challenged the many categorical binaries and presumed static structures of previous explanations. Thus the dynamics of "intersectionality," "identity fluidity," and "identity performance," for example, have entered the discourse on student development for the first time, with the goal of developing greater depth and nuance in the understanding of students' maturation and the role higher education plays in its progression. Further integral to these new understandings has been their emphasis on the privilege of dominant groups in society as both a powerful source of "normality" and a delimiter on the progression of those whose identities place them outside of its definitions. In addition this third wave of theories also tends to emphasize the social construction of identities and their susceptibility to changing contexts and circumstances.

Finally, noticeably qualitative in its orientation this emerging set of ideas has begun to outline a new holography of student development through a greater array of interconnected questions and methodologies. In doing so it has sought to uncover through idiographic portraits and case studies the simultaneous and mutual causalities of human development through the *emic* (that is, insider) perspectives of those immersed in them.

Anchored primarily in questions of identity development, this third wave of theory building has added significantly to an understanding of students' intrapersonal maturation in particular. Included among such scholars are those who have re-framed the discussion of identity development through new and critical distinctions; those whose work has explored the intersections of multiple dimensions of identity; those who have probed more deeply into variations of select expressions of identity; and those who have contributed to the mix new understandings of dimensions that have received only limited previous attention in the literature. In total these authors have moved the discourse on student development from an obvious to a more sophisticated perspective that better accounts for the realities students encounter in their quest for self-understanding.

The significance of this changing landscape of student identity is seen in Renn (2004), for example, who explored the complexities of race and ethnicity through five "identity patterns" associated with mixed-race students. According to her research some students embrace a monoracial identity ("I'm Black," "I'm Asian") or hold multiple monoracial identities, shifting according to situation ("I'm half white and half Chinese," "I am Mexican and Black"). A third pattern is evident in a multiracial identity ("I'm biracial," "I'm mixed"), and a fourth in extraracial identity: "deconstructing race or opting out by refusing to identify according to U.S. racial categories" ("I'm Jamaican," "I won't check any boxes," "I don't believe in having a race") (67). Last there are those who express a situational identity ("When I'm with my fraternity, I'm like them – white. When I'm with the Japan Club, I'm Japanese American. And when I'm home, I'm hapa.") (68). Furthermore, such patterns of identity were found to vary by gender, with women "less likely than men to choose a monoracial identity pattern and more likely to choose a bi- or multiracial pattern" (83). The contribution of Renn's model is its compelling story of post-secondary student identities as a function of self and society. Accordingly it affirms a constructionist perspective, holding that "racial identities are considered to have emerged from the tension between the definition of self assigned to an individual by out-group members and the definition of self constructed by that individual" and a symbolic interactionist perspective, asserting that identity is both a "reflexive process, influenced by both external constraints and individual agency" and a "negotiated process by which individuals understand themselves and others and evaluate their selves in relation to others" (Rockquemore 2002, 487–8, as cited in Renn 2004). This same dynamic applies as well to the development of other identity dimensions, such as gender identity and its relationship to sex, gender, and sexual orientation. Whereas once it was considered by most to be a simple binary choice, gender identity now is thought of as a complex of biological differences and socialized choices, themselves mutable distinctions across categories and time (Lev 2004). In the mix of all this, especially in the post-secondary setting, is the power of "peer culture ... [as] an important locus of identity construction and maintenance" (Renn 2004, 93). One implication of this claim is that when it comes to understanding students' identities, preference should be given first to how they self-identify, as well as exploring the dynamics of their own peer group in their expressions of how they see themselves.

Similarly Abes, Jones, and McEwen (2007) offered a reconceptualized framework of identity, which "more aptly captures the complexity of intersecting domains of development" (5). Based on the previous work of Jones and McEwen's (2000) model of multiple dimensions of identity, the authors considered how the salience of various domains of development and layers of identity might be influenced by an individual's cognitive meaning-making structures (e.g., dualistic, prereflective, received knowing). Thus, for example, one's identity as lesbian or Black might take on greater or lesser salience in the context of an environment that summarily supports or rejects such a distinction, if indeed an individual subscribes to or rejects the influence of externally defined sources (e.g., church, family). In articulating their revised model, Abes, Jones, and McEwen (2007) integrated the intra-personal, cognitive, and interpersonal domains of development to provide "a richer portrayal of not only *what* relationships students perceive among their personal and social identities, but also *how* they come to perceive them as they do" (13). Again, unlike second-wave identity work, grounded in fixed models of development, this holistic approach incorporates "contemporary perspectives of fluidity, per-formativity, and salience" (16) as it explains the evolution of social identities within the context of various structures of privilege and positionality. The importance of context in such development is fur-ther iterated in models of white racial consciousness (Rowe, Bennett, and Atkinson 1994), Latino (Ferdman and Gallegos 2001), Asian (Kim 2001), Canadian Aboriginal (Deer 2011), Native American (Horse 2001), gay and lesbian (Fassinger 1998), and gender identities (Lev 2004). Thus, the picture of human development arising from this third wave of ideas is anything but essentialist and particulate in its view of the maturation process; rather it is more holographic in scope, inasmuch as the complex of dimensions characterizing any individual is contextual, emergent, and timely.

In addition to the above clarifications, a number of newer itera-tions on the development of student subgroups have accompanied this recent wave of theories, expanding on as well as integrating various dimensions of growth and change. For example, Cross and Fhagen-Smith (2001), building on a previous model (Cross 1981), have integrated the development of nigrescence (or the "process of becoming black") within a lifespan perspective, yielding six "sectors" of development, evolving from "Infancy and Childhood in Early Black Identity Development" (sector one), "Preadolescence" (sector two), "Adolescence" (sector three), to "Early Adulthood" (sector four), "Adult Nigrescence" (sector five), and "Nigrescence Recycling" (sector six). At each point emergence of a Black self-concept occurs as a function of prior socialization and degrees of race salience or internalized racism. Rather than linear, Black identity is constructed as cyclical and open to personal revision as a result of various con-texts and circumstances. Identity then is seen as inherently fluid and dynamic, in contrast to second-wave iterations that tended toward the presumed fixed and stable aspects of development.

In addition to casting human development within a new and more complex frame of understanding, this third wave of theories has also contributed to the exploration of topics heretofore mostly ignored in the literature on post-secondary students. For example, Parks (2011) refocused on the journey of "faithing" or how young adults engage in meaning-making about the most comprehensive and ultimate dimensions of life. Although addressed previously in Fowler (1981), the advancement of *Big Questions Worthy Dreams* (Parks 2011) is realized in its integration of dimensions of spirituality with human cognition and forms of interdependence. Similar to other ideas in the current wave, Parks leans toward a more holistic explanation, if for no other reason than to reflect the complexity of life itself. All of this points clearly and repeatedly to the implications of differences in educational practice. To treat all students uniformly – while seemingly fair – is highly ineffective and fails to recognize the important distinctions of identity, especially at a time in the life of an individual – the post-secondary years – when experiences are most salient for their development. Understanding intergroup differences and within-group individual differences are both critical for. setting the conditions of success, and starting with how students personally construct those differences is a significant first step.

CONCLUSION

Although referring specifically to students in the US system, Pascarella and Terenzini (1991), in their first volume of *How College Affects Students*, suggested: "If there is a major future direction for research on the impact of college, it will be to focus on that growing proportion of students whom we have typically classified as non-traditional, although they are rapidly becoming the majority of participants in the American post-secondary system" (632). In the most recent version of their work (Pascarella and Terenzini 2005) the authors underscored a similar alert: "The increased heterogeneity of American undergraduates, particularly in race or ethnicity, spurred – indeed required – closer attention to what we have called conditional effects, or the possibility that any given college experience may have a different effect on different kinds of students" (626). Therein lies the importance of these subsequent waves of student development theory building. To the extent that the Canadian post-secondary system is similarly becoming more diverse, the need for student services staff to recognize and respond with a more finely tuned approach is paramount.

The evolution of a theoretical knowledge base that informs our understanding of the progression of students at the post-secondary level has been a distinctive development in the literature on higher education of the last half-century. First through theories presumed to be universal, then through models responsive to individual group differences, and now through frameworks that feature the integration and dynamic contexts of intrapersonal development, we have learned much by implication about the promise of education to effect the growth and success of post-secondary students. As the demographic and identity compositions of enrolments continue to shift toward a more diverse profile, it is imperative that educators in general, and student services personnel in particular, examine further the ideas presented here, especially those representative of this third wave of emerging theories, and embrace them as tools for more effective understanding and practice.

Section Two

3

Aboriginal Student Success

MICHELLE PIDGEON

"Okay, I'm here," thought Amber as she looked around. She is the first person in her family to attend university, and just getting to "here" is a milestone worth celebrating. Following registration the Admissions office put her in touch with the Aboriginal advisor and First Nations Centre. The Centre was warm, it smelled of sweet grass, and she noticed there was an Elders' room. "I wonder if it's okay I'm here," she thought to herself, still a bit nervous and uncertain about being a university student. At the Centre, she was welcomed by Stephan, who introduced himself as being from a nearby reservation and studying pre-med in his first year of university.

As an older single mom, Amber chose to live off-campus with the support of her aunt who helps take care of her son. Her uncle is studying auto-mechanics at a college nearby. Amber's return to post-secondary education has had its challenges, particularly in regards to funding. While talking with others in line at the Financial Aid Office, one student commented, "but I thought all you Indians got your education for free!" Amber, like many Indigenous students, does not have status and so is not eligible for Federal funding programs; neither does she have Band funding. She knew such a stereotype wouldn't be the only discrimination she would encounter; however, her prior experience with a college academic prep program helped her gain confidence to further her education. Grounded in her life experiences, her family, her dreams for her young son, and with First Nations Student

Centre support, she knows she will succeed in completing her university education.

INTRODUCTION

The above scenario is both fictional and real. Stephan reflects the growing Canadian Aboriginal population that completes high school and directly enters post-secondary education. Amber represents the Aboriginal student seen more frequently on our campuses – female, older than average, and a single parent. Such gender differences are readily apparent in Canada's post-secondary institutions. Statistics show that Aboriginal males typically attend a local trades college, like the uncle above, and Aboriginal females are more likely to attend university than are their male counterparts (Statistics Canada 2008a). In addition this scenario also highlights how some Aboriginal students rely upon intergenerational and community supports while attending university. In a June 2012 report (Aboriginal Affairs and Northern Development Canada 2012), the authors concluded:

> Three of the most prevalent challenges identified by Aboriginal students in their transition to post-secondary education are related to family and community: family pressure to stay home, family conflicts, and feeling disconnected from home and culture. It is clear that considerations pertaining to family and community are important factors in the post-secondary experience of Aboriginal students. Moreover, family and community have been shown to have a significant influence on student success. (26)

Student services practitioners need to become cognizant of these dynamics and of the diversity of Nations, cultures, languages, and identities of Aboriginal peoples. In addition, they need to consider the impacts of colonization (e.g., residential schools) on First Nations, Métis, and Inuit peoples' educational journeys.

Education is a provincial responsibility, and while Aboriginal education falls under the jurisdiction of the Federal government, it is ultimately a relationship between three entities: Aboriginal nations, provincial governments, and the Federal government. However the Canadian educational system can be a place of alienation for some, in this case Indigenous students, rooted in its history of failure to accommodate those from backgrounds other than the mainstream middle class culture (Battiste and Barman 1995; Battiste, Bell, and Findlay 2002; Bourdieu and Passeron 1990; Malatest and Associates Ltd 2004; Pidgeon 2008a; Royal Commission on Aboriginal Peoples 1996a). It is this challenge that is the focus of the present chapter. I have several aims: a) to discuss the characteristics of contemporary Indigenous students; b) to provide some rationale as to why we should consider the infusion of principles of *Indigeneity* in our institutions; c) to articulate the history and current landscape of Aboriginal student services; d) to outline some current issues and challenges facing Aboriginal students and student affairs practitioners; and e) to share some thoughts as to how more appropriate policies, practices, and understandings can transform post-secondary institutions to empower Indigenous student success.

Honouring Indigenous knowledge grounds Aboriginal student services, and is at the core of Indigenous student success. I raise my hand in respect and I acknowledge those in student services across Canada who persistently position Aboriginal student success at the forefront of post-secondary administration, policy-making, governmental action, and community support. This chapter is also for those Indigenous students who persevere and stand as a true measure of our "success"; it is written so that practitioners can broaden their understanding and inform their work based on a holistic Indigenous framework that honours the cultural integrity of all students.

HOLISTIC INDIGENOUS FRAMEWORK

Figure 3.1 presents a framework for understanding the complexities and intricacies of Indigenous ways of being and knowing. The framework acknowledges the centrality of place in the foundation of Indigenous ways of knowing and cultural practices (Battiste 2003; Battiste and Henderson 2000). Therefore, knowing the traditional territories upon which an institution is located is important to seeing the historical and contemporary connections to Indigenous peoples. You may see at your own institution or in events hosted by Indigenous peoples the explicit acknowledgement of territory and place. This cultural protocol respects not only place, but also the peoples from this place, and is a clear example of how one sees Indigenous ways of knowing being reflected within the higher education context.

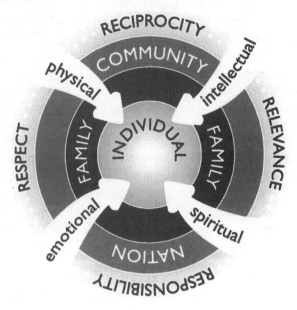

Figure 3.1 Holistic Indigenous framework

   This framework honours holism through the inter-connectedness
of the intellectual, spiritual, emotional, and physical realms; it also
values the interrelationships of the individual, family (i.e., immediate
and extended), and community (e.g., nation, university) as integral to
Indigenous philosophy, culture, and being (e.g., Battiste 2000, 2002;
Battiste and Henderson 2000; Brant Castellano 2000; Dei, Hall, and
Rosenberg 2000; Pidgeon 2008; Smith 1999; Sterling 1995; Weber-
Pillwax 1999).
   The 4Rs of *Respect* for First Nations' cultural integrity, *Relevance*
to First Nations perspectives and experiences, *Reciprocity* of relationships, and *Responsibility* through participation (Kirkness and Barnhardt 1991) provide guiding principles to ensure that post-secondary
institutions become successful places for Aboriginal peoples. One can
see that all are part of the Holistic Indigenous Framework; however,
the 4Rs must be understood from the emic (i.e., insider) perspective,
that is, one has not only sought understanding, but one also recognizes Indigenous knowledge and the contributions it has made to our
post-secondary institutions and the broader society. As in previous
work (Pidgeon 2008b), I argue that Aboriginal student services has

become one place within our institutions where such responsiveness to the 4Rs and Indigenous ways of knowing are apparent and influential on not only garnering support for Indigenous students, but also in changing institutional cultures, policies, and practices towards Indigenous peoples and their communities.

ABORIGINAL POST-SECONDARY STUDENTS

In Canada there exist over eighty distinct Indigenous peoples; consequently, one must examine distinct histories, places, languages, and cultures in order to understand Aboriginal students attending our institutions (Kidwell 1991; Pidgeon 2001; Royal Commission on Aboriginal Peoples (RCAP) 1996b; Smith 1999). In discussing Aboriginal education one must also acknowledge the complexities surrounding the colonization of Indigenous peoples and how this legacy continues throughout Canada's educational systems, policies, and practices. The Truth and Reconciliation events held across Canada in 2013 were aimed at not only documenting the stories and experiences of residential school survivors, but also at providing space for dialogue and learning for non-Aboriginal peoples, so that all can move forward as a nation, fully understanding the legacy and intergenerational impact colonization, and specifically residential schools, have had on our country (see www.trc.ca for more on this topic).

Canada's Indigenous people are commonly referred to as "First Nations," "Aboriginal," "Métis," and "Inuit." Each of these terms has historical and legal significance, being linked to Canadian federal legislation, such as the Indian Act 1867 and its amendment Bill-C31 (Graham, Dittburner, and Abele 1996; Royal Commission on Aboriginal Peoples 1996a; White, Maxim, and Beavon 2004). Such laws have left their mark over time on Canada's Aboriginal peoples. For example, prior to the 1985 Bill-C31, Aboriginal women who married non-Aboriginal men were disenfranchised, that is, they forfeited Federal recognition and rights afforded them in the preceding Indian Act. Such policies pervade the discourse of who identifies as "Aboriginal" and consequently shape in limited ways how Canadian society at large perceives Aboriginal peoples. Consequently, the question of "Aboriginal" identity needs to be re-centred and directly asked of Indigenous peoples themselves, acknowledging their inherent right to self-determine and self-identify by nation. More recently,

"Indigenous" is a label being used by Aboriginal peoples as a way of connecting to the global community of similar peoples and also politically reclaiming their rights as first peoples.

Student affairs professionals' knowledge of Aboriginal history and their own experiences with Aboriginal communities impacts how they advocate on behalf of students, as well as communicates their needs to the broader campus community (Pidgeon 2008b; Powell 1998); this is certainly true for serving Aboriginal students. In one study of Canadian Aboriginal student services, Pidgeon (2001) was told by a practitioner:

> It is important to remember that the Aboriginal students who will access your services are not homogeneous. You will have students directly from a First Nation, Urban Native students who have never lived on a reserve, [and] Aboriginal students who are only beginning to identify as "Aboriginal" and have never visited a reserve and do not know their heritage. [You will also have] Métis students and ... Aboriginal students who are Traditional, [as well as] those who do not participate in traditional ceremonies because they are Christian. In Aboriginal student services you have to understand and respect all Aboriginal students for where they may be on that continuum. That is also the key to success in Aboriginal student services.

The increase in numbers of Aboriginal students in Canadian postsecondary education has been attributed to their higher rates of high school graduation, the development of programs featuring Aboriginal content and Aboriginal faculty mentors, increased federal funding (e.g., Aboriginal Post-Secondary Student Support Programs), and scholarships, grants, and policies specific to Aboriginal students (e.g., admissions, housing, third party billing, and cultural ceremonies) (Battiste 1998, 2002; Battiste and Barman 1995; Battiste, Bell, and Findlay 2002; Danziger 1996; Human Capital Strategies 2005; Malatest and Associates Ltd 2004; Pidgeon 2008a; Royal Commission on Aboriginal Peoples [RCAP] 1996).

According to the 2006 Federal Census, one in three Aboriginal peoples had not completed high school, and 21 per cent listed high school as their highest educational achievement. Of those who went on to post-secondary education though, 14 per cent had attained trades credentials, 19 per cent college diplomas, and 8 per cent university degrees (Statistics Canada 2008a). As in the 2001 Census, the 2006 Census also showed that Aboriginal males are more likely than females to complete trades credentials, while Aboriginal females are more likely to complete college diplomas or university degrees (Statistics Canada 2008a), underscoring once again the gender differences noted above. Data from the 2011 National Household Survey (NHS) suggest modest recent gains, with almost 10 per cent of Aboriginal people reporting having completed a university degree, among the 48 per cent with a postsecondary qualification. Younger Aboriginal people were more likely to have completed a university degree than older ones and females more so than males, suggesting both a generational and a gender effect.

Despite these positive changes in educational attainment and aspirations, Aboriginal peoples are still underrepresented in most postsecondary institutions, especially in universities. For example, only 8 per cent of Aboriginal peoples, compared to non-Aboriginal peoples (23 per cent), have completed a university degree (Statistics Canada 2008a). In terms of Canada's post-secondary campus populations, the percentage of Aboriginal students, faculty, and staff do not reflect (in most cases) the provincial distribution of the Aboriginal population. In British Columbia, for example, the Aboriginal population is 10–15 per cent, while its post-secondary institutions typically report 3–4 per cent Aboriginal students. The exception to this case is the University of Northern British Columbia, where the Aboriginal student population is around 10 per cent.

The issues and barriers to Aboriginal student success articulated by the 1996 Royal Commission on Aboriginal Peoples (RCAP 1996a) persist even today – lack of funding, need for relevant programs and services, systemic prejudice, and limits of academic readiness for post-secondary education. An Association of Universities and Colleges of Canada report (AUCC 2010) speaks not only to the need for more funding of students' programs, but also for greater institutional support at the K–12 and post-secondary levels to enhance Aboriginal student success across the system. The challenge before educators and student affairs professionals is to develop a clearer understanding of the needs of Aboriginal students. The Indigenous Student Centre, should there be one available on campus, is the entryway for building relationships with and creating respectful practices for Indigenous students. Another route is through joining or volunteering at Indigenous hosted events (e.g., welcoming week, orientation, local movie night, cultural ceremonies, Elders' gathering, or graduation Pow-Wows). Such actions, done respectfully and reciprocally, not only benefit all participants, but also have wider implications for changing how institutions as organizations and places support Indigenous student success.

INDIGENEITY AND STUDENT SUCCESS

In understanding the holistic framework, one can begin to see the complexities of Indigenous student success (See "What I learned in Class today"). A December 2011 report issued by the Standing Senate Committee on Social Affairs, Science and Technology (*Opening the Door: Reducing Barriers to Post-Secondary Education in Canada*) noted in particular that:

> The educational paradigm reflected in post-secondary programs predominantly epitomizes learning as an individualized, competitive, testable process. In contrast, Aboriginal pedagogy prioritizes learning acquired through cooperation, storytelling, group discussions, modelling and observations. In many post-secondary institutions, the programs, curricula and presentation of content are misaligned with Aboriginal culture and pedagogy. (46)

Success therefore for many Indigenous students is not just an individual goal. While it's important, of course, that they attain their own aspirations and dreams, their career and educational aims are also often connected to being role models for others and/or giving back to their respective communities (Pidgeon 2008). For some it means simply attending and completing a course; for others it means pursuing not only an undergraduate degree, but continuing on to complete a master's and/or a doctorate degree. Ultimately, success for Indigenous students means coming to post-secondary education, where their indigeneity is valued and respected, and leaving an institution with their holistic selves enriched, not only intellectually, but also physically, spiritually, culturally, and emotionally (Pidgeon 2008a).

Research continues to demonstrate that Aboriginal support services empower students to fully participate in higher education and to attain their own successes (Dodd et al. 1995; Pidgeon 2008b; Royal Commission on Aboriginal Peoples 1996a; Wright 1985). Such engagement of Aboriginal students also enriches the overall culture of the institutions they attend (Martin 2001; Wright 1985; Moore-Eyman 1981; Tinto 1993). Instrumental in the achievement of all of this has been and continues to be the role of Aboriginal Student Services.

ABORIGINAL STUDENT SERVICES

Aboriginal student support services have been implemented on numerous campuses to address Indigenous students' unique academic, social, cultural, and psychological needs (Dodd et al. 1995; Martin 2001; Moore-Eyman 1981; Pidgeon 2001; Pidgeon and Hardy Cox 2005; Wright 1985). These services first appeared in Canada in 1972, with the establishment of so-called "Indian Student Services" at the University of Calgary. This evolved into "Native Student Services" and subsequently to the "Native Student Centre" between 1978 and 1982 (Pidgeon 2001). The University of Alberta began offering student support services to Aboriginal students in 1975, when Marilyn Buffalo was appointed to the position of "Advisor on Native Affairs," created by the General Faculty Council to establish an "Office of Native Student Services" (Pidgeon 2001).

The majority of Aboriginal student services in Canada were launched in the late 1980s-early 1990s, and some continued to emerge in the early 2000s. These services evolved from strategic policies constructed by various government entities (e.g., Provincial Advisory Committee 1990; Ministry of Training, Colleges and Universities 1999) and often extended from original academic support roles to the array of campus positions today that include Aboriginal academic advisors, counsellors, recruiters, and various Aboriginal student services positions. Such services established the foundation for the creation of many a centre on Canadian campuses dedicated to the needs of Aboriginal students.

"Aboriginal Student Centres" have been highly successful in providing an environment that fosters the legitimization of Aboriginal identity within mainstream institutions, and have facilitated First Nations student involvement in student life (e.g., student union, student representation on university committees) (Archibald et al. 1995; Martin 2001; Moore-Eyman 1981). Holistic and culturally appropriate services include academic and personal services, counselling, housing, financial advising/support, daycare services, Aboriginal student orientation, graduation ceremony, Aboriginal student advisors,

First Nations student organizations, student lounge/meeting place, study facilities and equipment (e.g., computers), outreach programs, Elders programs, leadership programs, cultural events/ceremonies, and volunteer opportunities (Pidgeon 2001).

The 1990 British Columbia "Report for the Provincial Advisory Committee on Post-Secondary Education for Native Learners" (Provincial Advisory Committee 1990) described the development of several centres with at least one staff person hired as an Aboriginal student support worker. Other than the Native counsellor position at Algoma University College (established in the 1980s and made permanent in 1987), no other university featured such a position until the Ontario provincial government funded Native Initiatives in 1991 (Pidgeon 2005). During the 1990s, the goals of these particular initiatives were to increase the participation of Aboriginal students in post-secondary education and to optimize completion rates. Government grants were made available to offset special costs of designing and delivering Aboriginal programs. In some provinces targeted funds were also made available to increase the number of Aboriginal counsellors and special support services. The expectation was that the operation of such programs, positions, and services become integrated into the institutions' main operating budget once the provincial funding expired. However, this was not always the case and some institutions continue to this day to rely upon such external funding sources to support Aboriginal initiatives and programs (Pidgeon 2008b). In some instances, Aboriginal student services remains only a part-time or contractual appointment or within an umbrella unit, such as an Office of Multicultural Student Services, where a specialized Aboriginal student counsellor functions as one member of a larger staff team. In other institutions Aboriginal student services have evolved into an institution-wide organization providing complete and integrated services, from recruitment to honouring graduation feasts (e.g., University of Toronto's First Nations House, University of Calgary, University of Victoria). It is also the case that increasingly so institutions are recognizing the importance of place and culturally relevant spaces to Aboriginal student success, as reflected in the architecture of the First Nations House of Learning constructed in 1993 at the University of British Columbia or the Aboriginal House built in 2008 at the University of Manitoba. Both of these centres create "homes away from homes" and stand as exemplar facilities for what can and needs to be achieved on behalf of Aboriginal students.

In addition to the above examples of government-rooted interventions, Aboriginal student services in some cases developed as a result of indigenous communities themselves recognizing the need to support its students while away from home and thus collaborated with the university to establish such supports. This was the case in Newfoundland and Labrador where, in 1991, a partnership between the Labrador Inuit Association (LIA) and Memorial University of Newfoundland resulted in the opening of the Native Liaison Office (NLO). The LIA initially began funding this office to support growing numbers of Inuit students leaving Labrador to attend the Native Teacher Education Program and other university opportunities in the capital city of St John's. The Native Liaison Office is currently funded internally by the university and is open to all students of Aboriginal ancestry attending the institution.

In 2001 a national survey of Canadian universities found that approximately half (49 per cent) provided some form of Aboriginal student services (Pidgeon 2001, 2005). By 2011, this figure had increased to 94 per cent of public universities and approximately 60 per cent of community colleges that listed services specific to Aboriginal students. The depth and scope of these services, similar to the 2001 findings, varied across provinces and were influenced most likely by local Indigenous demographics. Such interventions included Aboriginal-relevant academic programs, institutional mission and goal statements, government policy and funding initiatives, and creation of respectful student services. No denominational institutions in British Columbia or Manitoba provided specific Aboriginal student services. A more recent development in the field though has been the creation of Aboriginal consultant/advisor positions at a number of institutions to provide guidance and leadership to senior administrators (e.g., president or vice-president academic) concerning Aboriginal matters at the institution. This approach is found at the University of British Columbia, Simon Fraser University, and Memorial University of Newfoundland.

In 2004 the professionalization of Aboriginal student services underwent further change with the establishment of the National Aboriginal Student Services Association (NASSA) within the Canadian Association of College and University Student Services (CACUSS).

NASSA's mission is "to empower institutions of higher learning to become welcoming environments where Aboriginal Peoples can successfully pursue educational goals while maintaining their cultural identities" (see http://www.nassa.cacuss.ca/). The goals of NASSA are outlined further on its website: (a) to promote Aboriginal cultural awareness/participation within all areas of post-secondary institutions; (b) to increase abilities of all student services providers to respond effectively to the needs of Aboriginal peoples; and (c) to develop a national network of Aboriginal post-secondary student services providers.

Underlying all of these initiatives is the growing understanding, framed in the holistic model presented above, how various elements of the Aboriginal student experience contribute to their success. For example, cultural ceremonies (e.g., smudging, sweat lodge) not only provide for holistic wellness, but also ground students in what they know and provide balance to their academic lives. Elders also play a significant role in each realm, providing cultural support and guiding students academically, while reminding them of the balance of mind, body, and spirit. The infusion of Aboriginal knowledge and practices into other student services in addition assures that relevant services are also available in other campus spaces. For example, actions that support Aboriginal student success might include the role of visiting Elders and Aboriginal-specific housing policies; financial aid training and policy development relevant to specific Aboriginal funding options (e.g., third party billing); and availability of Aboriginal counsellors and/or training of non-Aboriginal counsellors to support Aboriginal client needs. While such efforts have greatly improved the situation for Aboriginal students in Canadian colleges and universities, a number of significant issues, challenges, and concerns remain and have yet to be addressed.

ISSUES, CHALLENGES, AND CONCERNS

First Nations Centres provide holistic services that empower Aboriginal student success. However, it is important to realize that in doing so some Aboriginal student services can remain marginalized within an institution. In addition, sometimes such services along with academic programs with Native-specific focus represent a limited space where Indigenous is "permitted" within the mainstream. This dynamic becomes particularly problematic at a time when decreasing expenditures engender a competitive culture of institutional cutbacks that, coupled with recurring negative perceptions of Native services, impact how people act, behave, and react to these services and Indigenous students, staff, and faculty. Such a dynamic not only affects individual institutions, but also the status of broader organizations committed to providing leadership in this domain. For example, the Canadian Association of College and University Student Services recently hosted a national dialogue and forum on its potential reorganization, where the need is critical for Indigenous student services practitioners to have a strong voice and representation. Continuing support for spaces specific to National Aboriginal Student Services Association members is important for ensuring their visibility and influence among the CACUSS leadership.

For the most part Aboriginal student services have remained resilient through recent waves of budget cuts, diminishing resources, and under-staffing. Due in large part to the efforts of dedicated staff, and with the support of activists lobbying, securing funding, and holding institutions and governments accountable, Aboriginal groups and their allies have continued to secure new academic programs and additional support services. Their degree of success in doing so however is influenced also by where in the institutional structure Aboriginal student services reside, that is, within an academic or student affairs portfolio. Both approaches have their respective issues and present challenges to success. Regardless, targeted "Aboriginal Student Services" provide a holistic framework based on Indigenous epistemology and culture, and are able to focus on issues of recruitment, admissions, retention, and other facets of service delivery specific to Indigenous students' needs. The relationship of Aboriginal Student Services to the larger institutional community also assures "awareness" by its very presence, and provides a resource locus where other community members can learn about Aboriginal peoples, their cultures and ways of knowing. Furthermore Indigenous student service providers can extend such a relationship to Aboriginal communities within and around an institution and/or province by engaging in liaison work between the Aboriginal community and the institution.

Regardless, to increase Aboriginal student achievement and success, mainstream institutions must offer a balance of Indigenous and non-Indigenous ways of knowing, pedagogical practices, curriculum, and policies. Institutions must also appreciate the diversity of their

own Indigenous student population and reflect such differences in
their programs, services, and facilities.

TOOLS OF CHANGE:
RESEARCH, POLICY, AND PRACTICE

The future of Aboriginal student services in Canadian post-secondary
education is unlimited. It is hoped that challenges to the funding and
justification of specialized services will diminish over time as institutions and their sponsoring governments recognize the reciprocal benefits of Aboriginal student services for the Aboriginal community and
for the institution itself as a whole. There are three means through
which this will occur: research, policy, and practice. Accountability
discourses across Canada's post-secondary system have many turning to research to guide the design and delivery of educational practices. Institutional research is critical for helping institutions evaluate
policies, standards, and interventions, to ensure that they are providing effective financial, political, and policy support for Aboriginal
students.

Education is the key to mutual understanding. While the resources
cited herein offer a helpful beginning to understanding Aboriginal
issues, they represent but a brief sampling of what is available on
the topic. Marie Battiste and Jean Barman's *First Nations Education
in Canada: The Circle Unfolds* (1995) is a foundational primer, as
is *Volume 3: Gathering Strength*, from the *Report of the Royal
Commission on Aboriginal Peoples* (RCAP 1996a). To understand
Aboriginal student experiences, the recent reports authored by the
Association of Universities and Colleges of Canada (AUCC) and
Council of Ministers of Education, Canada (CMEC) provide (AUCC
2010; CMEC and Statistics Canada 2010) a good overview as well,
although both overlook some of the key research being conducted by
Aboriginal peoples and allies that will help further guide practices
applying theory, research, and policy.

As institutions move to create and implement research programs
to address Aboriginal community needs, they are also moving forward in developing strategic plans to articulate institutional mis-
sions, goals, and objectives. Aboriginal issues and education must not
be an afterthought in this process. Some institutions are embarking
on creating specific strategic plans for Aboriginal learners. For

purposes of relevance and viability, the process of creating such policy documents must include participation of the Aboriginal communities both within and beyond the institution.

In terms of practice each reader would benefit from reflecting on the holistic framework presented above and considering carefully where their unit stands in addressing the needs of Aboriginal students. What relationship with the Aboriginal community on campus currently exists? How is it intentionally maintained and how can it be improved? The 4Rs (respect for First Nations' cultural integrity; relevance to First Nations perspectives and experience; reciprocity of relationships; and responsibility through participation) provide an important guide for individual reflections on current practices, whether by students, faculty, staff, or administrators. All are responsible for creating respectful, relevant, and reciprocal engagement in policies, practices, and designs of campus environments. The lessons learned in supporting Indigenous student success are in fact useful lessons in supporting all other students as well. Each new Aboriginal cohort deserves a warm welcome to campus as it brings unique gifts absent from the current system, and in doing so enriches and enhances the experiences of all engaged in the academy.

4

Serving Black Students

SUSAN McINTYRE AND BARB HAMILTON-HINCH

DeCosta, a recipient of an entrance scholarship, arrived at university the first day eager to start the next stage of his education and excited about the possibilities a degree would create for him and his community. He had the opportunity to visit the campus many times prior with his schoolmates, but never on his own. He aspired to complete an undergraduate degree, the first to do so in his family, and then pursue law school. He often dreamt about what this experience might be like, imagining himself walking across the stage at convocation someday with the pride of his family in attendance. However, DeCosta's first week of classes did not go as well as expected; he felt almost immediately that he was in over his head. The classes were large, with few students of African descent, and the requirements for reading and writing were overwhelming to him. At times he felt invisible as well. During one of his classes he met the only other Black student in the program – Simon, a returning student. Simon noticed how disengaged DeCosta appeared and so invited him to stop by the Black Student Advising Centre on campus. DeCosta had never heard of this centre and was concerned that it even needed to exist at a university. Simon explained that the centre was instigated several years ago by a group of like-minded Black students who shared a common alienation and desired to support one another in their campus experience. Simon's detailing of his own challenges in coming to university the year before rang true for DeCosta. He noted the date of the upcoming orientation and social and decided to attend. So it was not long after this introduction that DeCosta sensed he had found in the centre a home away from home. It was there, between classes, where he could catch-up with other Black students to share their experiences and strengthen their sense of connection. For the first time he also befriended at the centre a number of other Black students of varying ancestries. The Black Student Advising Centre also became a place where DeCosta and other Black students on campus could meet with an advisor, especially when they felt uncertain or became overwhelmed. Having access to this kind of support and community over time, DeCosta began to enjoy his university experience and his program of study. Following Simon's lead, he eventually became a regular volunteer at the centre, being a witness for other Black students to the welcome, support, and understanding he received in this place on campus like no other.

INTRODUCTION

Only three things are known about the two students in the above vignette: both are male; both are Black; and while one seems to have adjusted to university, the other one is struggling to do so. Although only alluded to, the most immediate source of concern for the one seems to be a feeling of disconnection and isolation, seeing very few other students who appear to share his heritage. Knowing that, however, only confirms the most basic distinction of a racialized difference – being Black. What is not known though is how that identity is situated within a myriad of social, historical, and ethnic contexts. Are either of these students of African descent, perhaps from recent immigrant families to Canada, or international students seeking new opportunities in a host country? Is one of them from a Caribbean island where a colonial legacy has shaped his sense of place and culture? Is one among the Black Nova Scotians whose heritage of slavery and oppression motivates him to succeed in what may be expected to be an uphill struggle? Is either of these from a family of Blacks rooted for generations in French-Canadian society, but reclaiming new connections to an African past? Finally, could one of these Black students be African-American, whose history of racism and discrimination predisposes him to expect similar treatment until proven otherwise? None of the above can be discerned without further engagement and interaction, but all of these possibilities present themselves within a racialized context of being Black.

Racial visibility, in this case Black, identifies increasing numbers of students in Canadian post-secondary education, whose backgrounds span a full range of contexts and characteristics. To assume that all are alike, due to visible similarity, would do injustice to each (Dei et al. 1995; Dei and Johal 2005). To conclude that none are alike, though, would be equally egregious, inasmuch as the effects of marginal status, as the above vignette illustrates, are consistent and undeniable. Most importantly, how being Black manifests among individuals or groups of students is a matter of self-perception, as one recent study concluded (Atkins 2012). Nevertheless, recruitment brochures often tantalize students with promises of a welcoming community, with faces appearing to represent a diverse student population and a campus environment that presumably values, respects, and nurtures cultural differences. However, many students arriving on campus discover that quite the opposite is true. For some, the experience is one of feeling lonely, isolated, unappreciated, and out of place, simply because of who they are. Furthermore, recent assessments have documented increasing incidences of racism (Canadian Federation of Students 2011; Chiang 2010; Crosby 2010; Queen's News Centre 2010; Ravensbergen 2010) on Canadian campuses, suggesting that Black students, regardless of background, may be at higher risk for negative or hostile experiences as members of a racial minority.

While the number of racially visible and ethnically diverse students has increased in Canadian post-secondary institutions, over the last two decades, overall enrolments remain mostly White. Consequently underrepresented students on campus don't always feel like they belong and neither do they have networks sufficient to underpin and support their participation in the post-secondary experience. Data on such questions are very limited in the Canadian higher education literature and are confined to a few recent select thesis projects (e.g., Atkins 2012; Paul 2012). Nevertheless, universities and colleges must adopt a more inclusive perspective in planning, policy, and practice, because the world is evolving rapidly into a multicultural and multi-ethnic society. Attending to the retention of an increasingly diverse student population on campus, especially among Black students, and the creation of communities of support are of urgent concern within student services today. This chapter considers the experiences of

Black students, the transitional issues and challenges they bring to campus, and some of the strategies employed in Canadian post-secondary institutions to meet those needs.

The potential distinctions among Black students highlighted above are necessary ones in engaging them on campus. While they may share a common racialized experience, they also bring unique heritages to the process of pursuing higher learning. For students of African descent the legacy of colonization and deep appreciation for the transcontinental history they represent may result in certain value commitments and traditions that are at odds with the dominant White, Western culture they encounter in our institutions. For students of Caribbean descent, being labelled Black as they enter university may be a first-time experience (Salutin 2008), while at the same time trappings of a Commonwealth education they encounter may appear quite familiar to them. Regardless, the impact of personal history, culture, norms, and socialization processes influence how people define, express, or explain perspectives on various issues and experiences; different cultures see the world in different ways (Lalljee 1981). Thus it is to be anticipated that the respective varying experiences of Black students will necessarily challenge the role of student services, and knowledge of their development of ethnic and racial identity (Evans, Forney, and Guido-DiBrito 1998; Evans, et al. 2010) becomes paramount in understanding how these students in general experience and cope with the post-secondary environment. In addition, it must be recognized that each student is also shaped by his or her unique circumstances.

In the following sections we survey some of the programs and practices used in Canadian post-secondary to address the needs of Black students on campus and we examine in greater depth through one exemplary model how an institution created intentional opportunities for students of African descent, in this case, to shape the design and delivery of student services for themselves. As will be explained, the key to that successful initiative is found in the collaborative ownership and responsibility of both student services professionals and the students being served.

A CANADIAN MULTICULTURAL SOCIETY

Canada's society is comprised of many ethnic roots; one very significant group includes persons of African ancestry, however that may be defined. There are many differences, too often overlooked, that are essential in gaining an understanding of the students who originate in the Black communities we serve. For example, people of African descent might also be Caribbean, American, Canadian, or African. Persons of colour in the multicultural Canadian context might also be relatively new immigrants, on the one hand, or individuals who have lived in the country for several generations. The historical Black population in Canada dates to the early seventeenth century. However, this term is also used to describe more recent people of African descent (e.g., African Nova Scotians). In addition, usage of the term "Black" has continued through the identification of a number of organizations in Nova Scotia, for example the Black Educators Association and the Dalhousie University Black Student Advising Centre. During the 1980s and 1990s African Nova Scotians came to be included as "persons of colour." However, this description includes other ethnic groups and is not exclusive to Black people. Some recent researchers also use the term "people of African descent." Perhaps the lessons learned in delving into this topic is that the naming of peoples is best left to those who subscribe to them, and effective student services depend on meeting students where they are, including how they choose to identify themselves. Rather than assuming, if an approach is to succeed, asking students to name and describe their own experiences and expectations is a fundamental first step.

The cohesion among persons of African descent is fluid at times, but solidifies more so over issues of oppression and racism. As services are developed and expanded for such students, it is important to acknowledge this cycle of fluidity and convergence from time to time. Many of the challenges encountered on campus are shaped by the solidarity of the diverse community of students of African descent on such concerns. The need for services to support students from those underrepresented communities is well documented. The Canadian Race Relations Foundation (2000) identified racism as a major barrier to educational success for racial minorities. There are, of course, many factors that contribute to the success of these students. However it has been found that exposure to racism significantly affects their health and well-being (Thomas Bernard 2004) and has a negative impact on their ability to succeed.

In the last two decades various collaborative initiatives have emerged and a number of Canadian institutions have created strategies to focus on the needs of the range of Black students who enroll in post-secondary education. For example, in Ontario, PRIDE *News* magazine offers a weekly digest of items relative to business, current events, public opinions, lifestyles, and sports and entertainment targeting the African and Caribbean Canadian communities. They also teamed up with the African Canadian Legal Clinic, Midaynta Community Services, the Coalition of Black Trade Unionists, the Ontario Federation of Labour, and the Canadian Labour Congress to promote the second African Canadian Summit, addressing the theme "Critical Crossroad and the Crisis in the African Canadian Community" (Armstrong 2015). Such initiatives have grown in concert with a range of campus-based steps that have served to advocate for students of various Black heritages. For example, at York University, the Centre for the Study of Black Cultures in Canada "endeavours to serve as a stimulus to and focal point for faculty, graduate and undergraduate students, as well as independent scholars who are pursuing research in African Canadian Studies at York and elsewhere" (http://www.yorku.ca/aconline/about.html). Numerous campuses have also supported the establishment of student advocacy groups, such as the Black Law Students Association and the African Students Association at the University of Toronto, the Black Students' Alliance at U of T Scarborough, and the Black Students' Network at McGill University. Similarly targeted groups have found organizational space at McMaster University, the University of Alberta, Concordia University, and the University of Waterloo. More focused groups have reached out to students of Caribbean descent, for example, at Concordia University, as well as through various non-profit organizations such as the African and Caribbean Heritage Students' Association (ACHSA) and the Jamaican Canadian Association (JCA). More direct student services have been channelled, for example, through the Black Canadian Scholarship Fund (BCSF), which offers scholarships and bursaries to support post-secondary opportunities for students so identified, and a number of institutions have framed a full range of educational and engagement opportunities to address campus issues of race and ethnicity, such as can be found on the Student Services website at the University of British Columbia (http://students.ubc.ca/campus/diversity/race). Finally, among other initiatives have also been those institutions that have established centres of integrated services for students from underrepresented racial and ethnic backgrounds, such as the one at Dalhousie University, to which we now turn our attention. The details of this initiative are offered, not only as one example for others to emulate, but also as an opportunity here to appreciate in greater depth the history and dynamics of how one institution sought to collaborate with students on the design and implementation of a culturally responsive facility on campus that addresses sensitively the needs of students who use it. While the experiences of other institutions noted above are worthy of consulting for ideas and approaches, the history of this one institution is perhaps indicative of what others might expect who are seeking potential guidelines for launching similar efforts. As with any unique case study, though, its ultimate transferability necessarily lies in the details articulated and adapted to each institution's context; generalizability is not presumed.

THE EXPERIENCE OF DALHOUSIE UNIVERSITY

The Black Student Advising Centre opened its doors at Dalhousie University in 1990, concurrent with the appointment of the first Black student advisor. This event followed a period of much discourse on Nova Scotian multiculturalism, a new force that would impact both academic and administrative policies and procedures in its post-secondary system. One of the legacies of multiculturalism then was the presumed understanding that each piece in the multicultural mosaic needed to be separately accommodated. This was a politically complex moment as many forces converged at the same time.

The political climate for investing in issues of this kind had long been established at Dalhousie by a series of task forces, academic studies, and numerous discussions at the University Senate and in student government. For example, in 1970, the university began the Transition Year Program (TYP) to redress historical educational disadvantages for the Mi'kmaq and Black Nova Scotian communities. It began as a one-year program for Black Nova Scotians and First Nations students who wished to enter university, but who did not yet meet standard entrance requirements. Over the last forty years a large cohort of Black and First Nations students have come through the TYP and gone on to take other degrees; many have made significant contributions at Dalhousie University, in their communities, and beyond. Following TYP, programs to encourage greater participation by Black Nova Scotian communities continued to expand at Dalhousie – in the areas of Social Work, the Sciences, Law and, more recently, in Dentistry and Medicine, and the nine Schools of Health

Professions. Academic staff and administrators were convinced of the requirement for resources to be allocated for enhanced accessibility. However, students struggled to convince the university that more was needed. In the end it was the strength of a growing Black community on campus, along with support from the University Task Force on Access for Black and Native Students (*Breaking Barriers* 1989) that brought pressure to bear on finding additional resources for a new service.

The service's mandate – to promote an awareness of the need for increased access and greater retention of historical Black students – was developed and clearly articulated by students and shaped by their experiences and knowledge. The Centre was a culmination of the *Breaking Barriers* report (Dalhousie University Presidential Task Force 1989), resulting in an important lesson about "the value, indeed the necessity, of consulting with the affected minority communities in designing and operating access programs" (152). Even professionals – and perhaps because they are professionals – overlook this important insight or believe they know what is best; at times they don't want to lose control or feel responsible and so on. However, the more students are engaged in the academic and social environment, the more likely they are to succeed (Kuh 2005). Research supports the idea that two factors are critical in engaging students:

> The first [factor] is student driven: The amount of time and effort
> students put into their studies and other educationally purposeful
> activities. The second is institution driven: how a school deploys
> its resources and organizes the curriculum, other learning oppor-
> tunities, and support services to induce students to participate
> in activities that lead to the experience and outcomes that
> constitute student success (persistence, satisfaction, learning,
> graduation) (Kuh 2005).

In turn, students' ability to participate is influenced by a number of other factors, including culture, race, socio-economic background, the environment, and more.

Related to this observation, one point warrants emphasis: the experiences of students of African descent do differ from other students; race and a cultural background that places a premium on family, community, and church set them apart in a predominantly White post-secondary institution. Such an institution does not automatically reflect or demonstratively appreciate students of African descent (Pounds 1989). Furthermore, these newcomers to the academy inevitably experience racism, as noted above – sometimes blatant and hard, other times subtle and inadvertent – but always sharpening their sensitivity to who they are and how they differ from the majority. The varying experiences of students of African descent, in this case, inform the way we develop and deliver programs and services.

Historically there have been significant tensions between recent immigrants and those with long-established histories in Canada. Acknowledging this dynamic becomes important in understanding how better to serve students with such varied backgrounds on our campuses. Persons of African descent in Nova Scotia reflect all those diverse communities: Caribbean, American, Canadian, and African. Achieving any sense of cohesion among them was complicated by the many waves of immigrants who had to learn to accommodate each other before they could challenge the dominant White population. Canada has persons of African descent who can trace their ancestry back more than 400 years. Some of their cultural beliefs provide a sense of continuity with their ethnic roots and identity, while others act as a barrier to full participation in Canadian society (Tirone, Caldwell, and Riddick 1992).

The early activities of people of African descent saw the church at the heart of numerous activities. Many African Nova Scotian families consequently were deeply rooted in the institution of the church. The strong belief that a family that prayed together, stayed together, was embedded in many African families (Paris 1993), and participation in church services and related activities were important ways for many of them to find release. Thus the church acted as a community centre, as well as a place of worship. Without its strong influence and support, the Loyalists, Maroons, Refugees, and Caribbean immigrants who eventually settled in Nova Scotia and Canada would not have been able to establish a focus for their community nor a place to express themselves. Overall, religion played a significant role in the African North American community (Boyd-Franklin 2003) and filled an important educational/cultural niche.

The church also became the driving force of community strength, and it instilled in African Nova Scotians a sense of pride, dignity, and hope. Regardless of the discrimination and exclusion they encountered in the larger community, the church was always able to provide a sense of acceptance. By working, sharing, and supporting each other they were able to abate some of the feelings of isolation so many experienced. While activities, such as sports, dancing, playing cards and other games dominated non-church organizations, singing and dramatics were the principal forms of amusement in church activities. In addition, participation in volunteer organizations also served to reduce such stress among people of African descent.

In Nova Scotia numerous barriers threatened the integration of people of African descent; most of the forty-eight Black communities were and continue to be located outside the societal mainstream, often removed from the metropolitan area. This added to the difficulties for people of African descent to access basic services such as opportunities for post-secondary education.

African cultures and value systems were also marginalized by a North American society that had enslaved African peoples in the past. Thus, "denying people the right to practice and maintain aspects of their culture [forces] them to develop other means of socialization and ways in which to continue to exist as a unique population within the larger societal value system" (Simms 1993, 6). The marginality hypothesis (Floyd, et al. 1994) emphasizes minority status as a causal factor in explaining "under-participation" among Black minorities and concludes that under-representation is related to limited economic resources that in turn are the result of historical patterns of discrimination (Floyd, et al. 1994; Washburne 1978). Thus, ethnic and racial differences in norms, values, expectations, and socialization patterns contribute to differences in participation or inter-group variations, and cultural processes seem to be important in explaining such variation (Edwards 1981; Floyd et al. 1994; O'Leary and Benjamin 1982; Stamps and Stamps 1985; Washburne 1978;) beyond socio-economic standing.

The legacy of this dynamic is that people of African descent have been excluded from many aspects of North American culture. According to Black feminist theory, seeing race, gender, and class as interlocking systems of oppression enables one to re-conceptualize the way in which domination and resistance are experienced in social relations. Such a perspective moves beyond simply giving oppressed groups new interpretations of their experiences, to revealing new ways of knowing and thereby empowering them to define their own reality (Collins-Hill 1990, 221). A case in point is found in the structures of some families of African descent that evolved out of a context of slavery, when members were separated and children sold from birth. Family structures and sense of home place were not always developed along bloodlines, but rather by location, most notably vis-à-vis the plantation. Thus, no matter who occupied it, they were all relatives or parts of one's family. The bonds of family were exceptionally strong and the concept of extended membership was quite prevalent in the African Nova Scotian communities. It didn't matter if one was related to another (that is, cousin, brother, friend, neighbour), but rather how one met each others' needs (Pachai 1987). The traditional African proverb, "It takes a community [village] to raise a child," is an apt claim for many African Nova Scotians, suggesting that their high degree of trust made for a very caring, loving community. Consequently, much of the energy of African families is put into community development and networking (Pachai 1987).

This analysis of people of African descent takes on an even more explicit meaning when giving consideration to what has been identified as the Afrocentric value system. Defined by Asante (1988) as the belief in the centrality of Africans in postmodern history, Afrocentricity places people of African descent at the centre of social and historical experiences, rather than peripheral to European ones (Thomas Bernard 1996). Asante (1988) stated that such a value system helps to change the way African peoples refer to themselves, their experiences in the present, as well as their past. Articulated in a framework, so called *Nguzo Saba*, Karenga and Karenga (2007) identified a set of seven Afrocentric values designed to: help African people work together; respect themselves and each other; and promote and celebrate their collective history, identity, and struggle. These principles are promoted by people of African descent primarily through *Kwanzaa*, an annual event (December 26 to January 1) first celebrated by African Americans and now by others in the Diaspora. These values also inform the operations of the Dalhousie Black Student Advising Centre. The following illustrate how these values help shape and direct many of the centre's student-focused activities and programs.

The first of these values is *Umoja* (unity) or striving for unity in the family, community, nation, and race. Within the Black Student Advising Centre at Dalhousie many students come from far away, often leaving loved ones (i.e., friends, partners, parents, and even children) at home. At the Centre they can readily discover a surrogate family, sometimes connecting with students who may be in the same program or classes, those who may be from the same country, community or town as theirs, or students who share similar life experiences, that is, being mature students with a family. The number of commonalties and connections made at the Centre are endless, and many of these connections last a lifetime. Regardless of where these students originate or their personal experiences, they know they have made it this far through the support of others and are, in turn, willing to help out and give back to the larger African Nova Scotian community.

One of the ways students give back is through participation in a Science Enrichment Program – Imhotep's Legacy Academy (ILA). This program was developed in partnership with the Physics Department under the direction of Dr Kevin Hewitt, an African-Caribbean professor at Dalhousie University, Mr Wayne Hamilton, the Chief Executive Officer for the Office of African Nova Scotia Affairs, and Dr Barb Hamilton-Hinch, assistant professor in the School of Health and Human Performance and a former Black student advisor at the onset of ILA. The Black Student Advising Centre recruits students of African descent who are studying Sciences and are willing to give back to the community. Historically many students of African Nova Scotian descent have not pursued professions in the sciences. In 2013 the historical African Nova Scotian community had not yet reached the target of twenty Engineering-graduated students from the former Technical University of Nova Scotia (now part of Dalhousie University), nor reached ten graduated students in Medicine, nor ten graduated students in Dentistry. With the implementation of Imhotep's Legacy Academy students of African descent are introduced to the importance and fun of the sciences in Junior High, in hopes of helping them realize that they can achieve success in such programs.

Students from the Centre are also involved in providing mentorship for students of African descent in the local high schools, through pairing with students in a discipline of their interest. As they develop relationships in the course of the year, these high school students are encouraged to visit the campus, attend classes with their mentors, and generate ideas about what university life might be like when they opt to enroll. Mentors also assist students in preparing their university applications, when necessary, and help complete any bursary or award applications. This program has been very successful in increasing the number of students of African descent on campus.

Another program that has experienced success since its inception is called Opportunities for Students of African Descent in Engineering. Previous surveys found that most students were unaware of the many facets of engineering and the opportunities available to them should they choose this profession. The Black Student Advising Centre, in collaboration with a number of academic departments, now provides personal tours of the Engineering department, informs students of the various financial supports available, and pairs with a mentor throughout the program each one who selects Engineering. In its first two years this program generated a rapid increase in the number of students interested and enrolling in this field. In 2005 five students of African descent enrolled in Engineering and in 2010 the university graduated its second African Nova Scotia-born female Engineer. The impact of *Umoja* is clearly adding value to the work of the Black Student Advising Centre.

The second principle, *Kujichaguila* (self-determination), emphasizes the need for people of African descent to define, name, create, and speak for themselves; indeed the Black Student Advising Centre initiative was launched on this principle. As one of the present writers and onetime member of the executive that advocated and presented at the conference Breaking Barriers and Access for Blacks and Mi'kmaq at University, my experiences then were like those of other students in the 1980s who were determined to carve out a space for themselves on campus and informed the university as to why this was necessary. Many students of African descent then in Nova Scotia had participated previously in a strong youth group called Cultural Awareness Youth Group (CAYG) of Nova Scotia, founded by Mr David Woods in 1983. This organization encouraged a strong sense of pride among students as people of African descent, taught them about their culture, which was absent in the school system, taught them how to debate and articulate their interest and their needs, and taught them how to advocate for their rights. Many of these same skills gained in CAYG primed students at the university for tasks involved in developing the Black Student Advising Centre. Students engaged in every significant aspect of the centre, including selection of its first and subsequent advisors. *Kujichaguila* ensured a level of participation that contributed to the positive outcomes of the Centre, as well as the means to achieve them.

Ujima (collective work and responsibility), the third principle, calls on members to build and maintain community together, to make the problems of others one's own, and to solve them together. Many of the aspects touched on above are also relevant here; however, the *Ujima* principle includes other aspects as well. For example, many students of African descent, while not financially secure themselves, are anxious to help out others in need. From 2002 to 2008 the Black Student Advising Centre solicited money, from September to December, to support a family in need or donate to the Akoma Family Centre, formerly known as the Home for Colored Children Annual Broadcast for Funds; at one time an orphanage, this facility now assists troubled youth of all races. The Black Student Advising Centre also established a food bank for needy students; it continues free and accessible to all students who wish to use it. Another initiative provides free clothing for students and families by sponsoring a winter coat drive. Many students in the Diaspora might experience winter for the first time while at Dalhousie University and the Black Student Advising Centre is there to help make that experience as comfortable as possible. The end goal of the principle of *Ujima* for the Centre is that students are successful in opportunities to achieve their dreams.

The fourth principle, *Ujamma* (co-operative economics) supports the building and maintenance of Black-owned shops, stores, and businesses, while profiting from them together. Throughout the academic year and especially during African Heritage Month (February) the Black Student Advising Centre strives to promote Black entrepreneurial activities within the community. For example, every Thursday at the Centre students order lunch from a small African Nova Scotian-owned restaurant. This provides the student with an opportunity to enjoy a cultural dish prepared in the community and to contribute financially to that community. Throughout the year the Black Student Advising Centre also reserves the Wall of Nostalgia, a presentation venue in the student union building, created to promote local businesses, display students' art work, and educate the university community on the experiences and contributions of people of African descent. Finally, consistent with the aims of *Ujamma*, the centre has developed a *Black Student Survival Guide* wherein Black-owned businesses and professionals are advertised, along with other services such as local churches, community organizations, and childcare facilities.

Nia (purpose), the fifth principle, seeks to make a collective vocation of the building and development of community in order to restore people of African descent to their traditional status of greatness. For many in the general university community, the Black Student Advising Centre (BSAC) remains the best-kept secret on campus. However, for most students of African descent, and to ensure the growth and development of one another, the B S A C is a familiar place, typically having been led there by another student who had already benefited from the connection. Participants in the B S A C often express how easy it is to just be themselves there, experience a sense of peace, and recoup from the challenges of being at times the only Black student in class or enduring the forms of overt and covert racism encountered among students and professors. For students of African descent who graduate from Dalhousie University, success is understood as a collective product bestowing honour not just on themselves, but on their immediate and extended families as well, including all participants in the B S A C. This principle of *Nia* underscores the conception that the achievement of one is the achievement of all.

The sixth principle, *Kuumaba* (creativity), expects everyone to leave their community more beautiful and beneficial than when they inherited it. Creativity is prized as B S A C students celebrate their history in a special way during Black History Month. Participants have been known to challenge the university community in a public contest-based forum on its knowledge of Black history and culture. Their creativity is showcased further through spoken word, music, dance, and monologues, promoting additional knowledge about the rich experiences of African Nova Scotians. *Kuumaba* serves to both strengthen tradition as well as support innovation.

The seventh principle is *Imani* (faith), the belief in people of African descent, their parents, teachers, and leaders, and the righteousness and victory of their struggles. While convocation is an important recognition for significant numbers of students, some for whatever reason may shy away from the celebration. Encouragement from an advisor can help students appreciate the significance of walking across the platform to accept their degree. The Black Student Advising Centre staff gently encourage students to remember whose shoulders they are standing on, and in doing so they are reminded of the strength of all those who have gone before and who are yet to come. This is not always an easy experience. For example one of the present co-authors of this chapter has participated for many years in Dalhousie's convocations, first as student, then as Black student advisor, and currently as a member of the teaching faculty. As she joins faculty and staff for the procession, she is reminded of just how important her role is, being a person of African descent. Ironically though, each year she is congratulated for successfully completing her degree by individuals who often assume it to be her first convocation. Such an experience perhaps illustrates an insidious form of racism, subtle but very real in its impact. At most convocations the Black Student Advising Centre staff is one of few persons of colour on the platform. In support of *Imani*, it is crucial for people of African descent to witness the accomplishments of these students, as well as for the larger community to see their ability and diversity.

Another example of this principle in action is seen in the BSAC's partnership with Connecting to Africa (CTA), a small NGO in Halifax, which helps to organize every two years learning projects for students and community members to visit a country in Africa. Beginning in 2003 this program has since exposed several dozen individuals to parts of West Africa who would have otherwise never previously considered such a journey. The BSAC is hoping to further develop a student exchange program with a university in Ghana so that students of African descent can also take advantage of study abroad programs by enrolling in universities in countries that are relevant to their culture and heritage. Many students have expressed a stronger sense of self since participating in the learning project, as one commented: "I remember getting off the plane and kissing the ground because I thought never in my life would this happen to me and here I was in Africa. WOW! Programs like this contribute so much to a student's learning and personal development." In the end, participants have reclaimed an appreciation for their cultural roots and the heritage they experienced first-hand during this opportunity.

The *Nguzo Saba* framework of seven values discussed here offers a model of positive aspiration for the community of African descent. As operational guides, they suggest ways Black students can become engaged in the work of their own achievement through collective action. They also serve to strengthen the organizational foundations of the Dalhousie Black Student Advising Centre by encouraging students within a safe space to take responsibility for their own successes at university.

The importance of this type of centre on campus cannot be overstated. Allen (1995) concluded: "Institutions need to provide services and programs that enhance the value of Black students' intellectual, social, cultural, and personal exposures and identify strategies to develop further their unique skills." In effect then, the BSAC serves as a critical "counterspace," "a home away from home, and a haven in a hostile territory" (Patton 2010, xiv), where people who are racially visible gather and feel safe, and are not judged by the colour of their skin or their cultural differences (Howard-Hamilton 2003). Furthermore, it becomes a place where students are able to safely explore issues of race and learn from their peers how to cope with instances of personal and institutional racism (Smith, Altbach, and Lomotey 2002). The Centre supports and helps them to validate who they are and why they attend university. In this context of support students readily draw on various aspects of their identity and student services can play a significant role in shaping that identity as it evolves. Under the guidance of the Black student advisor, they can focus their energies on survival and success. In this space they grow, discover more about the world in which they live, and learn how they impact that world – effecting change in a positive way. However, simply finding spaces for students of African descent on campus will not eliminate barriers to their learning. Programs and services in such spaces must also be designed to assist students in developing the skills to survive independently and successfully on campus and beyond.

CONCLUSION

Creating the Black Student Advising Centre at Dalhousie University involved taking risks – putting our experiences as student services professionals gently behind the students of African descent who were leading the development of a new campus, one that would welcome them, nurture them, give them an opportunity to grow and become leaders in their communities and throughout the world. In our case, the time was right for taking this risk, for letting go of the power that comes with position, and quietly giving students a stronger voice to champion the change needed on the campus that would enable them to succeed.

Today this vibrant Centre provides support for students of African descent. However, a work still in progress, the Centre continues to provide counterspace for students of African descent, but also reaches out in creating communities of support across the campus, acknowledging and celebrating the differences students bring to campus. Today those differences are seen as one of the strengths of the campus. We are helping to create responsible citizens for a diverse world. Services for Black students can provide a lead role in creating an environment on campus that welcomes and nurtures all students – particularly students of African descent. In the words of one student user, "It means having a spot in the school where I can rest assured I am cared for and people are able to relate to me and my issues," and another, "It is a place on campus where you can go to relax and get some advice and support that you can't find any place else on campus." In addition to the availability of safe space, where students can explore their identity, the B S A C is also a place where they celebrate their differences and offer support that comes directly from their understanding of those differences. For example, as one student explained: "During Ramadan, students were not permitted to eat their lunch in the lounge out of respect for the Muslim students, which I am one of. This showed so much respect to me and to my religion." Ultimately, the Black Student Advising Centre has become a community that supports students within a sometimes unknown, not understood, hostile, and harsh environment. Building communities such as this engages students in positive learning – inside and outside the classroom – and fosters their success (Strange and Banning 2015).

In conclusion, lessons learned in this one university's experience in responding to the needs of a particular group of students were both fundamental and institution-shaping. The fact that cultural differences related to race and ethnicity greatly influenced the course of learning for these students during their post-secondary experience was of no surprise to these authors. However, to see these differences acknowledged and implemented over the years into the form and substance of a virtual catalogue of responsive, student-led programs and initiatives was both instructive and inspirational. Meeting students where they are must be the starting point of any initiative intent on engaging and serving students, especially those whose heritage may have placed them out of reach of traditional circles of success. For reasons of equity and cultural diversity, as well as the success of all students in an increasingly multiracial, multicultural, and multiethnic world, this is an area of student services that is ripe for immediate improvement and ultimate advancement.

5

Francophone Student Services

CHANTAL JOY AND LOUISE LEWIN

Catherine is in her last year of high school and needs to make a decision as to which university to attend next year. She wants to major in business economics. Should she go to an Anglophone university, a Francophone one, or a bilingual institution? If she chooses an Anglophone university she is worried that she won't be able to maintain her French language and her culture. So either a Francophone or a bilingual institution might be a better choice for her. But those that offer her program of interest are located far from her hometown and parents, and attending them would drain her financial resources. And she has heard that, although one of those schools offers her program in French, the variety of course options isn't as rich as that offered at the English-speaking university. Where will Catherine decide to go? Marc is excited about his first year of post-secondary, but a little afraid to be in a new environment away from home and all that is familiar to him. He doesn't speak a lot of English and is excited to be attending a college where there is a French community. He had hoped that going through orientation would help him meet other Francophone students and get connected to the community. While the program provided has been a lot of fun so far, it has left him feeling more isolated than he imagined. He is finding that most of the activities and information are in English. Even at the social events, people mostly reverted to speaking English. And the materials he got at academic orienta-tion were also in English. Because he isn't as comfortable with the English language he is not sure he understands all of the information given to him. All this has made him feel a little lonely for home and wondering whether he made the right choice.

INTRODUCTION

Canada is a country with two official languages – French and English. The Official Languages Act in Canada states that French and English "are the official languages of Canada and have equality of status and equal rights and privileges as to their use in all institutions of the parliament and government of Canada" (Department of Justice 1985, 1). While both languages may have equal legal status in our country, in reality Francophones constitute a minority group in Canada and English is the dominant tongue. From one province to another, though, the landscape is more complex. For example, the province of Quebec is home to a Francophone majority and there French is the dominant language, although some would say that this is a relatively recent phenomenon and the product of some very intentional language preservation efforts. However, across other provinces Francophones are a linguistic minority, although there are a few stronghold communities where there exists a critical mass of French speaking people.

In regards to the application of the Official Languages Act beyond federal institutions, the Act itself stipulates that "the Government of Canada is committed to cooperating with governments and their institutions to support the development of English and French linguistic minority communities, to provide services in both English and French to respect the constitutional guarantees of minority language educational rights and to enhance opportunities for all to learn both English and French" (Department of Justice 1985, 2). What binding obligations this imposes on provincial governments and their institutions is a debate that continues even today. In education, being under a provincial jurisdiction yet the benefactor of Federal funding and a constitutional guarantee, the language debate is a very salient issue for practitioners. Yet how many, especially those in Anglophone institutions, address Francophone students as a distinct and unique population and provide services and supports reflective of their needs as a linguistic minority? And how is access defined? Such questions bear import for preservation of Canadian language communities where, for Francophones in particular, "ensuring inter-generational language and identity transmission" is a much greater challenge than for Anglophones (Pilote and Magnan 2008). Furthermore, as another study at the University of Ottawa suggests (Gingras 2005), "the sense of belonging to a linguistic community [is] more important for Francophone students than their Anglophone peers" (140).

What obligations then do provincial governments have in all this, and by extension institutions of post-secondary education, to ensure full access to French-language education? One recent study in Ontario (Lennon, Zhao, Wang, and Gluszynski 2011) found that uneven results persist, in that "a significantly higher proportion of Francophones pursued non-university postsecondary education (45 per cent compared to 37 per cent). Anglophone students were more likely to attend university: 50 per cent of them, as opposed to 40 per cent of Francophone students, chose this path" (9). A broader sampling (Labrie, Lamoureux, and Wilson 2009) reported that such opportunities are uneven at best across Canada, where for Francophone students,

> both distance and language combine to create barriers to PSE. While there are English-language universities in all Canadian provinces, there are far fewer French-language universities outside Quebec. The Association des universités de la francophonie canadienne (AUFC) represents 13 Francophone or bilingual universities in six Canadian provinces: New Brunswick, Nova Scotia, Ontario, Manitoba, Saskatchewan and Alberta. The situation is similar for colleges. Francophone communities in a minority setting have access to accredited colleges providing French education in only four provinces: New Brunswick, Ontario, Manitoba and Nova Scotia.

Finally, the implications of this analysis become clearer, as Landry (2014) argues that, "in a 'knowledge-based society' it is critical ... to ensure that all linguistic groups can contribute to the development of the country's economic prospects, while at the same time contributing to their respective linguistic community's development."

True educational equality means equal access to all types of programs, in various geographically convenient regions, and a full course of studies in French, from year one to completion, with a full offering of course options. The 2006 *Survey of the Vitality of Official Language Minorities* (Statistics Canada 2006) yielded data relative to such a goal, indicating that 43 per cent of Francophone students outside

Quebec attended university entirely in French in Ontario, in comparison to 80.2 per cent in New Brunswick, and 30.7 per cent on average in other provinces and territories. Furthermore, the data also revealed that Francophones in New Brunswick (19 per cent) and Ontario (20.3 per cent) are less likely than those in the other provinces and territories (28.4 per cent) to have completed a university program (with a certificate or diploma). It is not readily apparent from the data why this is so, but further research is warranted. Nevertheless it is imperative that provincial governments assume leadership in addressing these inequities, as for example in Ontario, where issues of access to higher education for Francophones have become key priorities of the government, with an associate deputy minister specifically appointed the responsibility of French language post-secondary education. The recent publication of a plan for development of French language post-secondary education in Ontario – "Direction des politiques et programme d'éducation en langue Française" (Théberge 2010, 2) is indicative of this kind of dedicated effort.

A conversation about access is not complete without talking about the experiences of those students once they are within the walls of our institutions (Dietsche 2010; Tinto 2005, 4). True access is also about equality of opportunity once through the front doors and equal chances at persisting to graduation. This of course implicates not just academe but student affairs and services as well. From the literature it is clear that students' ability to perform well academically and to persist to graduation is influenced by many factors, including many which bear directly on the work done in Student Services: academic advising, learning support, experiential education, orientation and transition support, and community connections (Dietsche 2000; Tinto 2005). Simply admitting students does not in and of itself guarantee equality of access. Institutions of higher education, and in particular student services staff, play a pivotal role in providing the conditions for success for all students including Francophones.

It is important that student affairs and services professionals in Canada engage in dialogue about the unique experiences of linguistic minority Francophone students in Canadian post-secondary institutions and reflect on their responsibilities to provide targeted supports that will ensure these students' persistence and success. This chapter is an effort to contribute to this dialogue, one that is virtually absent from our professional body of literature and the available research (Télévision Francophone en Ontario, Panorama – studio – Raymond

Théberge). We will discuss the diversity of this cohort, the pluralities inherent in the Canadian Francophone experience, and the complexities this gives rise to in offering a standard of practice for Canadian student affairs and services professionals. We are acutely aware of the irony of offering such a report and analysis in *l'anglais plutôt que le français*, given the focus being Francophone students and the inequity and marginalization of the French language. However we recognize the power of this platform and the importance of extending this dialogue beyond the borders of the Francophone community. With all that in mind, we explore the issues of significance to this cohort and, focusing on the Ontario context as a case in point, detail strategies available to student affairs and services professionals for responding to this cohort's needs in a meaningful way. We will comment on the applicability of our recommendations and observations to a broader context and discuss key issues that demand further inquiry and consideration.

FRANCOPHONE STUDENTS IN CANADIAN POST-SECONDARY EDUCATION

While Francophones are present in all Canadian provinces, their distribution is expectedly skewed, with the bulk of them in Quebec (84 per cent or 5,916,814), followed by Ontario (7 per cent or 510,240) and New Brunswick (3 per cent or 235,270). The smallest populations are found in Nunavut (390), Northwest Territories (1,000), and the Yukon (1,165). Other provinces with significant populations include Alberta (64,750), British Columbia (58,890), Manitoba (45,520), and Nova Scotia (33,705). Canadian Education Association data (2011) indicate that some eighty-eight Francophone school boards are distributed across nine provinces and one territory (i.e., Yukon). Sixty of these boards are located in Quebec, with twelve in Ontario; the remaining sixteen serve across the other eight provinces and one territory; no such boards exist in Northwest Territories or Nunavut. These boards collectively serve a total of approximately 7,000,000 so identified French-speaking people. Thus, very different circumstances establish varying contexts across the Canadian education landscape, setting the stage for highly variant experiences from one province to another.

Despite such differences, the number of French high school graduates wanting to pursue post-secondary studies continues to be on the rise. At a recent symposium on post-secondary access for Francophones in Ontario, the University of Ottawa reported seeing a 41 per cent increase in the enrolment of Francophones at the institution since 2000 (Houle 2010). According to research on access of Francophone students pursuing post-secondary studies in Ontario (Labrie, Lamoureux, and Wilson 2009), 20 per cent attended Francophone and bilingual universities and 36 per cent attended Francophone colleges (Labrie and Lamoureux 2010, 10). The debate persists as to whether Francophone students have choices comparable to those available to Anglophones. According to Ontario's associate deputy minister, they do not; only 22 per cent of first-year university programs in the province are offered in French (Théberge 2010, 7). Access to French-language education continues to be hindered by factors such as distance, financial barriers, and availability of programs (Labrie, Lamoureux, and Wilson 2009, 34). Access for Francophone students is one of the four key objectives of the Ontario Ministry of Training, Colleges and Universities (Théberge 2010, 2–3). While these expressed aims are affirming, a number of unique barriers continue to challenge Francophone students within our post-secondary institutions.

First is the failure to recognize the diversity of faces of Francophone post-secondary students in Canada. They may be Canadian-born, immigrant, or international and visiting students (Télévision Francophone en Ontario, Panorama – studio – Raymond Théberge). Diversity in place of origin also means, for example, diversity in mother tongue, dialect spoken, culture, educational preparation, and socio-economic status. For some, French may be their exclusive language; for others a primary language but neither exclusive nor their language of origin; and even for some a language that is spoken only in a select context (e.g., school or home). French may be their mother tongue or they may have learned it as a second language, but it is the primary language they speak. Many immigrants are not cultural Francophones but have learned French in their country as a first language. The Maghreb is a good example of this, as are Lebanon and Romania. There are a variety of ways someone may come to identify as Francophone; the definition is not absolute. For immigrants, this is further complicated as they interact with regional French cultures. Add to this the cultural differences arising from place of origin, including the geographical and regional differences that exist among Canadian Francophones, and the complexities of identity are amplified.

The institutions themselves, their structure and the communities within which these students are studying add further layers to a dialogue about how to serve the unique needs of minority-language Francophone students in post-secondary education. The experience of a Francophone student will vary based on whether they are attending a Francophone institution, a bilingual institution or an Anglophone institution, and their experience will be further impacted by the geographical location of that institution. For instance, issues faced by a Francophone student at an institution in Quebec will vary greatly from those encountered if they attend one in Ontario or in New Brunswick or Alberta. In fact, the experience may vary even within a single province. As further illustration, the experience of attending an institution on the Ontario-Quebec border will be very different from what one would have in attending a school in Toronto or in Northern Ontario.

The offerings of programs and services, the challenges, the opportunities, and the particularities of each community are simply too complex to address in a single chapter. That isn't to say there are no common denominators, because indeed there are. But clearly to speak of only the common denominators would mask the very real complexities inherent in serving this student population and the sensitivities required to do so effectively. The present authors acknowledge the difficulties in doing justice to this subject in a single chapter or generalizing to a single set of circumstances on a national level. Consequently the authors have instead opted to focus on the context most familiar to them, in Ontario, and to use it as a potential basis for discussion about Francophone experiences across Canada. Readers from other regions of Canada should observe caution in verifying the relevance of our digest for their own situations, prior to establishing precedent policies and practices.

SUPPORTS FOR FRANCOPHONE STUDENTS

In this section, we turn our attention to the historical developments that have shaped the post-secondary education options available in Ontario to Francophone students and reflect on the unique needs of Francophone students at Ontario universities and colleges. Taking a look at three different types of institutions, an Anglophone institution, a bilingual institution, and a Francophone institution, we will explore the challenges facing Francophone students as they pursue studies in those institutions and discuss the implications for student affairs and services staff. The authors will conclude with a discussion on how lessons learned in Ontario might inform a dialogue for student affairs and services professionals working with Francophone students across the country and the implications for further research.

Focus on Ontario

In order to understand the experience of Francophone students in institutions of higher education in Ontario, it is necessary to consider the broader historical and sociological context of French language existence in this province. As the original seat of British rule in Canada, Ontario has historically been dominated by the English language. English continues to be the dominant language in this province and as such, Francophones are a minority; yet the French language has a substantial foothold in this province. Francophone Ontarians make up 4.8 per cent of the total population of Ontario (Office of Francophone Affairs, Portrait of the Francophone community in Ontario). Its geographical landscape is dotted by a number of distinct Francophone regions and communities (Office of Francophone Affairs, Francophone population in Ontario), with the East hosting the largest number (242,055/41.5 per cent), followed by the Central (167,235/ 28.7 per cent), North East (130,820/22.5 per cent), South-West (34,395/5.9 per cent), and North-West (8,190/1.4 per cent) regions (Statistics Canada 2006).

Francophone Ontarians are an increasingly diverse group. The Ontario Trillium Foundation describes this cohort stating, "vibrant, complex and changing, this community in Ontario is comprised of Francophones born in Ontario, other parts of Canada, and increasingly, around the world. While they all share French as a common language, each group contributes to the unique heritage, cultural practices and settlement history of the Province of Ontario" (Association Française des Municipalités de l'Ontario. Profile of the Francophone Communities – Trillium 2009).

The increasingly diverse city of Toronto itself is home to a growing immigrant Francophone community (Farmer 2001). In an article written in 1995, François Paré refers to this community as "une nouvelle élite multiculturelle francophone" – a new multicultural elite – that according to him appeared suddenly beginning in 1985 (Paré 1995, 174). Ontario is also home to our nation's capital city, and that inevitably gives French as an equal language a strong foothold in this province. Its shared border with Quebec means that Ontario's language landscape is inevitably influenced by that proximity.

Francophone education has a long history in Ontario (Sylvestre 2010); in fact, Canada's very first French school was established there in 1786 at l'Assomption du Détroit (Sylvestre 2010, 132). However, in 1912, French education was eliminated and it took fifteen years of battles to bring back French schools. By 1968, one year before the Federal Official Languages Act was passed, the Ontario Government adopted legislation that paved the way for the creation of French elementary public schools in this Province (Labrie 1995). What followed was the emergence of a French secondary school system that, of course, necessitated the creation of French-language options at the post-secondary level. Ontario is home to more than four hundred and twenty-five public and Catholic primary and secondary schools, eleven colleges and post-secondary institutions that offer a French language experience to their students.

It is important to distinguish between the post-secondary French-language instruction options available to students attending Anglophone institutions and the options provided by either a Francophone or a bilingual institution. Francophone and bilingual institutions aim to provide their students with options to study a variety of subjects in French and to experience campus life in French. This is not to diminish the contributions to French language education that may be made at many of Ontario's Anglophone institutions, but it is important to identify those institutions expressly created to respond to the educational needs of Francophone and bilingual citizens.

Students in Ontario thus have a number of in-province choices when they complete high school. They can decide to enroll in an all-English institution, an all-French institution, or a bilingual institution. Their choices are somewhat limited by the subject they wish to study. While there are over two hundred and fifty programs of study offered at Ontario's Francophone and bilingual post-secondary institutions (Ontario Ministry of Training, Colleges and Universities, French language and bilingual colleges and universities), there are still some programs of study that are only available in English. In some cases, students' choices may be further complicated by the fact that their program of choice may only be offered in French at an institution outside of their geographical area, thereby necessitating a significant relocation. For example, Toronto students who wish to pursue studies in the sciences in French must go to University of Ottawa or Laurentian University, or do their studies at an English institution. The same applies for community colleges. Collège Boréal offers only eleven programs at its Toronto campus (Collège Boréal, full-time studies). A student wishing to complete any of the other programs offered by that institution would have to relocate in order to attend one of their six other campuses.

Francophone students make choices that will affect not only their educational and career direction but also the retention of their heritage and their language, and in the end, the bilingual and bicultural fabric of Canadian society. These choices then impact their expectations coming in. We can reasonably anticipate that students choosing a Francophone or a bilingual post-secondary institution have expectations that they will be provided with an intensive French experience. A recent study on the student experience of a Francophone cohort in Ontario post-secondary education confirms this, revealing language supports as a priority concern, with respondents identifying wanting more French course options and access to more French documents and materials (Dietsche 2010). Just as one might reasonably anticipate, Francophone students selecting an Anglophone institution have relatively few expectations that their French language or culture will be fostered. Those expectations are by and large what guide our practice as student affairs and services professionals delivering an educational experience in those varied contexts. We look to the students for a sense of what we need to provide to create a fulfilling experience for them and to gain insight into the needs we must meet. Having said that, as a profession whose aim is to foster student success and enhance the student life experience, we also have an obligation to delve deeper, beyond students' expectations and examine what unique responses may be necessary to promote their achievement.

Anglophone Institutions

Clearly, there are Francophones who choose to attend English institutions in Ontario (Labrie and Lamoureux 2010, 10; Théberge 2010, 7). Their reasons for doing so are likely quite varied, but one can reasonably expect that in some cases program options played a role in the decision and still others might have done so hoping to improve their English language skills. No doubt geographical proximity influenced the choice of others. While they likely enter these institutions with few expectations vis-à-vis their language and cultural needs, this does not absolve us of our responsibilities to pay special attention to this cohort.

If student success is the goal, then we must ask ourselves what if any barriers might exist for this particular cohort to succeed in our institutions. Critical to such a goal is a student's ability to "get involved, to participate and integrate into the life of the institution" (Tinto 1997, 600). Those working in English institutions must recognize the potential challenges that exist in the environment that could make it more difficult for a Francophone student to establish connections and feel that they belong in the community. Many Francophones will experience "culture shock" as they join Anglocentric communities (Dietsche 2010, 22). Depending on their level of proficiency in English, they may find themselves under-prepared for the university/college experience which, of course, could significantly impact their ability to succeed (Engstrom and Tinto 2008, 3). It is likely that most will experience some level of cultural disconnect, and they may find differences in how people communicate with one another. Additionally, they may experience a void of representation when it comes to their history, their foods, their holidays, and their customs, and they may even find there to be a disconnect in social mores. The "culture shock" will no doubt be more pronounced in cases where a student has come from a different country, but what must be understood is that Canadian-born Francophones might experience this cultural disconnect as well. For some it will be significant enough to impact their adjustment to the post-secondary environment, while for others not. However, a note of caution suggests that even if there is no obvious impact, it does not mean there is no impact at all. Given what is known about the loss of language and culture that can occur to Francophones as a minority immersed in a majority environment, even where students may not recognize it, there is likely a toll exacted on them (Tardif and McMahon 1989).

It has become common practice in the student services field to provide additional supports to international students in helping them adjust and persist in the face of cultural and language adjustments. Practitioners have also worked to develop a variety of responses aimed at other "at risk" populations attending post-secondary institutions in an effort to improve their chances of persistence and their likelihood of success. But the reality is that, on many campuses, such initiatives are not designed with the Francophone student in mind and this cohort's needs remain largely unaddressed. Surprisingly, there are no public data available on the persistence of Francophones in English institutions in Ontario, but given what is understood about their experience as a minority group in the province, it is safe to assume that the minority experience is inevitable inside an English institution. We first need to work to ensure this cohort is making the connections necessary to persist at our institutions. We would argue however, that we also have some responsibility to take steps to help these students preserve their language, their heritage, and their culture. As public institutions in a country with two official languages, it is incumbent upon us to be role models in nurturing bilingualism in our society.

At minimum, student affairs and services professionals in English institutions have a responsibility to conduct an assessment of this cohort's needs. In an informal survey the authors conducted with colleagues in Ontario, we found only about 40 per cent of the schools serving Francophone students on some scale conducted some sort of needs assessment. Is there a critical mass of Francophone students on your campus that might warrant a response? When we collect data on our students, do we conduct an analysis to help us determine whether needs and use of services vary between Anglophone and Francophone cohorts? And when we evaluate existing initiatives, do we examine differences in the success of those initiatives for these two cohorts so that we might better determine whether alternatives need to be offered? For obvious reasons, an English institution located in a community where there is a substantial population of Francophones is more likely to be engaged in this practice, but this exercise is equally necessary where that is not the case. Some institutions may draw a high number of Francophones in spite of their location in a primarily Anglophone community because they offer academic programs that are not widely offered elsewhere, or in some cases proximity to a student's home community may play a role. It is dangerous to assume we intuitively know if we have a critical mass of Francophones at our institutions. In fact, we may well discover that we do not have a critical mass, but at the same time our assessments may reveal that because we do not, Francophones are even more at risk – particularly when limits of language are compounded by other factors that may put them at risk (Engstrom and Tinto 2008).

Student affairs and services professionals have to make a commitment to this cohort. To increase the odds of success (Tinto 2000, 6)

for Francophone students at Anglophone institutions, we need to
explore methods for creating connections among peers in this cohort.
We can be intentional in grouping Francophone students at orientation to facilitate a sense of belonging, of sameness. Mentorship programs – whether peer-to-peer or those involving faculty, staff, alumni,
or community members – can provide continued support and assure
these students that they are not alone in their experience. We need to
find ways to give visibility to the French language and culture that is
an inherent part of the Canadian fabric, through multicultural festi-
vals that include displays of Francophone Canadian culture or stand-
alone events that celebrate French Canadian customs and/or holidays
(Culture Francophone; French for the Future). Remembering that
this is a marginalized group on campus, we must explore ways to
provide positive space for Francophone students, where they can
express their culture and communicate in their language. Living
learning environments focused on the French language and cultures
are great examples that exist on some of Anglophone campuses.
Other initiatives can be effective as well, such as French clubs,
Francophone guest speakers addressing issues of significance to the
Francophone community, and theatre trips to Francophone produc-
tions. Expanding usual offerings to provide this cohort some important opportunities to keep their language and heritage alive in their
studies and in their work is also key. For example, where we offer
community service or work placements, we might look for placements where they can use their French. Students may be provided
with a list of staff and faculty members who speak French and are
willing to help them if necessary. Another common example is career
and educational fairs where Francophone opportunities for post-
graduate education and employment are featured. Initiatives such as
these will not only enhance their chances of persistence at our institutions but will also contribute to the preservation of their language
and culture.

   Last but not least, it is important that in our assessment, we take
time to review this cohort's experience in using some of our existing
services. Do they feel welcome? Do they feel understood? We need to
ensure, for example, that academic advisors are alerted to the possibility that a student manifesting with academic difficulty may be experiencing adjustment issues specifically related to being Francophone in
an English institution. A comparative analysis of responses to the
1994 Student Information survey administered at eight Canadian

Universities revealed a number of significant differences between Francophone and Anglophone students in how they rated their experiences both with academics and student services (Joy 1996). Francophones in this study placed greater importance on financial aid, class size, sense of community, and international study opportunities than their Anglophone counterparts (Joy 1996). Replicating such studies could help us understand this cohort's needs and what areas to focus on to maximize the impact of various interventions.

Bilingual Institutions

Bilingual institutions, such as Glendon College (Glendon College) and the University of Ottawa (University of Ottawa), offer a unique educational experience. They offer their students an opportunity to study in both of Canada's official languages and an educational environment that promotes bilingualism. Depending on the institution, students may be asked to choose their language of study and then take courses from their language stream of choice, or they may be presented with the opportunity to fashion a fully bilingual course of study in their field of choice. But the bilingual experience these institutions aim to offer extends beyond the formal curriculum. They work to create an environment where both languages and the associated cultures can flourish and one that fosters a truly bilingual community. Glendon College at York University is an example of this, stating that its goal is to "provide French-speaking and English-speaking students with as wide a range of high-quality educational services in both languages, while giving cultural support to students in both their cultural backgrounds" (Garigue 1985, 943). Bilingual institutions hire staff that can support both languages and offer the range of typical student services in the language of students' choosing. They provide co-curricular programs in both languages and structured experiences that aim to foster bilingual interactions. This is a unique environment for Francophone students and their experiences in each type of bilingual system will vary somewhat, but there are obvious commonalties.

The Francophone cohort at bilingual institutions typically will include a certain percentage of Franco-Ontarians. Labrie, Lamoureux, and Wilson (2009) showed in their research that between the years of 1998 and 2006, Ottawa received 55 per cent of Francophones and Glendon only 1.6 per cent (Labrie, Lamoureux, and Wilson 2009, 23).

These institutions also count among their students French Canadians from other provinces – Quebec Francophones, immigrant Francophones, and international and exchange students from Francophone countries; their educational preparation will have varied widely. What results is a very diverse student body, a virtual mosaic of French cultures.

Their reasons for choosing a bilingual institution are as varied as their origins. They may be looking to sustain or strengthen their French language skills. In many cases students attending bilingual institutions are looking to make themselves more marketable for when they enter the workforce. All of these factors inform a whole set of expectations these students have of their educational experience, especially relative to choice and equal access (Labrie 1995). They expect to have a choice of taking courses in French or in English; they expect to have a choice to be served in French or in English; they expect to be provided a choice of resources in either French or English; and they expect to have options and opportunities in both languages, not just during their time at the institution, but beyond. More importantly, they expect that the institution will deliver these opportunities. Of course they also expect to be provided a social and cultural context reflective of both English and French heritages.

Francophone students attending bilingual institutions in Ontario face some unique challenges. While such institutions provide more support conducive to their success, Francophones in this environment are still in the minority and, as such, continue to experience the effects of that. By virtue of living where English is the language of the majority, students' access to French resources is limited. For example at Glendon College, approximately 30 per cent of their library holdings are French compared to 69 per cent English, with the remaining 1 per cent being in Spanish (Julianna Drexler, personal communication). The reasons limiting access to academic resources in French are not all exclusive to the French language itself but certainly it is part of the picture. The reality is these resources and others, such as internship opportunities, may not be so readily available in a primarily Anglophone province.

The demographics at these institutions are such that there may not exist a critical mass of Francophone students. This impacts student life and student learning in innumerable ways. For example, from past research, we know that Francophones in a majority Anglophone environment are at risk of experiencing some loss of their French language (Tardif and McMahon 1989). Creating opportunities to build connections between Francophones at the institution may also be hampered if critical mass does not exist. For example, the practice of grouping Francophones together at Orientation in an effort to build community among the group is frequently stymied by the reality that Anglophone groupings outnumber Francophone groupings, an imbalance which can further isolate this cohort. Another common example is the struggle faced by bilingual mentorship programs and language buddy programs in finding a sufficient number of Francophones to match with the Anglophone demand for such pairings. The absence of a critical mass also makes it difficult to offer targeted programming.

The profile of the Francophone student body at bilingual institutions is diverse, and while it enhances the experiences of students on that campus, it can also pose some obstacles when it comes to creating a sense of community among Francophones. The French they know and speak most readily may itself vary depending on their place of origin; there are variances in the language even across Canada. Differences in accents, dialects, and vocabulary are common regional nuances. Students may also have come from different Francophone cultural contexts, yielding differences in holidays, customs, and mores. Even within Canada there are variances in cultural practices and observances between the various Francophone communities (Office of Francophone Affairs; Fédération Culturelle Canadienne-Française; Centre francophone de Toronto). This diversity will no doubt enhance a students' knowledge of Francophone language and culture, yet it may also make it difficult for them to have the opportunity to nurture their own heritage within the particular university or college. It is not uncommon to see such students join external community groups in an effort to satisfy this need. Unfortunately, this may in turn detract from efforts to create a positive student experience on campus within the institution's community.

Bilingual institutions have as their primary aim to promote bilingualism. In and of itself this makes room for Francophone expression in a way that is simply not available at Anglophone institutions. However, French in this context can still become marginalized by virtue of the fact that we are situated in an English province. Bilingual institutions must work hard to ensure that Francophone students are offered opportunities equal to that of Anglophones, to give French equal billing to English. To meet this objective, bilingual institutions must work to provide all services and programs in both languages. Counselling, career advising, financial aid, campus life, security, residence life, for example, all have to be able to serve and advise students in both languages, provide materials in both languages, and offer their programs in both languages. Where it is not possible to do so, there must be a certain balance achieved where the French offerings are just as numerous and substantive as English offerings. French social and cultural events need to be offered just as frequently as English ones. Speaker series need to feature at least as many French speakers as English speakers. In instances where one language must preside over the other, such as during committee meetings, institutions must explore strategies that will ensure French is not undermined. This might mean alternating the language of choice at each meeting or at minimum allowing members the choice to express themselves in French. It is important for bilingual institutions to nurture the French language and culture on their campus. Francophone students need to feel congruence with their educational context to be successful learners. They also need to experience a sense of connection, with peers, staff, faculty, and the institution as a whole. Coordinating peer and alumni mentor programs that allow Francophone students to connect with other Francophones is an effective method for building meaningful connections that can enhance their experience as students and in turn their success.

As bilingual institutions work to meet their obligations to the Francophone cohort on campus they face some challenges of their own. Creating an environment where French has equal status to English requires constant effort. Those bilingual institutions located in Anglophone regions, for example Glendon College, will face greater challenges resulting from lack of direct access to a surrounding community of Francophone resources. Offering all services and programs in two languages is a tremendous amount of duplication that requires careful planning, strategic use of resources, and creative methods of delivery. It requires a versatile staff complement and an investment in their continuous development. Having to do everything twice is stressful on the staff and a significant challenge to resource. All of the staff working in student services must, in addition to demonstrating the qualifications necessary for the work of a particular service, also be bilingual. Yet compensation for their work is typically no greater than, or only nominally so, that of their counterparts working in only one language. Recruiting staff for this context can be challenging, as it requires specialized language skills that exist in limited supply within an Anglophone province. The work itself is demanding and can tax the staff, since materials for committee meetings must be in both languages. Staff advising students must be prepared to do so in either language as well. All publications must be done twice, and consequently everything takes twice the time it would in a unilingual context.

Documents and publications of any sort often require the use of translation services. This includes posters, web postings, pamphlets, surveys, and official documents. Translation is a specialized skill distinct from bilingual communication skills, so typically staff members are not equipped to translate materials from one language to another. Making use of outside translators is costly and rarely accounted for in funding formulas. It also still requires staff time to coordinate those transactions and to proofread the final products. This means having to build extra time into project timelines to allow for these additional stages of production.

Programming for this student cohort is also a complex undertaking. Meeting the needs of this very diverse Francophone student cohort requires offering a larger than usual range of programs and events and finding ways to appeal to multiple needs with each. It is a careful balance as one also needs to ensure critical mass for the program to have optimal impact. Attendance at French programs tends to be lower than the English ones, yet it is important to persist in offering French activities. Recruiting Francophones to participate in mentor programs and language buddy programs is a challenge because of their minority representation at the institution. Recruiting Francophone alumni to participate in programs and events is equally challenging. Providing French groupings at Orientation or as part of any program offering is not always effective as their numbers are overshadowed by the English groupings and it may further isolate the Francophone students rather than making them feel supported; it also accentuates their minority status. Additionally there may simply be times when it is not feasible to offer a program twice, to accommodate both languages, or the resources, such as speakers, are not available to do so. Committee meetings involving students are further examples that give rise to the dilemma of having to choose one language of operation. The diversity and the reality of existing in a majority English province can also make it difficult to provide a cultural atmosphere for Francophone students. Staff at bilingual institutions must be prepared for the fact that French activities will require more effort to plan and to market if they are to be successful.

Another unique challenge that arises from serving the Francophone cohort on this type of campus lies in the ability to provide students in this cohort with opportunities for campus employment. A portion of this cohort includes international students and landed immigrants. Their English may not be adequate enough to work in a bilingual or English position and the number of positions, both on and off campus, requiring French only is limited; there simply is not enough of those opportunities to meet the needs. For those who can only work on campus this may even be less likely, especially given requirements that the staff be bilingual.

Francophone Institutions

Ontario is home to a handful of post-secondary Francophone institutions, including Laurentian University, University of Ottawa, La Cité, and Collège Boréal, whose aim is to deliver post-secondary education to Franco-Ontarians. Typically these are grassroots institutions that serve a specific region and the Francophone communities therein. Many of these schools operate campuses in regions where Francophones make up anywhere from 30 per cent to 85 per cent of the population (Statistics Canada, Population by mother tongue and age groups). For the most part, program offerings at these institutions are from the arts and social sciences, although there are a few locales that offer science-based studies. Some of these schools do offer on-campus accommodation, although most operate as commuter institutions. Most offer the usual range of student services and programs but employ non-traditional methods of delivery that better suit their structure, the regional contexts, and the students they serve. Many of these institutions play important roles in the promotion of the French language and cultures as centres of activity within their respective communities.

Clearly, Francophones are in the majority on these campuses; however, their exact makeup varies depending upon the institution's location and is reflective of the community where the particular campus resides. Although it again varies by institution and by region, a large proportion of the students attending these institutions are commuting non-traditional students – mature students, students with families, Aboriginal students, and distance learners (Contact North; Centre Francophone de Toronto). Their reasons for choosing a

Francophone institution are complex. In some cases, proximity to home communities dictates students' choices, while for others it is based on language proficiency. A portion of this cohort is also looking to secure language skills to ensure their marketability in the workforce. Others no doubt select this option as one that provides a context conducive to maintaining their language and culture. But it is important to note that while the need to preserve their French heritage exists for this cohort as well, the need is perhaps not as urgent, especially for those students attending campuses in Francophone communities. The expectations that flow from their choices include, of course, that they will be provided a full-service experience in French. Some may also be expecting to be offered a network and a sense of community, in essence a connection to the Franco-Ontario community. Many are expecting that completing studies at a French institution will ensure them employment.

Francophone students on these campuses, being in the majority, simply do not experience marginalization to the extent their counterparts at bilingual and Anglophone institutions might. Thus they are able to more readily achieve a sense of connection and belonging, both important factors in student success (Strange and Banning 2015). We must however recognize the two big challenges that exist for these students. The first is that, while they may be in the majority on their campuses and in some cases within their immediate community, they are all still part of a marginalized group in Ontario. Like their peers at bilingual and Anglophone institutions they too may, for example, have difficulty accessing resources and materials in French that they need to complete their study. Their choices with regards to all sorts of things including programs of study, opportunities for post-graduate work, and employment may be limited as well. They will experience differences between their campus lives and those outside of campus, and that disconnect will in some instances be quite taxing on them personally and professionally. The second challenge flows from the diversity of this cohort. Across the system and even within institutions, this cohort has many faces. Their background, their heritage, their needs, and their situation as students vary greatly. It may be quite difficult to build meaningful connections across such divides. With commuter populations or distance learners these divides can be compounded further.

There are some key strategies that have been employed by these institutions in setting the stage for success among the Francophone student cohort. Their very structure and location is perhaps the most significant of these. All operate in key Francophone regions with a very grassroots approach to the delivery of education. Larger institutions have used a de-centralized model with smaller satellite campuses located in the heart of key Franco-Ontarian communities in order to achieve that level of outreach. Most also offer distance learning which facilitates even greater levels of participation from Franco-Ontarians (Ontario Ministry of Training, Colleges and Universities, French language and bilingual colleges and universities). For example, Collège Boréal offers video conferencing programs accessible to Francophones in twenty-five sites across Ontario, an initiative funded by the Ontario Government in order to increase access to Franco-Ontarians in remote areas (Collège Boréal, Éducation permanente). The University of Ottawa also offers a Bachelor of Education in two remote sites; Toronto and Windsor using the video-conferencing method as a means (University of Ottawa, Faculty of Education). While these are sound decisions from a business standpoint, they have also increased the odds of access for students. However, how the use of distance learning impacts the success of this cohort is unclear. Tinto (1997) concludes that student success is impacted by a combination of factors such as the structure of educational activity in the classroom, student involvement, and the quality of student effort (Tinto 1997, 614–15). These factors are perhaps less easy to achieve in distance education. On the other hand, distance education provides access for Francophones to the programs they want without requiring a change in location, which may be preferable as well.

Another key strategy employed by many of these institutions involves partnerships with the community to deliver services and programs. They might work with local employment centres or recreation facilities to provide service to students. Clearly this benefits the institution from a resource standpoint, but again, students also gain. Regardless of the size of the institution or distance between satellites and the main campus, students are provided access to important support mechanisms and to more of them, as the partnerships make it possible for those institutions to offer a broader range of services and programs. Not only that, but the service is delivered in places already familiar and comfortable to them.

Another popular form of partnership for some of these institutions is one where they have collaborated with each other and with local businesses. Some schools have partnerships with larger universities or with professional preparation programs. In fact, some schools are engaged in networks that involve a number of institutions. For their students this means they have the opportunity and flexibility to tailor their own course of study. It provides students with more options overall and facilitates their access to avenues for furthering their education and training. For Francophones this is important because post-graduate choices in French are limited and gaining access to such opportunities can be challenging. Institutions that have built such partnerships with local organizations and businesses are able to offer internship and training opportunities to their students as well. Again, such partnerships enhance the number of opportunities available to Francophone students to participate in programs that will enhance their likelihood of success and to have those experiences in a Francophone context.

However, serving the Francophone student cohort at Francophone institutions in Ontario is not without its challenges. The high proportion of commuters and distance learners among them presents barriers to building those valuable connections between students and students and the school. This is compounded on some campuses where the number of non-traditional learners, such as mature students and students who have families, is higher. Campuses located in communities where the Francophone population is lower have fewer community resources to tap into; in such locales, the cultural context is somewhat diminished. Francophones in an Anglophone centre will tend to resort to speaking English rather than French. Cultural activities featuring Francophone heritage are fewer in number and opportunities for internships, co-ops, and skill development in a French context are harder to come by. As part of an Anglophone province the Francophone institutions also face similar limitations to those faced by bilingual institutions. Francophone resources and materials may not be readily available and the range available may be restrictive. Institutions are then left to invent them, which can be costly, or make use of English materials while assuming the costs of translation. In a province where Francophones are in the minority, it can also be challenging to find the staff and faculty needed.

ISSUES AND CHALLENGES

There are of course challenges to providing support to this cohort of Francophone students. We rely on students to self-identify, and for a variety of reasons not all do so. And when we survey them we typically request they specify language of preference, which does not always yield reliable data on their primary language. This makes it particularly difficult to target them directly; it also impacts our ability to assess their needs. Limited resources are another common challenge that diminishes our capacity to plan and offer a response. In fact, it came up as one of the most common obstacles to serving this community in our informal survey of Ontario student affairs and services staff. And it is difficult to make the case for funding if critical mass does not exist and if we don't have data supporting what we have identified to be the needs of this cohort. Beyond this, we also may be limited in terms of our accessibility to Francophone resources. Some of us, by nature of our locations, may be able to partner with neighbouring Francophone and/or bilingual institutions or community agencies, thereby facilitating the creation of initiatives. For example, College Boréal offers sixteen joint programs with Ontario universities, including Laurentian, Hearst, and Guelph (Annuaire 2011–12, 25). Where we are able to mobilize and offer programs and services that specifically address the needs of this cohort, we face further challenges in engaging these students where their diversity at times defies unification.

There is also a gap when it comes to research and data on Francophones in higher education. While this has been changing rapidly over the last ten years with the efforts of the Ministry, the work of the Centre for Research in Education of Franco-Ontarians, and other interested scholars (Labrie, Lamoureux, and Wilson 2009), most of that research has focused on questions of access. There are very limited public data available with respect to persistence rates of Francophones and their overall student experience. We know very little about their needs and how to engage them in a meaningful way. There also seems to be little that speaks to their experience of marginalization and best practices for promoting student success among this cohort. We need more research about how to engage Francophones at our institutions, be they Anglophone, Francophone, or bilingual in design. We would also benefit from research about how to make them feel part of a community where they are the minority. Finally, a discussion of challenges would not be complete without addressing the issue of resources when it comes to serving Francophones in our institutions. The availability and cost of materials in French is often prohibitive. There are heightened costs of doing business, including those supporting translation services, sufficient staffing, and access to appropriate materials and activities that must be duplicated at some institutions in both French and English.

Student affairs and services practitioners need to recognize Francophones as a unique cohort in our post-secondary system and begin to take a serious look at what our role is in fostering their success. Francophone institutions have to form partnerships with other institutions to expand the academic program offerings for students. Bilingual institutions need to find ways to sustain and grow the choices they offer in French in order to fully meet the needs of Francophones in this context. All of us need to do a better job of surveying these students about their needs, their experiences, and their expectations.

While it is clear that there is a growing provincial dialogue in Ontario on the issue of Francophones in post-secondary education, it seems that few student affairs and services professionals, beyond those in recruitment and admissions, have been engaged in such exchanges. The time has come for student affairs and services professionals to step into the conversation, to share data, common lessons, and best practices for serving this cohort. We need to create opportunities either within the existing dialogue or in a separate forum for student affairs and services professionals in Ontario and across Canada, to discuss issues of relevance to Francophone students at our institutions and share ideas for how best to respond to their needs. Our professional organizations need to take a leadership role in creating such opportunities for the exchange of information and ideas on the subject of serving Francophone students. They also play a critical role in fostering research in this area and publishing relevant data at regular intervals, perhaps in sync with their yearly conventions. Given their current role in the development of professionals in higher education, they could also be a key partner in spearheading the creation of a course or training modules for student affairs and services professionals with an interest in advancing their knowledge of this cohort and how best to enhance their success in our institutions.

CONCLUSION

We have made a case that Francophone students, as a linguistic and cultural minority in Canada, experience post-secondary education from a place of disadvantage, from initial access to graduation and beyond. This chapter is also in many ways a call to action. Student affairs and services professionals in Canada have a critical role to play in the success of Francophone students at their institutions. By extension, student affairs and services professionals also have a critical role to play in nurturing bilingualism as a core value of our country.

In Ontario, that call to action is echoed by the Ministry of Training, Colleges and Universities, which has a clear mandate to offer equal opportunities for Francophones choosing to obtain post-secondary education, and an associate deputy minister dedicated to providing such opportunities. This has created a unique climate in the province and ignited dialogue across the various institutions on how to improve access to post-secondary education for Francophones and facilitate their success in those pursuits. It is through that lens that we have identified in this chapter the factors that impact the success of this cohort and strategies we can employ in student affairs and services to foster such success.

There is no doubt that each province is a unique jurisdiction and that each has a distinctly different vantage point on the subject of Francophones in post-secondary education. Indeed the experience of Francophones will, as we have discussed above, vary from province to province. Hence, where the context is different, so might the issues for these students vary and the supports needed take on a different shape. We nevertheless maintain that many of the issues raised here – and many of the methods suggested – have relevance beyond Ontario. Even in Quebec, where Francophones are the majority, challenges persist around the breadth of programs available in French. Clearly, many of the barriers to success identified for Francophones in Ontario will be the same in any place where Francophones are a linguistic minority. Our strategies to make sure that this group succeeds are also not altogether different.

Across Canada we need to do a better job of understanding this cohort, tracking its persistence, assessing its needs, and identifying best practices in fostering its success. We need to engage with one another and share best practices to a much greater extent than we currently do. We need to recognize their unique experiences. Finally, we need to reflect upon our responsibility to act and meet the needs of this cohort to ensure that they have a positive educational experience and they succeed.

6

LGBTQQ Student Services

AMIT TANEJA

A discussion group is about to begin in the basement of the Student Union building, where Steve, a Residence Director and advisor to the lesbian, gay, bisexual, transgender, queer, and questioning (LGBTQQ) student group, is facilitating the meeting. Students settle in and start sharing their stories. Matt, a first year student, shares that he is questioning his sexual orientation, and that he feels confused and scared. Loretta, a junior student, adds: "I felt that confusion too because we were told that we had to pick sides – man or woman, gay or straight. I just don't believe in that view, so now I just accept myself as queer." Venice agrees, stating the importance of "safe spaces" on campus where students can feel welcomed and affirmed. She felt that her residence hall was generally a safe space for her to come out, but a few isolated incidents of harassment were enough to create a chilly atmosphere for her and other LGBTQQ students. Hong, an international student, shares that one of his peers made a gay joke in class, and the lack of response from the professor made him feel uncomfortable and devalued. Yousef, a Muslim student, states that he is out on campus, but he has to be completely closeted within his faith community. Helena, a transgender student, responds angrily to Yousef asserting that he was at least accepted on campus as a gay man. Helena reports that people started giving her the cold shoulder ever since she started transitioning, and recounts instances of harassment where campus police questioned her use of the female bathroom. Melanie, the president of the LGBTQQ student group,

notes her frustration with campus policies regarding transgender individuals, and asks if people are interested in organizing
a protest outside the president's office. An hour later Steve calls
the meeting to a close and reminds everyone to pair up with
others since last year an out gay student was assaulted and
abused while walking alone on campus at night.

INTRODUCTION

The preceding account illustrates the variety of issues faced by lesbian, gay, bisexual, transgender, queer, and questioning students on
post-secondary campuses today. While achieving the independence
such a setting offers, many students focus on exploring their own
sexual orientation and gender identity during this time (Evans and
D'Augelli 1996; Rankin 2003) and seek connection with others who
share the same thoughts and feelings. During the post-secondary
years, gay, lesbian, and bisexual students might also be concerned
about their own physical and psychological safety, and may choose
to live dual lives where they are out to some people and not to others. Transgender, gender queer, and gender non-conforming students
often face even more significant challenges, especially while they are
exploring variations of their own gender identities and expressions
(Bilodeau 2009).

LGBTQQ students have long been subject to unacceptable treatment both within and outside the classroom (Peter, Taylor, and
Chamberland 2015). Peer-based harassment, threats, vandalism,
intimidation, exclusion, and other negative behaviors constitute the
greatest challenges for members of the LGBTQQ community in
exploring and expressing their sexual orientation and/or gender
identity; such behaviors are often even more damaging when they
originate from faculty and staff. A negative climate for LGBTQQ students still prevails on many campuses today and can lead to diminished academic performance, undue stress, and feeling disconnected
from the institution among this cohort; for some, such conditions
may even lead to their withdrawal from school (Rankin, Weber,
Blumfeld, and Frazer 2010). One recent survey of twenty-one public
universities in Ontario revealed that "sexual and gender minority
students, staff, and faculty were three times more likely to seriously
consider leaving their university when experiencing campus environments as uncomfortable/unaccepting, and twice as likely to consider

doing so when experiencing harassment based on sexual identity, gender identity, and/or gender expression" (Tate, 2014, ii). Conversely, the same study also found a positive correlation between the campus climate (for institutional equity and inclusion) and student educational outcomes (intent to persist) and employee experiences (career consequences).

The need for institution-wide efforts to address these concerns is urgently apparent. Strange and Banning (2015) asserted that inclusion and security of all students are prerequisites of campus engagement in supportive learning communities (see chapter 12). Thus full and equitable involvement of LGBTQQ students can only occur once these basic needs of inclusion and safety have been satisfied to some degree. It is imperative that faculty and staff take on the responsibility to create a more supportive learning environment that enables LGBTQQ students to be successful both personally and academically. A significant step has been achieved in recent years on some campuses with the establishment of student services designed to address such shortcomings. This chapter explores the emergence of LGBTQQ student services within Canadian higher education institutions with reference to the cultural and legal status of LGBTQQ citizens in Canada, their identity development, and the role campus services can play in ensuring the integration and success of these students. In addition, the chapter considers implications for policy development and practice emanating from current and emergent issues affecting LGBTQQ students on campus.

LGBTQQ STUDENTS ON CAMPUS

Delving into the issues that concern the LGBTQQ community on campus is hindered significantly by the fact that Canadian post-secondary institutions do not collect demographic information pertaining to students' sexual orientation or gender identity. Furthermore, while several studies have been undertaken in recent years at the Canadian secondary school level (e.g., Kitchen and Bellini 2013; Taylor and Peter 2011), as well as one national survey of Canada's "gay landscape" (National Post Forum Research Poll 2012), there is little to no research done to investigate the scope and presence of LGBTQQ students on Canadian college and university campuses. Eyermann and Sanlo (2002) suggested that demographic information on such students is difficult to find because surveys rarely collect

information on sexual orientation, and when they do, students may
not self-identify with the concepts of gay, lesbian, bisexual, or transgender, as defined by the survey itself. In fact, as suggested in Table
6.1, the language of sexual identity and gender expression is a complicated matter and subject to varying interpretations as well as misun-
derstandings. Consequently, there are no firm estimates of the
percentage of post-secondary students who self-identify as LGBTQQ.
However, despite these challenges, some studies conducted at American colleges and universities assert that 4 to 10 per cent of students
self-identify as gay, lesbian, bisexual, or questioning their sexual orientation (Ellis 1996; Longerbeam, Inkelas, Johnson, and Lee 2007).

Despite the lack of any systematic approach, several institutions
have made an effort to collect data regarding the experiences of
LGBTQQ students on campus. The first such initiative was launched
at York University (Grayson 1994), where information collected was
used by the President's Task Force on Homophobia and Heterosexism
to make recommendations for a more inclusive campus environment
(York University 1996). Another example of a comprehensive climate survey can be accessed through the website of University of
Victoria's Committee on the Status of Sexual Minorities (University
of Victoria 2000).

Some institutions have also investigated for their own campuses
the attitudes of heterosexual students towards LGBTQQ students
(Evans and Heriott 2004; Mohr and Sedlacek 2000; Simoni 1996).
Wilfrid Laurier University, for example, conducts an annual survey
of their incoming students' attitudes, and has included questions
regarding perceptions of students towards LGBTQQ issues (Pepper
and Ellis-Hale 2004). Another study was conducted at the University
of Windsor regarding attitudes of students towards gays and lesbians
(Schellenberg, Hirt, and Sears 1999). These studies found that students enrolled in social sciences, in comparison to science and business, typically tend to have more positive attitudes towards LGBTQQ
students (Schellenberg et al. 1999). Furthermore, students typically
are more accepting of lesbian women than of gay men. Such studies
have painted a relatively consistent picture of the campus climate for
LGBTQQ individuals. Most commonly, LGBTQQ students report
some instances of harassment or non-inclusive behaviors within the
campus setting, and such behaviors occur both within and outside
the classroom (York University 1996). Lesbian, gay, and bisexual students also acknowledge the positive impact of support services and

Table 6.1 Glossary of terms related to LGBTQQ people

Term	Definition
LGBTQQ	A common acronym used to indicate a community of identities, including lesbian, gay, bisexual, transgender, Two-Spirit, queer, and questioning people.
Gay	A male who is attracted to persons of the same sex. Sometimes used as a common term to reflect same-sex desires regardless of the person's gender.
Lesbian	A female who is attracted to persons of the same sex.
Bisexual	A person who is attracted to both men and women.
Transgender, trans, trans-identified, or trans*	A person whose identity or behaviour fall outside of stereotypical gender norms. The addition of the asterisk at the end is a reminder that the term serves as an umbrella, and that many different identities fall under this term.
Heterosexual/straight	A person who is exclusively attracted to members of the opposite sex.
Sexual identity or orientation	A person's deep-seated feelings of emotional, romantic, and sexual attraction to another person.
Closeted	The experience of living without disclosing one's sexual orientation or gender identity, often also referred to as being "in the closet."
Coming out	Becoming self-aware of one's own sexual orientation or gender identity, and disclosing it to others.
Gender	A social construct based on a group of emotional and psychological characteristics that classify an individual as feminine, masculine, androgynous, or other.
Gender expression	All of the external characteristics and behaviours an individual chooses to present or explain their gender, including dress, speech, mannerisms, etc.
Gender identity	A person's internal, deeply felt sense of being male, female, or somewhere other than or in between the two extremes
Cisgender or cissexual	Where individuals' experiences of their own gender agree with the sex they were assigned at birth.
Homophobia	The irrational fear of homosexuals or homosexuality expressed as negative feelings, attitudes, actions, and institutional discrimination.
Transphobia	The irrational fear of those who are perceived to break or blur stereotypical gender roles.

Table 6.1 Glossary of terms related to LGBTQQ people (*Continued*)

Term	Definition
Queer	A term used to refer to lesbian, gay, bisexual, and transgender persons (used both as a slur and as a term of pride). Sometimes the term is used to indicate identities that are not normative, but also do not align with typical representations of LGBT people. The term has been reclaimed as a term of pride, most commonly amongst young people.
Questioning	Uncertainty of one's sexual orientation and/or gender identity.
Androgynous	A person who may exhibit traits traditionally associated with, or appear as, both male and female, or neither male nor female, or in between male and female.
Sex	The genetic, biological, hormonal, or physical characteristics, including genitalia, which are used to classify individuals as male, female, or intersexed.
Intersex	An umbrella term used to describe a variety of conditions for persons born with chromosomes and/ or sexual anatomy that mixes male and female characteristics, or is otherwise atypical.
Transitioning	The process of beginning to live as a gender other than the one assigned at birth. May include changes in clothing or speech, taking hormones, and/or attaining sex reassignment surgery.
Transsexual	A person who identifies with a gender different (or opposite) to the one assigned to them at birth. Many experience intense personal and emotional discomfort about this. Some transsexuals may undergo treatments (i.e., sex reassignment surgery and/or hormone therapy) to physically alter their body and gender expression to correspond with what they feel their true gender is.
Two-Spirit	Some Aboriginal people believe that some individuals are born with both male and female spirits within them. Often, these people were regarded as having special or healing powers. Many Aboriginal people today choose to use this term instead of LGBTQ.
Gender queer or gender non-conforming	A term used to describe people whose gender is fluid and does not align with stereotypical notions of male or female.
Gender-neutral pronouns	A set of pronouns that do not assign or assume male or female gender. Commons examples are "they," "hir" (instead of him/her), and "ze" (instead of he/she).

straight allies (University of Victoria 2000). L G B T Q Q students therefore experience a wide range of reactions towards their sexual orientation and gender identities from the university community, including
complete acceptance, celebration, and inclusion on one end, to
instances of bias, discrimination, and violence on the other.

Although researchers have yet to breach the topic of L G B T Q Q students on Canadian post-secondary campuses, beyond a select number of institutional assessments, Rankin et al. (2010) have published
the most comprehensive national study on L G B T students, faculty,
and staff at colleges and universities in the U S A. This report confirms
other findings indicating that L G B T Q Q students face significant
obstacles that negatively impact their living and learning environment on campus. Furthermore, L G B T Q Q students with other marginalized identities (e.g., people of colour, gender non-conforming
students) also face significantly compounded challenges in their
educational journey.

Research regarding transgender students' experiences within
higher education is even rarer. Beemyn (2003) noted that in spite of
transgender students becoming more visible on college campuses,
higher education literature has largely ignored them. A select number
of case studies though have highlighted issues faced by transgender
students, including issues with bathroom usage, residence hall environments, violence on campus, negative interactions within the classroom, challenges undertaking name and gender changes in official
institutional records, and inclusive health care needs (Beemyn 2003;
Bilodeau 2009; Nakamura 1998). The bifurcation of some campus
opportunities along traditional gender lines also further complicates
the choices for many transgender students.

Overall, reliable data on the demography of Canadian post-
secondary students of differing sexual orientations and gender identities continue to elude higher education researchers. However, a
deeper understanding of these students has emerged nonetheless in a
recent evolution of theories (see chapter 2) that have attempted to
map out their progression of identity development during the post-
secondary years.

LGBTQQ IDENTITY DEVELOPMENT

Identity development models can be useful for student services professionals as lenses through which to understand the developmental

processes of various students. Within this line of inquiry a number of models of LGBTQQ identity development have appeared in the literature, approaching the topic from one of several perspectives (see Bilodeau and Renn 2005): (a) stage models; (b) lifespan and other nonlinear models; (c) diverse perspectives on sexual orientation and gender identity; (d) medical and psychiatric perspectives on gender identity; and (e) feminist, postmodern, and queer perspectives.

Initial research in this area emphasized stage and lifespan distinctions of LGBTQQ identity development (e.g., Cass 1979; D'Augelli 1994). Accordingly, they identify sequential steps individuals progress through as they move across time from phases or stages of unawareness through encounters leading eventually to awareness and full integration of their identity. Such models have been critiqued as overly simplistic, partly because they essentialize identities as homogeneous, thereby overlooking and minimizing the impact of other intersecting identities such as race, class, and abilities (Bilodeau and Renn 2005). Furthermore, many of these models also explain sexuality and gender as innate aspects, rather than focusing on them as social constructions that are produced and reproduced through everyday discursive practices.

Although limited in their explanatory reach, medical, stage, and lifespan perspectives have nonetheless opened the doors for inclusion within higher education of inter-disciplinary feminist, post-modern, critical studies, and queer theory perspectives of LGBTQQ identity development. At a fundamental level, such perspectives challenge conceptions of sexuality and gender by questioning the veracity and value of male/female and gay/straight binaries (Butler 1993; Feinberg 1998; Halberstam 1998). Furthermore, identity is now viewed as contextual and "fluid," so that one's current identification may not be permanently fixed as new situations and experiences are encountered.

Queer theory, although initially conceptualized in related disciplines, has recently been adapted to student affairs research to shed a more critical light on the experiences of LGBTQQ individuals (Abes and Kasch 2007; Renn 2007). Instead of arguing for an increasingly complex developmental stage model, queer theory focuses on how identities are socially constructed to provide power and privilege to one societal group at the expense of another. Instead of relegating identity development to internal processes, queer theory not only recognizes the importance of context, but it adds to the explanation of how privilege and marginalization are enacted on bodies through everyday actions. Given the importance of peer culture on college and university campuses and the complex social dynamics of young adult maturation, this theoretical perspective offers much promise for student affairs practitioners (Abes and Kasch 2007).

Recent conceptions of LGBTQQ identity development have also focused on the social, political, cultural, and historical understanding of what it means to be non-heterosexual. Students do not construct their own LGBTQQ identity in a vacuum, but do so within a socio-cultural context that describes LGBTQQ people, for example through media, politics, and religion. Many media representations of LGBTQQ people have been narrowly limited to primarily white, middle class, educated gay men. Such homo-normative representations render many within the LGBTQQ community politically and socially invisible in mainstream society. Consequently such narratives do little, for example, to inform how a Latina lesbian comes to concurrently understand her gender, race, and sexual orientation within this larger societal context?

Some researchers have focussed on the impact of formulaic constructions of identity on LGBTQQ students, relying on popular understandings of what being LGBTQQ means. Such theoretical models have argued that, while students may start with these preconceived notions of how they are supposed to negotiate the world as non-heterosexual people, their conceptions of "normal" and "LGBTQQ" begin to shift over time as they increasingly come into contact with others who deviate from the stereotypes (Abes and Jones 2004). This shift may allow students to move from external constructions of identity (for example by emulating clothing or speech of popular LGBTQQ media characters) to a more internally defined identity (Taylor 2008).

Emerging research on identity development of LGBTQQ students also emphasizes the interconnectedness of dimensions of sexual and/or gender identity with other areas of development, such as cognitive, moral, interpersonal, and intrapersonal growth (Abes and Jones 2004; Renn 2007; Taylor 2008). As exemplars of the third wave theories discussed in chapter 3, these theorists have conceptualized models of multiple dimensions of identity development that demonstrate the interplay between context, meaning making capacities, and multiple identity dimensions, such as race, class, and abilities. (Abes, Jones and McEwen 2007; Jones and McEwen 2000). Furthermore, they argue that race, gender, and sexuality are distinct identity

dimensions that are linked to one another. However, Black feminist
and intersectionality theory scholars have argued that these identity
dimensions are not discrete, but rather a part of a core concept of self.
In other words, additive analyses of "race + class + gender + sexual
orientation" will overlook the complexity that each layer of marginalized identity brings, and as a result not fully capture the lived experiences of multiply marginalized individuals (Bowleg 2008; Collins
2000; Crenshaw 1991). In sum, the literature on the development of
LGBTQQ students has done much in recent years to advance an
understanding among student services professionals of the complexities these students encounter in the resolution of their identities, and
thereby to suggest strategies in support of their success.

WORKING WITH LGBTQQ STUDENTS

The roots of LGBTQQ student services in Canadian higher education
are strongly linked to the legal and cultural status of LGBTQQ individuals within Canada. While a comprehensive overview of this subject is outside the scope of this chapter, a brief interpretation is offered
to highlight the historical and socio-political climate towards
LGBTQQ rights in Canada.

LGBTQQ Rights in Canada

The LGBTQQ rights movement gained momentum in the late 1950s
and 1960s through the decriminalization of "homosexual acts," even
though the prevailing social attitudes towards homosexuality
remained chilly and condemnatory (Warner 2002). Several grassroots organizations emerged in the 1970s and collectively garnered
national attention. In 1982, the Canadian government incorporated
the Canadian Charter of Rights and Freedoms into the Canadian
Constitution. Subsequently, the enforcement in 1985 of section 15 of
the Charter (i.e., concerning equality rights) set the stage for legal
and political debate regarding the status of LGBTQQ individuals in
Canada (Smith 1999). The Charter led to various court cases that
increasingly afforded legal protection to LGBTQQ individuals.
Progressive movements in the 1990s also led to inclusion of sexual
orientation as a protected class under several provinces' human
rights codes (Smith 1999). The Charter of Rights and Freedoms,

court cases, and the human rights codes established a platform for policy change to occur in both the private and public sector in regards to legal protections offered to LGBTQQ individuals (Warner 2002). Recently, the debate for LGBTQQ rights has focused on the legal recognition of same-sex relationships at the federal level by affording gay and lesbian individuals the right to marry same-sex partners.

LGBTQQ Student Groups

As LGBTQQ individuals acquired greater legal recognition within Canada, by the 1970s students on campuses began forming various support and advocacy organizations (Rynor 2004). One legacy of this period is the University of Toronto's student group, LGBTQQOUT (University of Toronto 2016), which celebrated its fortieth anniversary in 2010. In the 1970s and 1980s LGBTQQ student organizations were acknowledged by their respective institutions as recognized student groups and were afforded the same rights and responsibilities as other student organizations. However, there was very little or no institutional staff support for these efforts (J. Tate, personal communication, 15 February, 2005), despite their value.

LGBTQQ student groups serve numerous purposes on campus. First and foremost, they provide an essential service for LGBTQQ students to meet others and make connections on campus. Such groups offer valuable mentorship and support for students in the coming out process through weekly support groups and formal and informal social events, and they connect students to university resources when appropriate, such as student health and the counselling centre (Browning and Walsh 2002). This peer support network is also invaluable following public acts of hatred, such as a campus assault on an openly LGBTQQ individual (Bochenek and Brown 2001; Nesmith, Burton, and Cosgrove 1999).

Second, LGBTQQ student groups also offer educational programming for all students by inviting speakers to campus, holding events like "out week" in celebration of LGBTQQ individuals, and creating educational panels or speaker series for classrooms and residence halls. Third, these student groups offer advocacy for the rights of LGBTQQ students, faculty, and staff by working with supportive administrators to effect appropriate policy and protocol changes (Sanlo, Rankin, and Schoenberg 2002). Lastly, leaders of LGBTQQ

student groups can additionally form inter-group coalitions by working with other like-minded organizations or influencing the leadership
of other student groups (Sanlo et al. 2002; Winters 2002).

Emergence of LGBTQQ Student Services

Encouraged by these earlier initiatives, LGBTQQ student groups in
the late 1980s began mirroring the advocacy work of community
LGBTQQ organizations to establish a stronger presence on campus.
Evolving cultural trends made it increasingly more acceptable for
LGBTQQ students to publicly identify with their sexual orientations
and gender expressions. Furthermore, the changing political and
legal status of LGBTQQ Canadians created a need for policy review
and greater administrative attention to claims of discrimination.
As a result, by the early 1990s, staff charged with equity work on
campus also began serving as policy advisors and mediators for
LGBTQQ faculty and staff (J. Tate, personal communication,
15 February, 2005). It should be noted, however, that even though
equity office staff initially assumed an official role in assuring the
rights and benefits of LGBTQQ faculty and staff, students were still
very much left to fend for themselves.

As the 1990s progressed, the need for student advocacy and support became even more prevalent, and faculty and staff began taking
on advisory roles for LGBTQQ student organizations (O. Dryden,
personal communication, 12 February 2005). In addition those staff
within equity offices assigned to work primarily with LGBTQQ faculty and staff, by extension also started providing support to LGBTQQ
students and their organizations. Typically, such work was done in
addition to any full-time teaching or administrative responsibilities
held and without institutional recognition.

The University of Toronto was one of the first to organize an institution-wide effort to address concerns brought forth by LGBTQQ
students, faculty, and staff with the formation in 1989 of the
Committee on Homophobia (Rynor 2004); other institutions followed suit shortly thereafter. Additionally, while there were no official staff members charged with the responsibility of working with
LGBTQQ students, several offices within Student Affairs – Residence
Life and Counselling Services in particular, by the 1990s had become
more attuned to the needs of these students. At some institutions,
staff within these offices had also become more aware of LGBTQQ

services offered at American institutions, and began mirroring advocacy programs, for example, at the University of British Columbia, where the Residence Life Safe Space Program was initiated in 1993. "Safe space" programs include the provision of a safe-zone marker, such as a sticker or magnet, which identifies on-campus allies for LGBTQQ individuals who are knowledgeable of LGBTQQ issues (Sanlo et al. 2002b). York University, for example, was a trendsetter in this regard by implementing a "safe space" program in 1998 that required individuals to participate in mandatory training prior to their posting a safe space marker. This training ensured that allies were knowledgeable and sensitive to current LGBTQQ issues. Following its initial success York University's program was subsequently adopted by several other campuses (York University 2000).

By the mid 1990s, many Canadian post-secondary institutions started taking a more active role in supporting the experiences of LGBTQQ students through conducting campus climate surveys focusing on LGBTQQ issues. Additionally, faculty and staff garnered institutional support to form ad-hoc committees on sexual orientation and gender identity issues to guide institutional leadership on these concerns and to create more accepting environments through policy change (K. Ellis-Hale, personal communication, 28 February 2005). The need for institutional support became increasingly apparent as various campus climate studies and committee reports concluded that there was a need for staff within student services to serve LGBTQQ students more directly. Furthermore, following the examples of fifty-eight American institutions, which had created LGBTQQ centres by 1999 (Consortium of Higher Education LGBTQQ Resource Professionals 2010), a combination of such factors set the stage for Canadian institutions to create staff positions dedicated primarily to working with LGBTQQ students.

The first dedicated staff position for LGBTQQ student services in Canadian post-secondary education, albeit on a part-time basis, was created in 1999 by the University of Toronto's Division of Student Affairs (University of Toronto 2003) and funded through a joint venture between Student Affairs, Academics, and Human Resources (J. Tate, personal communication, 15 February 2005). The overwhelming success of this office, coupled with high demand from students, led to the expansion of the position to a full-time basis in 2000 and further extension to support and advocate for faculty and staff in 2003. The establishment of this position set a trend in Canadian higher education, and several institutions (e.g., McGill University, Ryerson University, Queen's University, York University, University of Calgary, and University of British Columbia) have since established similar L G B T Q Q coordinator positions building on the experience of the University of Toronto.

The Role of LGBTQQ Student Services on Campus

The field of L G B T Q Q student services is relatively new to Canadian higher education, and as a result there are no formal standards of performance set for its implementation. There are however models within other systems (e.g., United States higher education) that can be very beneficial to Canadian professionals. The primary professional organization for L G B T Q Q student services professionals is the Consortium of L G B T Q Q Resource Professionals in Higher Education (2016). The consortium offers a variety of resources for L G B T Q Q service providers through their website (www.LGBTQQcampus.org). Another valuable resource is the Council for Advancement of Standards (C A S), which offers standards and guidelines for a variety of student services specialties, including lesbian, gay, bisexual, and transgender programs (www.cas.edu). These standards, along with self-assessment guides, can assist institutions in evaluating areas of growth in their L G B T Q Q student services.

Data collected from US institutions (Ritchie and Banning 2001; Sanlo et al. 2010) indicate that L G B T Q Q student service providers assume a variety of roles, including:

- Assessing needs of L G B T Q Q students on campus
- Assessing attitudes of heterosexual students
- Assessing campus climate and policies for L G B T Q Q students, faculty, and staff
- Developing a strategic plan, mission, and vision for L G B T Q Q services on campus
- Providing a safe space for L G B T Q Q students to gather on campus
- Establishing advisory boards for L G B T Q Q issues
- Creating educational programs, such as speaker series, safe-zone programs, and ally training
- Advising L G B T Q Q student groups and providing programmatic and financial support to these groups

- Creating peer-counsellor or mentoring programs for LGBTQQ students
- Providing advocacy and support services for LGBTQQ individuals
- Connecting with the academic leadership on campus to ensure inclusion of LGBTQQ content in the curriculum
- Serving as educators through the university judicial system for students engaging in homophobic behaviours
- Establish working relationships with LGBTQQ faculty, staff, and alumni
- Celebrating the contributions of LGBTQQ individuals on campus through programming and events like LGBTQQ graduation ceremonies
- Conducting fund-raising on behalf of the institution
- Supporting advocacy and activism work of students, faculty, and staff
- Reviewing campus policies for equity and compliance with national and provincial human rights codes
- Acting in an advisory capacity to other institutional offices on matters concerning LGBTQQ individuals
- Serving as mediators or policy advisors on complaints of discrimination
- Maintaining connections with other LGBTQQ service providers at other institutions

Together, these roles and strategies are focused on responding to individual and student group needs, as well as influencing those who shape institutional policies and practices. The goal is to create an ecology of acceptance and support on campus so that students who identify as LGBTQQ can succeed in spite of the challenges of their marginalized status.

CURRENT ISSUES AND TRENDS

Providing services to LGBTQQ individuals on campus engenders a number of issues that must be addressed. First and foremost, institutions that currently do not offer such services should consider establishing professional staff positions dedicated to working with LGBTQQ students, staff, and faculty. The primary struggle in this area revolves around funding concerns related to salary, operating, and programming costs for LGBTQQ centres. Sanlo et al. (2002) suggest that since LGBTQQ centres typically serve a broad constituency – students, faculty, and staff, funding should originate from different sections of the campus community (an excellent example of such collaboration was noted above in the University of Toronto LGBTQQ coordinator position).

Second, there is a strong need for assessing campus climate for LGBTQQ students, faculty, and staff at both the institutional and national levels. The importance for professionals to document the experiences of LGBTQQ students, along with the educational needs of heterosexual students, cannot be overstated. Campus climate data can be useful in establishing educational programs aimed at addressing homophobia, transphobia, and heterosexism, thereby contributing to the success of graduates who are prepared for a diverse work environment. Current information on the experiences of LGBTQQ individuals on Canadian post-secondary campuses is extremely limited in scope and nature, and further ignoring such voices could negatively impact institutions in the long run through unnecessary student attrition and potential alumni/ae regret. Regular intermittent assessment of campus climate for LGBTQQ students can help fill the gap in understanding their status and contribute to the development of more effective institutional environments.

Third, there is a need for review of institutional policies and practices that affect LGBTQQ individuals on campus. More specifically, the current trend of LGBTQQ rights in Canada suggests the need for proactive review of policies to be inclusive of all individuals. Institutions would be wise to review their non-discrimination policies to ensure that they include sexual orientation, and gender identity and expression among their delimiters. Student codes of conduct and policies regarding campus housing should also be reviewed with the same intent. Institutions could benefit from consulting leaders in the field, specifically in regards to transgender issues, since these concerns are relatively new to higher education circles. A particularly useful resource can be found in Bilodeau (2009) wherein the author offers a series of pragmatic concerns and proposed solutions to accommodate transgender and gender non-conforming students, faculty, and staff. A recent case at the University of Manitoba (CBC News 2013) suggests that more work needs to be done in that respect.

Fourth, professionals need to review emergent literature and policy implications regarding the experiences of racial and other minorities within the LGBTQQ community. The LGBTQQ community as a whole is not isolated from racism, ableism, sexism, transphobia, and ethnocentric viewpoints (Hidalgo 1995; Purdie-Vaughns and Eibach 2008). Students who also self-identify as people of colour, as transgender, as intersexed, as international, or as individuals with disabilities face additional challenges within both mainstream and LGBTQQ communities. Staff working with these students should understand their unique needs, and engage the campus community in dialogue that promotes understanding and acceptance of these individuals.

Lastly, institutions should create opportunities for a campus-wide collaboration between students, faculty, and staff to address LGBTQQ issues. The creation of a LGBTQQ centre does not eliminate the need for other professionals to become advocates and allies to LGBTQQ individuals. Furthermore, student affairs staff need to work with faculty to ensure the implementation of an LGBTQQ affirming curriculum. The inclusion, safety, and success of LGBTQQ students are institution-wide responsibilities, and ultimate solutions can only come from the participation of all campus constituents.

CONCLUSION

The LGBTQQ community is an integral part of higher education, and it is important for professionals to take steps to meet its needs. LGBTQQ students grapple with identity issues, homophobia, and heterosexism on a frequent basis, underscoring the critical need for support, advocacy, and education. Campus policies that are inclusive and supportive of LGBTQQ individuals assist in the creation of a positive learning environment for all. Current best practices in post-secondary education suggest that institutions would benefit from designating professional staff members to work specifically with LGBTQQ students, faculty, and staff. To achieve this it is imperative for institutional leaders to connect with other professionals and resources to determine how their campus can be more inclusive and supportive of LGBTQQ individuals. In the end, it can only result in a more inclusive campus supportive of the abilities and talents of all students – by celebrating all the identities they bring to the institution.

7

International Students

TAMARA LEARY, KEITH HOTCHKISS,
AND ALANA ROBB

"Finally, I'm here," thought Ming as she made her way from the taxi into the university residence – her home for the next eight months. She was exhausted and scared – it was quite a trek from China to Nova Scotia and having just spent a great deal of time at the airport trying to arrange a taxi she was beginning to question why on earth she left the comforts of her home. She approached the front desk and stood behind another student being served by the clerk. As Ming rooted through her knapsack frantically looking for the bundle of paper she assumed she would need she could overhear the conversation between the other student and the clerk. There was laughter and free-flowing conversation as the student signed papers and took a key before heading off with what appeared to be a group of family members and friends helping with the move-in. Ming proceeded to the counter. "Can I help you?" said Jim, the clerk. As she stumbled to find the right words Jim repeated his question – this time louder as if she didn't hear him the first time. "Register please" said Ming. After completing the paperwork Jim provided Ming with a large folder entitled International Student Information. "You will need to be at the international student orientation program which starts this afternoon – in fact you might want to hurry to get there," said Jim. "Oh no," thought Ming. She was beyond tired from the long journey and feeling overwhelmed and very nervous. Jim said, "You just go through these doors, turn right at the flag, pass four buildings, and take a left and then a right and you will see lecture hall 101 – it is in there." Too nervous and intimidated to admit she didn't fully understand what Jim had just said, Ming simply smiled and nodded her head politely. As she gathered her belongings and made her way down the hallway to her room, she could hear other students arriving at the counter with much laughter and conversation. Ming flicked on the light to her new room. There were two bedrooms that shared a common living area. One of the bedroom doors was closed and Ming thought she could hear someone in the room. She proceeded to move her things into her room and closed her door. She lay on her bed and reflected on the last seventy-two hours – packing, saying good-bye to her family and friends in China, travelling, almost forgetting her passport on the last plane, Jim, the other students she heard and the excitement that surrounded them. She was scared – what would this university world be like? What would Canada be like? How would she make friends? What if she failed her courses? What if the professors didn't like her? What would her roommate be like? Where was the nearest grocery store and mall? Would she need a special permit to work part-time? Where will she go over the winter holidays? Do they celebrate Chinese New Year here? She sat up and started rifling through the large file of information. "What does all this mean?" thought Ming. Gathering every bit of energy she could, she debated what to do next.

Ming didn't realize that in the bedroom next to hers, Alicia, her roommate, was lying on her bed somewhat terrified to move. She had just woken up from a nap having arrived from Calgary earlier that day. She didn't know anyone here, and although the front desk attendant gave her the information about the orientation events that night, she was too scared to go alone. Alicia wondered what this university world would be like as well. How would she make friends? What if she failed her courses? What if the professors didn't like her? What would her new roommate be like? Where was the nearest grocery store and mall? How soon could she go home for a visit? Could she get hired at Starbucks here given that she worked at one in Calgary? She pulled herself up and turned on the computer to review the new student information and to figure out her next steps. There was a knock at the main door of the unit: "Hello, anyone in there?" called Amanda, the resident life assignment. Both Ming and Alicia sprung from their beds and reached for their doorknobs at the same time.

INTRODUCTION

The above two first year students from different countries share a number of similarities in the challenges they face as they transition into the post-secondary world. There are indeed differences between the students as well, some of which are cultural. The institution has actively recruited both students and must ensure that supports and services are provided to each in a meaningful and effective manner. This requires an institution to reflect on existing practices and policies and to make informed adjustments or changes necessary to provide equitable and appropriate services. This is especially true for the emerging market of students from other countries.

Kunin and Associates (2012) concluded, in its review of trends in international student recruitment, that as recently as the early 2000s,

> international students were still primarily seen as a source of revenue for educational institutions, an asset for the internationalization of Canadian campuses and "ambassadors" for Canada in their country of origin. In the space of a few years, they have become a sought-after source of immigration for different levels of government (Hawthorne 2005). Public discourse and policies make no effort to hide the strategy of drawing on the human capital of students by offering to facilitate the transition process leading to permanent residency and turning them into ideal candidates for economic immigration (Alboim and Cohl 2012; Baas 2010; Papademetriou and Sumption 2011; Picot and Sweetman 2012).

Competition between Canadian post-secondary institutions for international students is fierce (Healey 2008; Madgett and Belanger 2008; Mavondo, Tsarenko, and Gabbott 2004). In addition to providing an increased source of tuition revenue, as well as considerable economic benefits to those communities where they enroll (Kunin and Associates 2012), international students bring a wealth of talent, knowledge, and awareness that institutions want their students to prosper from and, as a result, be better prepared to work in global environments. Canadian post-secondary institutions want to be associated with this calibre of graduates (McCormack and Labi 2007; Taras and Rowney 2007). After all, how an institution responds to the political, socio-economic, religious, racial, and cultural diversity in today's student population will directly impact its ability to sustain itself in a global society (Talbot 2003). Finally, as noted in Kunin and Associates' 2012 report, international students are often seen as cultural agents capable of helping small communities evolve toward values of openness to and respect for cultural diversity (Mosneaga 2013; Wade and Belkhodja 2012; Walton-Roberts 2011).

During the last three decades Canadian higher education has witnessed ebbs and flows in international student enrolment, ranging from approximately 21,470 students in 1975 to current enrolment levels of over 293,500 across all levels of study, making Canada the world's seventh most popular destination country hosting 5 per cent of internationally mobile students (CBIE 2014). In CBIE's *A World of Learning: Canada's Performance and Potential in International Education 2014*, it is estimated that this group accounts for 8 per cent of undergraduate university enrolments, 16 per cent of graduate enrolments, and 26 per cent of doctoral level enrolments. Overall the last decade (2003–13) has witnessed an 84 per cent increase in the number of international students in Canada, with an 11 per cent increase in 2012 alone. While some 194 countries of origin are represented among them, more than half of all international students in Canada are accounted for by enrolments from China (95,160), India (31,665), South Korea (18,295), Saudi Arabia (14,235), and France (13,090) (CBIE 2014). Such rapid increases across Canada have challenged many post-secondary institutions to adapt, adjust, and develop services and programs to meet the needs and expectations of this increasingly culturally diverse student body. The fact that Canada included among its international education strategies the doubling of the number of international students choosing to study in its colleges and universities by 2022 (IES 2014) suggests that this area will only grow in importance in the immediate future for Canada's post-secondary system.

Education is a provincial rather than federal responsibility in Canada, and legislation at both levels of government can and has significantly affected the status of international students studying in Canada. The Council of Ministers of Education for Canada (CMEC) is an intergovernmental body mandated to provide leadership and guidance to Canadian provinces and territories to ensure that their constitutional responsibilities are fulfilled. International relations has been identified by CMEC as a key area in need of a collective voice and one that is complicated by the clear division between the provincial and territorial jurisdiction of education and the national authority over foreign affairs.

A HISTORICAL PERSPECTIVE

The Canadian Bureau of International Education's (CBIE) Commission on "Foreign Student Policy, the Right Mix" (CBIE 1981) commented on the impact of government policy on "foreign students," as they were then called. Prior to 1973, international students could work and study in Canada with very little restriction, other than having the financial resources to pay their fees and living expenses. In fact, a student could apply for landed immigrant status from within the country. In 1973, federal legislation required that individuals must apply for this status from outside the country. At the same time, foreign students were restricted from having a job in Canada unless they were issued a work permit, and then only if a qualified Canadian were not able to fill the job. As costs of post-secondary education increased, this had a dramatic effect on international students' ability to finance their educational expenses. In 1978, a new immigration act required international students to obtain Student Authorization prior to coming to Canada; such authorization was specific to the student and to the institution of study, and it required regular renewal at an annual cost to the student.

Provincial governments also had a part to play in Canada's international education marketplace. In 1976, differential fees were first introduced in Ontario and Alberta. As reported in CBIE's Commission on Foreign Students (1981), both provinces justified the increase by arguing that, "foreign students should be making a larger contribution to the cost of their education, since neither they nor their parents made a substantial contribution to the provincial treasury through taxes" (20). In 1977, the government of Quebec followed suit and finally, in 1979, New Brunswick, Nova Scotia, and Prince Edward Island introduced differential fees (CBIE 1981). Currently, differential fees are assessed in each province.

Notwithstanding these measures, the number of international students increased from 21,470 in 1975 to 30,850 in 1983, followed by four years of declining enrolments that bottomed out at 23,335 in

1987. This decline caused Stewart to predict that "the international student at Canadian universities may well be going the way of the dodo bird" (1988, 8). Fortunately, this prediction did not materialize; however, Stewart went on to say,

> In light of this decline, this is sad news indeed. Our institutions and our domestic undergraduate students need an international student presence if they are to begin to understand the dimensions of our interdependent world. Homogeneity in our institutional student bodies is no way to prepare our youth for life in a pluralistic community of nations. (ibid)

International students then arrived in increasing numbers, once again reaching 37,034 by 1991. However, numbers began to decline the following year prompting Jim Fox (Humphries 1995) to state, in the 1994 CBIE National Report, that both internal and external factors were affecting this decline. Internal factors included tuition fee increases, additional health insurance costs, declines in scholarship funding, and a lack of promotion. "Externally," Fox suggested, "aggressive recruiting by the U.S.A., the U.K., and Australia were affecting Canada's numbers" (2). The notion of a national policy for international education became a hot topic within the Canadian international educational community once again, as did institutional expansion in international recruitment. About this time, the term "Internationalization" was becoming popular on university campuses, and in doing so really embraced the spirit of Colin Stewart's call for a larger international presence on campus to enhance the educational experience for all. Jane Knight (1994) observed that "the purpose and meaning of internationalization varied from institution to institution, but typically involved a range of activities, policies, and services that integrate an international and intercultural dimension into the teaching, research, and service functions of the institution" (2). At about this same time, Canadian universities began developing strategies to attract more international students to their campuses. International entrance scholarships were introduced, international recruitment was expanded, and more resources were committed to the support of international student functions on campus.

By the late 1990s international student enrolments in Canada began to rise steadily, and its composition had significantly changed since the 1970s. At present, the Asian student population represents the majority of international students in Canada, with approximately

150,000+ students compared to the mere 213 Asian students in Canada in 1975. It remains to be seen whether the composition of international students in Canada will continue to change. China is rapidly expanding its post-secondary capacity and the European numbers are steadily increasing. Currently though, many European countries are moving from a free tuition system to a user pay system. This may prompt senior university administrators in Europe to increase international recruitment as a means of increasing revenues, hence adding even more competition in the international student marketplace. Growth in North American numbers has also increased during this same period and US and Caribbean students are included as well in this group. By virtue of the fact that students in the North American market speak English and that the Canadian dollar provides a comparable cost advantage, this may well be the market that Canadian universities will have to seriously target in terms of future international recruitment. Africa's growth during the past three decades, while smaller, has been steadily growing. Given many of Africa's ongoing internal struggles and financial challenges, Canada and its universities must ensure that African countries are included in future internationalization plans.

According to most recent data (Education Facts 2012), the Province of Ontario enrolls the greatest number of international students (111,171), followed by British Columbia (68,321), and Quebec (38,114), collectively accounting for almost 75 per cent of all international students registered in Canadian universities. Institutions that develop aggressive recruitment strategies, while simultaneously increasing resources for support staff and scholarships, will most likely be more successful in attracting international students to their campuses. Perhaps emboldened and guided by the recently released *Canada's International Education Strategy* document (2014), greater numbers of institutions will seek to engage international markets for purposes of recruiting students and diversifying their campus enrolments. Should they do so, significant resources will need to be dedicated to their inclusion and matriculation.

CHOOSING TO STUDY IN A FOREIGN COUNTRY

The Right Mix (CBIE 1981) defined a "foreign student" as:

> an individual temporarily in Canada for the purpose of study, in most cases under the authority of a Student Authorization issued

by the Canadian Employment and Immigration Commission. Foreign students can come to Canada when they have been accepted by a Canadian educational institution and when they have demonstrated to Canadian Immigration authorities abroad that they have such an acceptance, have sufficient funds to finance their studies in Canada, and are of good character and not medical risks. (3)

In the early 1980s, "Foreign Student Advisors" advocated to be called "International Student Advisors" and "foreign students" to be called "international students." This, they argued, was a more positive expression. An international student was defined as "a non-Canadian student who does not have permanent resident status, and as such has received permission from the Canadian government to enter Canada for the purposes of study. Permission is usually granted in the form of a student authorization, and international students are expected to return home upon completion of their studies" (Queen's University International Centre 1992, 2). Most recently, however, Canadian Immigration has issued an open student permit allowing students to switch institutions without having to renew their authorization. Furthermore, Canada has begun recently to actively recruit international students as prospective candidates for permanent immigration, inasmuch as they can bring a high level of skill to fuel an emerging economic profile and contribute to the continuity of an increasingly global community (Kunin and Associates 2012).

Why does an international student leave the comfort of home to seek post-secondary education in a foreign country? More specifically, why do they come to Canada? The Canadian Bureau of International Education (CBIE 2014) reported that 80 per cent of students indicated that living in a safe country was important in their selection of a Canadian institution, and 78 per cent cited having access to a high quality education as being an important reason for studying in Canada. Other reasons include prestige of a Canadian diploma, lower cost compared to other countries, attractive conditions for admission, availability of scholarships, and the fact that their parents or friends studied in Canada. Based on what some students have told these authors, they come here because due to cost and limited spaces a quality education is unavailable to them in their home country – or is even nonexistent. In addition, a particular field of study they wished to pursue may not have been available at home. In some countries academic opportunities for women are scant. They want to learn about a subject area – business, for example, from a "Western perspective." Their intention may be to stay here permanently or merely obtain work experience upon graduation. They may wish to bring home their Western expertise and English language skills to improve business practices in their home country. They might also be on scholarship from their home country or international agency such as the Commonwealth Scholarship program. In such cases they will be obliged to return to contribute to their home country. Some, not many, may be using the student permit route to escape a dangerous situation at home and intend to apply for refugee status upon arrival. Others are avoiding compulsory military service. Not all come willingly; some students are pressured by their families.

Although international students have been a presence on Canadian campuses for many years, it is within the last two decades that they have been perceived as an integral part of the internationalization process. Such students contribute to internationalization, in effect, by bringing the world to the campus. Having a diverse student population, especially in less diverse regions of the country, enriches academic life by introducing new perspectives and allowing domestic students to develop cross-cultural skills, thus better preparing them for the emerging knowledge-based global society and economy. However, just having a healthy percentage of international students is not the only feature of an internationalized campus. In fact, more recent assessments of such an expected outcome has yielded somewhat disappointing results, with one study indicating that relatively few international students reported having developed friendships with Canadian students during their stay in the country, with those from the United States (84 per cent) most likely to do so and those from the Middle East and Northern Africa (28 per cent) least likely (CBIE 2014).

Subsequent to her earlier work, Knight has since updated her 1997 definition of internationalization from "the process of integrating an international/intercultural dimension into the teaching, research, and services functions of the institution" (Knight 1997, 8) to "the process of integrating an international, intercultural, or global dimension into the purpose, functions or delivery of post-secondary education" (Knight 2004, 11). The updated definition is inclusive of all sectors of post-secondary education – the academic and non-academic, as well as policies and practices. Knight's focus is on the general organizational approaches to internationalization rather than the myriad details needed for faculty and staff to internationalize their curriculum and services (Qing, Schweisfurth, and Day 2010; Sanderson 2008).

Hamrick (1999) categorized higher education's conception of internationalization into four discrete views, each with a specific goal:

a *International studies* – to educate students about the various cultures, languages, political views and sociological perspectives in the world;
b *Student mobility* – to introduce and engage domestic students in international relationships and experiences with other students and faculty;
c *Sharing expertise and development* – for faculty to share expertise and skills with foreign faculty and students in other parts of the world; and,
d *Education* – to ensure students are adequately prepared to live and work in an international and culturally diverse world.

All four views are important and one could argue that the first is the most traditional and the fourth captures the more current trend. The increasing growth of an international student body and a domestic student body looking for the international experience, in addition to current political, social, and economic global realities, have heightened the urgency of responding effectively to the current internationalization trend (Healey 2008).

ISSUES FACED BY INTERNATIONAL STUDENTS

Given the well-established correlation between student engagement and student success (Gardner 2007; Kuh et al. 2005; Pascarella and Terenzini 2005), the importance of understanding the experiences of international students is obvious. Issues like student transition (Edgeworth and Eiseman 2007; Hayes and Lin 1994; Poyrazli and Grahame 2007; Ren, Bryan, Min, and Wei 2007; Ramsay, Jones, and Barker 2007); culture shock (Brown and Holloway 2008; Zhou, Jindal-Snap, Topping, and Todman 2008); discrimination (Hanassah 2006; Poyrazli and Lopez 2007); use of support services (Tidwell and Hanassah 2007); student satisfaction (Gatfield, Barker, and Graham 1999; Mavondo, Tsarenko, and Gabbott 2004); and student well being (Bartram 2007; Sovic 2008; Rosenthal and Russell 2008; Russell, Thomson, and Rosenthal 2008) are well documented, with the bulk of the research having been conducted in the United States, United Kingdom, and Australia. How a Canadian university responds to or supports international students through their transition into first year is not as well understood. Neither has any significant attention been paid to the correlation between international students' university experiences and their educational outcomes.

In addition to the routine pressures domestic students face during their first year of university or college, international students are also faced with a new culture, new education system, and significant language barriers (Ren et al. 2007). Researchers have responded by investigating the various aspects of international students' academic and personal experiences. The correlation between international students' experiences and their level of success however has not been sufficiently explored in Canada (Grayson 2008) nor in other parts of the world (Madgett and Belanger 2008; Ramsay, Jones, and Barker 2007). According to Dao, Lee, and Chang (2007), transition experiences for international students are affected by three variables: acculturation levels, English fluency, and perceived levels of social support. All three variables can contribute to a heightened sense of psychological distress (Dao, Lee, and Chang 2007; Flaitz 2003) or success. Each of these points warrants some attention.

Acculturation

When an individual enters a new culture, it is natural, inevitable, and desirable to experience some level of culture shock (Brislin and Yoshida 1994). The term "culture shock" dates to the 1950s, when anthropologist Kalervo Oberg first defined it "as a disease suffered by individuals living in a new cultural environment" (Chapdelaine and Alexitch 2004, 276). The term, as defined here and still widely used today, has been questioned and challenged over the years (Sovic 2008). With so many variables factored into what can influence students' transition experiences it is unrealistic to expect only one term to accurately reflect the process in its entirety.

Seele describes culture as "a frame of reference consisting of learned patterns of behaviour, values, assumptions, and meaning which are shared to varying degrees of interest, importance, and awareness with members of a group" (1996, 9). Anderson asserted that "culture along with genetics is the most enduring, powerful shaper of human behaviour" (1999). A common analogy is that of the iceberg (Althen 1995). Obvious aspects of culture such as language, dress, art, and music are the visible tip of the iceberg. However, it is those things that lie hidden deep beneath the surface – values, assumptions, and meanings – that are at the heart of the dynamics of culture shock.

Culture shock occurs when a visitor's culturally laden and most often tacit vision of the world clashes with that of the host culture (Barker, 1990). It is likened to playing a game with no knowledge of the rules (Chapdelaine and Alexitch 2004). Nothing makes sense; patterns of behaviour that were learned from infancy no longer apply. This process of acculturation has been described as a U-shaped curve comprising several stages (Barker, 1990; Pedersen 1994). Although this theory has been criticized as oversimplified and unsubstantiated, it offers a vivid picture of the emotions involved (Pedersen 1994). The initial exhilaration of the honeymoon stage gives way to depression and typical symptoms of stress. Later, hostility sets in as newcomers are overwhelmed by negative feelings about the host culture and the odd behaviour of the locals. Eventually the newcomer overcomes many of the obstacles and develops a sense of pride and independence. In this last stage, the new culture is recognized as a different but acceptable way of life.

Gochenour and Janeway proposed a more complex seven-stage process necessary for cross-cultural interaction (1993, 3). Success is defined as the "degree to which a person is able to enter into respectful, appreciative relationships (though not necessarily admiring) within a culture other than his or her own." The first three levels involve establishing contact and observing what is going on. The fourth level is a bridging stage where a role is established within the society. It is interesting that at this stage an individual can reach a level of comfort and function quite well. However, to progress to a higher level of establishing meaningful relationships, it is necessary to develop a conscious knowledge of oneself as a cultural being and recognize that we are "products of one culture, yet affected and enlarged by our involvement in another" (ibid., 8).

Gochenour and Janeway's stage theory supports the notion that meaningful interactions with the host culture are a necessary part of the adjustment process, an idea that concurs with Chapdelaine and Alexitch's (2004) research on Canadian graduate students suggesting that interaction with the host culture decreases as cross-cultural differences over friendship, marriage, educational system, and language increase. In addition, as the size of the compatriot group increases, interactions with hosts tend to decrease. This does not necessarily mean that students should avoid their compatriots who can provide emotional support especially in the early stages (Lyakhovetska 2003). Similarly, work by Tompson and Tompson confirmed that students identify the development of a social network as the most difficult aspect of adjustment: "Loneliness and the fear of not fitting in kept students mentally preoccupied until an acceptable level of stability in the social domain was achieved" (1996, 54). These authors also observed that the next most difficult challenges were experienced in regard to language and cultural norms concerning classroom behaviours and interactions with peers, professors, and staff.

Academic Challenges

The most obvious and arguably the best understood challenge international students whose mother tongue is not English encounter in English speaking universities is language proficiency (Dao Lee and Chang 2007; Ren et al. 2007; Sovic 2008; Wang et al., 2008). In addition to posing difficulties in the academic component of a student's experience, not speaking or understanding English well interferes with the social aspects of the student experience and can contribute to social isolation (Ren et al. 2007).

Ren et al. (2007) cautioned institutions' use of language-based measures, like the Test of English as a Foreign Language (TOEFL) and the Graduate Record Examination (GRE), as indicators of graduate international students' ability to cope well with the transition into the foreign school or program of study. Instead the authors urge policy makers and administrators to incorporate student interviews into the admissions process. They concluded that the one-to-one communication would serve as a more reliable proxy indicator of the student's potential for academic and personal success.

According to a study conducted by Beykont and Daiute (2002), students' values, expectations, and assumptions of what constitutes a good class is influenced by their prior learning experiences. International students taught in an elementary and secondary school system that valued a more traditional pedagogical framework, in which the teacher is central to the learning, found the transition into a student-centred post-secondary classroom challenging. International students described post-secondary education in their country of origin as also being traditional, with the professors being the unquestioned deliverers of knowledge and students the information receivers. Beykont and Daiute found that the international students preferred classes in which the professors offered an equitable and safe learning environment – one in which the professor maintained control of the discussion, but solicited diverse student input and comfortable exchanges. Classes that the international students described as less than comfortable included seminar formats in which the professor permitted the students, or a select few, to dominate the class discussion and wherein the professor offered little structure or leadership.

Social Support

International students like domestic students indicate a positive relationship between levels of support and level of adjustment to the post-secondary experience. In fact they prioritize social relationships as having the most significant impact on their successful matriculation (Ramsay et al. 2007; Zhao et al. 2005).

Madgett and Belanger (2008) analyzed data from an online survey examining the role of the university providing relevant information to international students pre- and post-arrival. Overall, Canadian universities are meeting the expectations of international students. In some cases, such as technology support, institutions are even surpassing expectations and in other areas, such as assisting with finding accommodations, learning where to shop for groceries, and transport from airports or bus stops upon arrival are falling short of expectations. These personal connections set the foundation for the international students' experience and the authors strongly recommended that administrators invest the resources necessary to ensure that international students receive these types of supports.

Abel (2002) recommended that international students find ways to become actively engaged in their learning (in the classroom) and social life in order to be successful in the classroom. The onus is on the student to seek out appropriate tutors and professors rather than assuming that the help will come to them. There is recognition that there are differences between, in this case, American and international academic structures, although the author assumes that an international student will be confident and familiar enough with the host culture to proactively address their potential areas of difficulty. However, Briguglio (2000) reported on a group of international students in Australia who preferred not being left on their own to figure out how things worked. It takes time to learn the expectations of a new culture and time to adjust; having someone provide information and assist in the transition could make the experience much more enjoyable and successful.

In addition to adjustment and adaptation to a foreign university campus, international students often face discrimination. Hanassah (2006) found that international students attending an institution of higher learning in the United States faced varying degrees of perceived discrimination, depending on their region of origin. Ensuring that international students have the supports and services necessary to assist with their transition into a foreign university also requires higher education institutions to challenge existing cultural stereotypes and ignorance on campus, as well as in the community. Simply accepting international students into a university alone does not make that institution diverse nor free of the injustices that international students sometimes encounter.

First-Year Transition

There is little doubt that student engagement – the degree to which students are involved with the academic and non-academic components of their post-secondary education – positively affects a student's academic and personal learning experience (Pascarella and Terenzini 2005). Research has consistently demonstrated that the highest rate of student attrition occurs during a student's first year of enrolment (Feldman 2004). Universities and colleges fully recognize the importance of supporting and engaging their first-year students (Cuseo 2004; Pascarella and Terenzini 2005). The National Resource Center for the First Year Experience and Students in Transition (http://www.sc.edu/fye/) continues to be a valuable resource and leader in research and literature on the importance of higher education initiatives aimed at supporting first year students, and others, through the various periods of transition inherent to the post-secondary experience.

Brown and Ward (2007) refer to the 1993 work of Vincent Tinto, and to his use of the phrase "academic and social integration" (303). Students who have a higher quality of experiences in and out of the classroom are 50 per cent more likely to graduate. The meaning of Tinto's work for higher education professionals is "institutions that consciously reach out to form personal bonds between students, faculty, and staff and that emphasize frequent and rewarding contact beyond the classroom are the most successful in promoting student persistence" (ibid.). Pascarella and Terenzini (2005) have consistently documented that what happens outside the classroom is the greatest predictor of student academic and personal success.

Johnson et al. (2007) argued that, while relationships first-year students develop within their academic and social community directly impact their success, the emphasis tends to be on the student to make this happen rather than the institution to ensure the opportunity; for students of different racial and ethnic groups, as well as international students, this can present a great challenge. Such studies have implications for student services professionals as the connection is made between acculturation, academic challenges, and the need for social support.

THE ROLE OF STUDENT SERVICES

Drawing from extant literature (Guo and Chase 2011; Moores and Popadiuk 2011), there is little question that international students require supports that can exceed what is traditionally offered their domestic peers transitioning into post-secondary education. With the increasing international student enrolment in Canadian higher education there is urgency for senior administrators to understand the needs of this particular group of diverse learners and to respond in a manner that will result in positive student experiences and successful retention numbers.

With only limited Canadian research providing a best practices framework to support international students with their transition into higher education, the obvious question is: who is responsible for coordinating and developing existing and new supports and services? The natural custodianship should rest with student services professionals, already well versed in responding to the expectations of a changing student population (Dalton and Gardner 2002). How an institution recruits and retains international students will be influenced by the practices, programs, and expertise the student services unit offers. Given the relationship between student engagement and student success (King 2003; Kuh 2003; Pascarella and Terenzini 2005) and the expertise in student development that student services offers, there is a natural expectation for higher education to position student services as a key provider of service and support for international students.

International student centres staffed by dedicated advisors are common among Canadian universities. The centres are usually housed within the student services sector of the institution, and typically report to the senior administrator responsible for student services. Such centres have the unique challenge of discerning the needs and providing services to students at times from fifty or more countries. It is virtually impossible to know the cultural perspective of each and every student, especially as international students are individuals as well as cultural beings. However, it is possible and advisable to become familiar with the abundant literature on inter-cultural communication. In addition, there is no harm in sensitively asking students specific questions about their background. Althen (1995, 84) suggested the use of questions that address status, friendship patterns, verbal interactions, and male-female relationships. Talking with students in an open nonjudgmental way is a very rewarding part of an international student advisor's job that can also profoundly deepen cultural understanding.

Any discussion of intercultural sensitivity should include the work of Bennett (1993), who maintained that such a quality is not inherent. Bennett created a developmental model hypothesizing that intercultural competence involves "phenomenological knowledge" that relies on experience to develop skills for understanding intercultural interactions. The six stages of his model begin with an "ethnocentric" state and advance towards an "ethnorelative" orientation. At the one end, ethnocentric stages of avoidance, protection, and minimization progress from extreme levels of rejection of other cultures to a minimal acceptance of other cultures without acknowledging different world views. At the other end of the model, ethnorelative stages of acceptance, adaptation, and integration recognize that communication and values are embedded in the cultural context and necessarily involve learning to respect the different opinions and values of others.

To prevent cultural misunderstanding, it is crucial that International Centre staff understand the cultural basis of verbal and non-verbal communication styles. One such theory distinguishes between individualism and collectivism (Brislin and Yoshida 1994) to explain the fundamental differences between North American/European societies and those of Africa, Latin America, and Asia. Researchers generally agree that individualists value self-reliance, competition, and reward, and are interested in pursuing their personal goals, distrust people in power, and are not always loyal to their workplaces. Collectivists, on the other hand, value loyalty, sharing, social interaction, conformity, and specifically the advice and direction of family members. Their own goals are secondary to those of the group. These and other fundamental differences have implications for student services personnel.

Student development theory must be applied with caution to international students because it has been based primarily on research with North Americans (Althen 1995). Kodama et al. (2002) noted that psychosocial theory, in particular, is grounded in an emphasis on individualism, self-exploration, and achieving independence, whereas Asian students' cultural values are based on collectivism. Chickering and Reisser's (1993) theory of seven vectors of development, one such example, would apply differently to international students pressured by family expectations; should they seek counselling they may be reluctant to make independent decisions. Emotional development may be such that it is difficult to interpret cues that might signal distress in personal counselling situations.

BEST PRACTICES

Knight (2000) recommended that advisory and support services for international students include trained staff and designated admissions officers. There should also be orientation and re-entry programs, social cultural and peer programs that involve international and domestic students, counselling on visa, health, and employment issues, as well as academic advising, links to the local community, and an emergency assistance plan. McBride (1998) recommended that, "money spent on ensuring that services to international students are good may be the best investment in a recruitment strategy" (31). In addition to the above emphasis on the first-year experience and acclimation, services and opportunities for international students should include personal counselling, a place to practise religion, a place to gather, such as an international centre, scholarships, and evaluative procedures, as well as some flexibility with regard to fee payments and a facilitative demeanour among business office staff and administration. Standards have to be met and maintained and appropriate services have to be established. Knight (2000) made the case for both qualitative and quantitative tracking measures, including benchmarking – an evidence-based quality management tool that embraces measurement, comparison, and identification of best practices and improvements.

As most colleges and universities are members of the Canadian Bureau of International Education (CBIE), international staff members have excellent opportunities to network with colleagues from across the country through listservs, online seminars, conferences, and regional workshops. This support system is especially useful for anyone who has just entered the field because they have access to a wealth of expertise. CBIE has set an ethical code of practice in international education that is an excellent guide to follow.

It is important to recognize that, first and foremost, international students as such have many of the same academic and personal needs as domestic students. In addition to common transition challenges, the needs of international students are further complex and multifaceted with the additional range of cultural, social, educational, and logistical concerns. A comprehensive international student service model is most successful when it accommodates these needs in a systematic and integrated manner, from the beginning to the conclusion of the student experience. Although such services might appear as an added cost to the institution, the initial outlay may be worth the expense in terms of bolstering international student retention and enriching the global and multicultural dimensions of the institution.

Orientation

Orientation, welcoming, and reception may be the most important function of an international student services office. However, only 36 per cent of university and 50 per cent of college-bound international students surveyed in Canada have reported attending such a program (Canadian Bureau of International Education, 2004) (CBIE). Apparently, some may not attend orientation for reasons ranging, for example, from not knowing about the opportunity in the first place to not being able to secure timely study permits or flight arrangements. International centre advisors must underscore the importance of effective orientation programs as vital tools for helping international students adjust to campus and community life. Clearly, when such students do miss out on important information, confusion is inevitable, as is the frustration of those who are assigned to assist them. Ideally, incoming international students should be met at the airport, although rising enrolments will continue to make this a more challenging task. At the very least, a reception centre should be set up at the institution to help address any immediate concerns upon arrival. Most importantly, orientation should provide arriving students with the opportunity to settle in and begin establishing a network of friends, a step so vital to their satisfaction and success. The most effective programs are therefore the ones that use experienced student volunteers and succinct communication, which helps prevent students from becoming overwhelmed by the large amounts of information that they are expected to absorb under conditions that are often stressful or detrimental to their full attention (e.g., overcoming jet lag).

Requiring all new international students to attend an onsite program is a matter of institutional policy and resources, although it may be neither practical nor desirable to do so. However, there are other ways to reach these students. It has been suggested that orientation should start before students arrive and continue beyond the first week of classes by offering both pre-arrival information and follow-up sessions (Althen 1995; Anderson 2002). Most institutions send out pre-arrival information and feature extensive website resources. Murphy, Hawkes, and Law (2002) suggested several ways that websites could be designed to "initiate, complement, or extend pre-departure training by offering a virtual introduction to a campus and a community" (38). A comprehensive site should include information on immigration, workshops, cultural societies, job opportunities, community programs, academic and personal support, personal safety, a student message board, and links to a currency converter, home newspapers, and tourism contacts.

Many Canadian universities offer orientation programs specific to international students. Prior to students arriving on campus international advisors will contact students to provide information pertaining to arrival, international student office and advisor contacts, schedule of events for orientation, student handbook, and information pertaining to academic registration. While frontloading resources and programs is critical to effecting initial adjustments of international students, services also need to be extended to support them as they encounter new experiences throughout the academic year. Follow-up orientation sessions on various topics, such as the academic system, study skills, employment, and Canadian culture can all be offered throughout the year once students have passed the initial adjustment phase. Such contacts can also generate more complex questions and concerns that, in turn, benefit from additional follow-up. Adaptation to a new culture and learning experience is an on-going process that often progresses through predictable steps, requiring different resources at each stage. Ultimately, the delivery of effective international student services depends on the quality of rela-tionships established from the start. A positive and supportive initia-tion should connect students to their peers and prepare them for accommodating the most immediate challenges of a new culture and a new educational experience. Such an effort might include informa-tion and advice concerning immigration regulations, financial aid, employment, counselling, health services, housing, and other needs, as might be addressed by various programs and interventions. The importance of such programs was underscored in the 2014 CBIE Report, where several exemplary models were featured, including a newly designed International Student Orientation Program at Capilano Univeristy, a Pre-Arrival Orientation Webinar series at McGill University, a College of the Rockies International Week, engaging international and domestic students in an introduction to the local community, and a Culture-to-Community Program at Memorial University of Newfoundland.

Immigration Advising

It would be correct to say that most staff time in any International Centre is consumed with assisting students with immigration con-cerns and questions. Furthermore, if the office provides these services to "English as a Second Language" (ESL) students, this will require an even greater amount of time. Students need accurate information and assistance with the completion of forms to extend their study permits, to obtain temporary resident permits, and to secure post graduation work permits. The Canadian Citizenship and Immigra-tion website (http://www.cic.gc.ca/english/index.asp) is the most reli-able source of information for international students and advisors. Although it is desirable for students to take responsibility for them-selves, immigration is complex and forms not completed perfectly can result in additional cost and inconvenience. As international student numbers increase it is imperative to find strategies to continue a high level of personal service in that regard. For example, institutions might consider offering bi-weekly workshops to assist with completing renewal of entry visa and study permit forms until such needs are met. Self-service information guides that can be downloaded to a laptop computer or mobile device (e.g., cellphone, iPad) might also relieve some of the confusion associated with such a process.

Financial Aid

The CBIE (2004) reported that 50 per cent of international students experience financial problems during their post-secondary stay. Differential fees for international students are applied at all institutions, resulting in tuition fees that are often double those for domestic students. Scholarships and bursaries are generally offered through university financial aid offices or admissions, but resources are often limited. Although students are made aware of the cost prior to coming, and in many cases have to prove to Canadian Immigration authorities that they have the necessary resources, many students arrive with insufficient funds to support themselves. Technically an international student cannot be in financial need, having had to prove financial security, and as such should not qualify for university financial need bursaries. To compensate, some universities have responded to the financial need for international students by developing awards and scholarships based on scholastic achievement and extracurricular activities.

Employment

The CBIE (2004) also reported that three out of ten international students work on campus, an opportunity that has been very helpful for many students who are short of funds. However, it cannot finance their entire tuition and living expenses. Furthermore, it usually takes several months for the new student to acquire a part-time job that in most cases is just above minimum wage. In 2007 the Canadian federal government initiated a pilot project to provide off-campus work permits to international students studying at particular public and private institutions. Currently there are public and private institutions from all ten provinces and one territory participating in the Off-Campus Work Permit Program. Such permits authorize students to work up to twenty hours per week during regular academic sessions and up to full-time during scheduled breaks. In addition graduates can participate in the Post-Graduation Work Permit Program, allowing them to work for a period equal to the time they studied in Canada. If a student graduates from a four-year university program then he or she could be issued up to a three-year work permit; an eight-month diploma program could result in an eight-month work permit, and so on.

Students can benefit from workshops on finding local employment. Student employment offices need to understand the challenges that face students as they begin the job search process. Spencer-Rodgers and Cortijo (1998) reported that international students identify work experience, job search skills, and career planning and preparation as their most critical career development needs. Major barriers to succeeding in the workplace for them are the differences in cultural behaviours and expectations and the notion of self-promotion, or the need to emphasize their strengths, engage in self-assessment and decision making, and understand office corporate culture, as well as various local work practices and customs.

Counselling

It is often challenging to deal with mental health issues as they pertain to international students. Sue and Sue (1990) identified characteristics of counselling that can be misinterpreted when applied to clients from different cultures. Culture-bound values associated with counselling include an individualistic worldview, an emphasis on self disclosure, linear and analytic thinking, separation of the mental and the physical, and the importance of discussing one's feelings. International students may be reluctant to seek personal counselling as some cultures do not see the value in seeking mental health treatment or disclosing personal information beyond their immediate family circle. Nevertheless, international students are under a great deal of stress, are subject to many of the same mental health problems as domestic students, and are far away from family support. Ideally, international students should have access to counsellors with cross-cultural expertise.

Health Services

International students need to have health coverage upon arrival. As health care is a provincial matter, each province handles it differently.

Due to costs, dental care is generally excluded, which is unfortunate, since many international students are at an age when typical dental problems, such as the emergence of wisdom teeth, often occur. Many students arrive, never having visited a dentist, only to find that the cold temperatures aggravate existing cavities. It is very useful to have emergency medical funds to assist students with extra expenses in that regard.

Housing

Finding suitable accommodation on arrival is one of the prevalent concerns facing international students. They often apply late for on-campus residence, only to find that they are offered a place on a waiting list unless the university has reserved spaces for them ahead of time. Quite often, if they remain on the waiting list, they stand a good chance of obtaining a bed space during the first week of classes. However, reluctant to take such a gamble, many arrive without permanent accommodation. If the institution does not have an off-campus housing office, the International Student staff needs to provide assistance in these matters. This can be a stressful experience for everyone.

Universities that have a well-organized residence life program can provide an excellent means for students to make friends, improve speaking and listening skills, and learn about Canadian culture and youth culture in particular. When international students are dispersed throughout the residence, it can be a wonderful learning experience for everyone that is further enhanced when Canadian roommates take an international student to their home communities for holidays. Conflicts will of course arise; therefore, resident assistants have to be appropriately trained with these potential issues in mind.

Programming

Finally, the International Student Centre will, as time allows, engage in a variety of programs. It is advantageous for the Centre to have a mission statement and goals to guide programming, based on student needs, current theories associated with cross-cultural adaptation, intercultural sensitivity, and student development. To reiterate, Bennett's (1993) work suggests that program planning should address the audience's level of cross-cultural sensitivity as they move along a continuum from *ethnocentric* to *ethnorelative* orientations. Klak and Martin used Bennett's theories to evaluate a semester-long, large-scale celebration of Latin American culture on one campus and found that "progress toward greater intercultural understanding seems possible through a combination of special events, related courses, and a supportive campus environment" (2003, 445). When a wide range of events is offered, students can pick and choose those appropriate to their current intercultural perspective. Events developed and delivered by institutions across Canada include: social programs, e.g. an international student night celebration; exploring the local community; academic events, e.g. a speaker series on topics specific to diversity and inclusion; curriculum designed to bring a global perspective to the topic at hand; and the development of institutional policy and practice specific to the inclusion and needs of the international student population.

Many Canadian institutions sponsor an International Development Week. At the University of Prince Edward Island (UPEI), for example, this annual event held in January is organized by a working committee comprised of representatives from Student Services, UPEI faculty and staff, the student union, and the international student body. Both Saint Mary's University in Halifax and the UPEI "International Development Week" offer a wide variety of events planned collaboratively with faculty and Canadian and international students alike. Although such events require a tremendous amount of work, with the International Centre playing the lead role, they provide a much-needed venue for international awareness and celebration.

International Student Centres also assume the lead in the design and delivery of peer programs for international students. Abe et al. (1998) found that participation in a peer program helped students feel more adjusted and enhanced their interpersonal skills, and noted that Asian students seem to have the most difficulty with such adjustment. Lastly, the researchers concluded that peer programs have a significant impact on adjustment and they suggested that such programs could be used effectively for other purposes, such as teaching academic skills and encouraging volunteer experience. Regardless, the successful adjustment of international students is best facilitated when a variety of proactive programs and services anticipate their concerns and respond with options supportive of the variety of needs they present.

Post-College/University Plans

Meeting the matriculation and social and academic needs of international students constitutes an already full agenda for any International Student Centre staff. But the demand for additional services to help effect the successful transition beyond the college or university will likely increase. In the 2014 CBIE Report, 50 per cent of all international student respondents indicated their intention to apply for permanent resident status in Canada in the future. Given the new emphasis on recruiting international students as potential contributors to Canada's emerging global economy (see the 2014 release of *Canada's International Education Strategy*) it makes sense to organize various sources of information that can facilitate the next steps once students have completed their degree programs. Relevant opportunities highlighted in the 2014 CBIE Report include Post-Graduation Work Permit Program (PGWP), Federal Skilled Worker Program (FSWP), Provincial Nominee Program (PNP), and the Canadian Experience Class (CEC). All of these programs are designed to match the education, skills, and/or work experience of applicants with Canada's labour market needs. In no uncertain terms, Canada's Minister of International Trade averred, "International education is critical to Canada's success. In a highly competitive, knowledge-based global economy, ideas and innovation go hand in hand with job creation and economic growth. In short, international education is at the very heart of our current and future prosperity" (IES 2014, 4).

To the extent that campus International Student Centre advisors see themselves sharing in this mission and supporting international graduates to do the same, it becomes important to identify this as yet another way post-secondary institutions can serve their constituents.

TRAINING AND PREPARATION

Canadian student services look to organizations like the Canadian Association for College and University Student Services (CACUSS) for guidance and resources to develop the profession. Founded in 1973 as an umbrella organization to the University and College Placement Association (UCPA) and the Canadian Association of University Student Personnel Services (CAUSPS), this association recognizes and supports Canadian student services professionals (Hardy Cox and Strange 2010). The education, experiences, and professional credentials for a student services professional working with international students are consistent with those for working with domestic students. Such preparation might include knowledge, skills, and training in student development, social services, community development, and leadership in post-secondary education; equally relevant is having personal and professional experiences and skills working with diverse populations of learners, exposure to a variety of cultures, the ability to support students during periods of transition, and a solid understanding of international student needs and expectations. An international student advisor is not expected to be certified in all qualifications that traditionally support students – advisors are the point of contact for international students to help navigate the broader services and supports available to them within the institution.

Student service professionals working with international students also inherit – often by default – the responsibility of championing internationalization efforts of the institution on behalf of students and staff. Love and Estanek identified actions for Student Service professionals to adopt a global perspective, including conducting research on global issues in student services (2004, 183). The authors described the limited research that exists on student services work and internationalization in higher education as "anecdotal and exhortative" and recommended that student services work with faculty to research and develop models and theories from a global perspective (183).

We know that the recruitment and retention of international students is a vital component of internationalization within higher education. How a university responds to the academic and personal needs and expectations of international students will directly influence the students' experience. Positive student experiences correlate positively with engaged and successful students. Student service professionals play a pivotal role in supporting international students and as such have a wealth of experience and expertise to offer to researchers and higher education leaders in the development of best practices models for international student centres.

This is an ideal and timely opportunity for student services to assume responsibility for the development and delivery of international student supports and services across Canadian campuses. Kuh (as cited in Komives et al. 2003) offered this appropriate metaphor:

Working on a college campus today is like white-water rafting. To negotiate the rapids, one must use a variety of psychological and behavioral skills to change direction. One must also take into account as many variables as possible: the current, eddies, rocks, the laws of physics, other rafts and paddlers, and so forth. Moment by moment, student affairs professionals must decide when to let the river have its way and when to use their professional knowledge, judgment and skill to change direction. To survive in the white water of the coming decades, student affairs staff must embrace ambiguity, risk taking, team building, and continuous learning. (291)

Internationalization, of which the recruitment and retention of international students are significant components, is the current: student services professionals are best poised to navigate the waters.

8

Students with Disabilities

JOAN WOLFORTH

In 1988 Chris enrolled in the faculty of arts at a large Canadian university. His admission grades were stellar. Chris required his reading in Braille or recorded on to a 4-track cassette tape. He produced his own Braille documents on a manual stylus or special typewriter and dictated them to his mother, who typed them in regular print. A counsellor from Student Services read exam questions to him and he dictated his answers to a scribe. Sometimes he used an electric typewriter but he couldn't correct his typing errors. At their first meeting his history professor told him he shouldn't be in university because he couldn't read. There was no service to help him obtain the help he required to succeed in university. He relied heavily on an outside specialist agency for this. He met few other students and was very lonely and eventually dropped out of university. His nephew had the same genetic vision loss disorder. He achieved stellar admission grades and entered the same university in 2008. He could read Braille but preferred to use a laptop computer with a voice screen reader. The university now had a well-staffed service including an adaptive technology computer laboratory. He obtained digital format books direct from the publisher, or the service digitalized reading materials with a high-speed scanner and adaptive software. He loaded his reading material on to his iPod. He wrote his exams himself using appropriate technology. At his request, the university provided exams in Braille. He received funding from his province to pay for specialized materials and services. Professors no longer questioned his right or his capability to be in university.

INTRODUCTION

The above case illustrates the revolution that has taken place over the past twenty years in the lives of post-secondary students with disabilities. Institutions now accept that students with disabilities have a place in the academy. This has not only changed the lives of students themselves but has also resulted in the development of a new group of professionals charged with providing service for these students. Initially, students who received support tended to have visible disabilities, but in more recent years a much larger number of students with invisible disabilities have also sought assistance from disability services. In Ontario, where the total number of university students self-identifying as persons with disabilities quadrupled between 1992 (4,045) and 2008 (17,002), those who identified as having mental health issues increased 128 per cent in just four years between 2004 and 2008 (COU 2010). Similar proportions have been found in recent studies of students with disabilities, such as Fichten et al. (2014), where 611 students enrolled in ninety-eight different colleges and universities across nine provinces reported most commonly (about 57 per cent) impairments of a psychological/psychiatric nature, followed by a learning disability (LD), and attention deficit hyperactivity disorder (ADHD). This precipitous rise reflects both a broader definition of disabilities and a greater understanding of how disabilities can shape the post-secondary experience for students.

The same period has also witnessed an evolution in the aspirations of students with disabilities and in community attitudes towards them. Even much of the language and terminology used to describe people with disabilities has been reassessed in both of Canada's official languages; such usage now reflects more positive attitudes towards these students. Even though services have developed over a relatively short time, initial theories underlying service provision are already being questioned, and challenging new perspectives are being proposed. The underlying factors that have created this revolution for students, service providers, and institutions alike are discussed below.

Post-secondary education in Canada is a provincial responsibility, which means there is no nationwide agency charged with compiling statistics on participation rates for students with disabilities, although a few studies have given an indication of national trends. Killean and Hubka (1999), using responses from sixty-six colleges and universities nationwide, reported an average of 163 students per institution. Fichten et al. (2003) reported results from 183 colleges and universities, estimating that 41,879 students with disabilities were enrolled countrywide. They suggested an average enrolment of 211 students per college and 217 for universities, but cautioned that discrepancies between institutions were substantial. They also confirmed that a higher percentage of students were registered at the college level. In a more recent survey of 117 institutions, Wolforth and Harrison (2008) reported that 45 per cent of their sample had registered more than 500 students with disabilities and a further 20 per cent had between 300 and 500 students.

One of the key issues in determining the magnitude of numbers enrolled is an operational one: what is the definition of a student with a disability? A comparison between Ontario and Quebec, for example, illustrates the effect a lack of uniformity in definition can have. The two neighbouring provinces use different criteria when they define a student with a disability. In Ontario, institutions tend to use a broad, inclusive definition based on the provincial human rights code. In Quebec, the definition is very medically based and therefore quite restrictive, with emphasis on functioning, such as the level of vision or hearing loss. It is not as broad as that implied in the Quebec Charter of Human Rights and Freedoms. At the time of this writing, two major categories of students recognized elsewhere – students with learning disabilities and those with mental health disorders – are not officially recognized as students with disabilities by the Ministry of Education, Leisure and Sports.

The effect of these two definitional approaches on numbers of registered students seems apparent. Ontario, with the largest number of colleges and universities in the country, reported in 2001–02 that 8,188 students with disabilities were enrolled at the university level, and 13,549 at the college level for a total of 21,737 students (Ontario Human Rights Commission 2003). As the data above demonstrate however, those numbers in Ontario have continued to increase (COU 2010). Several years later, in an environment that operated from a more restrictive definition, the Quebec Association of University Disability Service Providers (AQICESH 2010) reported only 3,538 students registered for service at the university level, while in autumn 2008 the Ministry knew of only 1,757 students at the cégep (college) level (MELS, personal communication to author 7 November, 2008). Fichten et al. (2003) estimated there were ten times fewer students with disabilities in Quebec cégeps than in colleges in the rest of the country (i.e. 0.5 per cent in Quebec versus 5.5 per cent in other provinces). This considerable difference in numbers between two neighbouring provinces of course raises questions about the effect of how one defines the status. In Quebec more students may be enrolled than the data imply, simply because many students don't fit into an accepted classification and therefore aren't counted. At a more profound level, as Ebersold (2008) contends, certain definitional models may discourage students with disabilities from post-secondary education because they translate into different levels of support, and ultimately perhaps more pejorative attitudes.

The statistics provided rely on reports from disability service providers. This limited source of data collection may also result in an unrealistic statistical picture. Fichten et al. (2003) and Jorgensen et al. (2005) pointed out that, if figures are based on reports from service providers alone, they are likely to be underestimates since they only include self-identified students. They also suggest that only between 25 per cent and 50 per cent of students with disabilities on campus register with the disability support office. Unknown is whether this is the result of fear of self-identification due to potential stigma, or because of a well-adapted campus where students can function without registering for specific supports. Although determining the magnitude of students with disabilities registered at Canadian post-secondary campuses remains elusive, there does seem to be a general impression that their numbers are continuing to grow. Such increases perhaps have been fueled by several factors: better support services delivered in an inclusive educational environment at earlier levels of education; the availability of appropriate services at universities and colleges; and changes in societal attitudes towards the aspirations of people with disabilities, in terms of goals they themselves set as measures of success.

When institutions first began to make changes to include students with disabilities, most of the students came with mobility, vision, and hearing impairments, and campuses concentrated on improving restrictive facilities, often dated to a much earlier era. Ramps were added, washrooms were renovated, and entrances were modified for people with mobility impairments. Gradually technological innovations in hardware and software facilitated the inclusion of students with vision or hearing impairments and eventually those with various learning disabilities. As new buildings were constructed on many campuses, access elements were included in designs and building codes were modified to ensure compliance. The inclusion of elements such as standards for signage and lighting, stair demarcation, and acoustical environments began to take better account of the presence of people with sensory impairments. A myriad of academic accommodations, such as various methods of note taking or the provision of modified exam conditions were also developed and implemented, and adaptive technologies became available on campuses. In addition, federal and provincial governments established financial support programs targeted at both individual students and institutions.

As colleges and universities worked to accommodate students with visible disabilities, the diversity of students requiring accommodation widened. Current studies report that students with "traditional" visible disabilities have now been overtaken in numbers by those with invisible conditions such as learning disabilities, attention deficit disorder, and chronic medical conditions (e.g., Mullins and Preyde 2013; White, Summers, Zhang, and Renault 2014). More recently students with a range of mental health disorders have enrolled and requested support. The most recent of these is the arrival at universities and colleges of students requesting accommodations for various autism spectrum disorders (for example the condition formerly referred to as "Asperger's Syndrome") (e.g., Anderson, Shattuck, Cooper, Roux, and Wagner 2014). It is encouraging that most institutions seem to clearly recognize their obligation to provide support services that permit equal access for all students with disabilities.

The arrival of the first students with disabilities often predated the presence of any systematic services to support them. Their self-advocacy proved to be a powerful impetus for their initial establishment. In the late 1980s they set up national, provincial, and local support and advocacy groups. Thus, the National Educational Association of Disabled Students (NEADS) was formed in Ottawa in 1986, and it continues to provide a strong voice on behalf of its constituency in government, education, and employment sectors. At the same time, groups of students at the provincial level and at individual universities began to advocate on their own behalf (e.g. the Association québécoise des étudiants ayant des incapacités au postsecondaire [AQEIPS], British Columbia Association of Disabled Students, Access McGill, Able York). Perhaps encouraged by similar movements in the United States, such groups in the Canadian system were able to galvanize fellow students to support their demand for services. In the university community the actions of students at Berkeley, for example, led by Ed Roberts – a hero of the disability movement, provided a critical turning point for university access in the wider North American context. Roberts, afflicted during the polio epidemic of the late 1950s, was excluded from the University of California because he was confined to an iron lung. He was eventually successful in persuading the university to admit him, and graduated in 1962 (Shapiro 1993). This event provided a model for what could be accomplished when pressure to change was applied to university authorities.

As the demands of student groups and their allies succeeded in persuading institutions to support students, it became clear that a disability service as an entity was required to adequately address such needs. At first, institutions tended to address the issue by appointing an ancillary professional from another office to provide service on an ad hoc basis to individual students. As numbers requiring services increased, and diversity of need grew, a more systematic approach became necessary and the new field of disability service provision was born, generally established within the student services framework. Since no professional education route for disability service providers existed, professionals came from a variety of backgrounds such as counselling psychology, rehabilitation sciences, and other health professions. Wolforth and Harrison (2008) reported from their survey of disability service providers at 117 post-secondary institutions that 15 per cent of their respondents held a doctoral degree; 52 per cent had a master's degree in science, education, social work, or rehabilitation, with the largest group being from education (35 per cent); and the remaining group held a bachelor's degree from a variety of academic fields.

This diversity of background and the need for constant learning perhaps enhanced the urgency to establish a peer-based reference group for disability service providers. While unable to issue a national licensing qualification, an organization was required to provide the opportunity for professional development and, however informal, the acceptance of a common core of national practice expectations. Until the mid-1990s disability service providers in Canadian post-secondary education relied primarily on informal meetings as venues for sharing their experiences, but no professional body united them in their efforts. In the United States, the Association on Handicapped Student Service Programs in Post-secondary Education (since 1992 called the Association on Higher Education and Disability) was still a relatively small organization, but nevertheless offered leadership beyond its national borders. The biannual conference of the student group, NEADS, eventually became a venue for exchange and professional development for service providers. Gradually those disability service providers attending the annual conference of the Canadian Association of College and University Student Services (CACUSS) found each other and met informally, and then more formally, to discuss the founding of a professional association. Without a doubt, the seminal event in the pan-Canadian development of disability service provision was the 1997 founding of the Canadian Association of Disability Service Providers in Post-Secondary Education (CADSPPE) and, in 1998, its transition into a division of CACUSS. The CACUSS annual conference has become the pre-eminent forum for service providers from across the country to meet, attend professional development sessions, share experiences, and encourage the development of professional standards of practice. The beginning of each academic year brings new students and frequently new accommodation demands to assess and solve, but with common themes frequently appearing at the same time across the country, service providers are able to draw upon their collective wisdom to address new concerns; a national listserv facilitates this sharing.

In addition to the national organization, the desire for cooperation and information sharing among service providers themselves is reflected in the work of provincial organizations such as AQICESH in Quebec, IDIA in Ontario, and the Disability Resource Network in British Columbia. Such groups have recognized the need for a consistent connection with their respective provincial governments, to ensure that inclusive regulations are applied in post-secondary education. As an example, with the establishment of the Learning Opportunities Task Force (1998–2002), the Ontario government and post-secondary disability service providers cooperated to develop a better understanding of how to best serve students with learning disabilities. In addition to governments, service providers also cooperate with community resources willing to provide expertise and advice. A good example of community cooperation occurred when, with input from many disability service providers, the Canadian Mental Health Association (2004) produced a comprehensive guide to assist their target clientele navigate the post-secondary experience.

Even though universities can act as agents of change, and probably did so in terms of advancing the position of people with disabilities in Canada (Neufeldt and Egers 2003), changes in post-secondary education do not, of course, occur in isolation from changes taking place in the wider society; this is certainly true of the inclusion of students with disabilities. Social justice movements that came to prominence in the 1960s on the heels of the Civil Rights movement in the United States, and which empowered disadvantaged groups, informed social action within the disability community in Canada. By the 1970s significant groups of people with disabilities had begun to organize to demand control over decisions that affected them, and to advocate for their full inclusion in society. The social justice perspective began to change the focus from what is termed "the charity model" of disability, where people with disabilities are perceived as deficient, limited in ability, and the recipients of charity, to a "rights model," where people with disabilities are treated with dignity and included through the imposition of legal guarantees of social and economic equality (Disability Rights in Canada 2003; Loewen and Pollard 2010; Shapiro 1993). The activities of groups such as the Canadian Association of Independent Living Centres (1986), ARCH (1980s), and the Coalition of Provincial Organizations of the Handicapped (1976) (now called the Council of Canadians with Disabilities), led to a greater awareness about the rights and expectations of people with disabilities on the part of governments and other critical social entities (Neufeldt 2003).

By 1980, federal and provincial governments had begun to take active note of their citizens with disabilities. The United Nations declared 1981 the "International Year of Disabled Persons," an occasion to raise awareness and emphasize the rights of people with disabilities to take part in the development and activities of their societies. The adoption of human rights legislation at the international, national, and provincial levels was also of paramount importance. In Canada, Section 15 of the Constitution Act (1982), generally referred to as the Charter of Rights and Freedoms, specifically prohibited discrimination on the basis of disability. Canada remains the only western country to have enshrined the concept of equality minority rights in its constitution. Provincial human rights charters, many of which predated the federal charter, included equivalent anti-discrimination imperatives. In 2010, Canada became one of eighty-nine countries that ratified the United Nations International Convention on the Rights of Persons with Disabilities, a further reflection of its commitment to the inclusion of all citizens.

However, legal directives and changes in societal attitudes did not result in equivalent changes within post-secondary education.

Throughout the 1980s and the early 1990s institutions and provincial governments were sometimes slow to develop policies and establish supports to enable those with disabilities to enter higher
education. Until the late 1980s inclusive education at the primary
and secondary level was not well supported (Smith and Foster 1996),
and students educated in "special schools" were often not qualified
academically to enter colleges and universities. Gradually, from the
mid-1980s, Ministries of Education began to look seriously at the
needs of students with disabilities and the inclusion movement in
education began. In the late 1980s the Quebec government commissioned provincial reports on students with disabilities at both the
college (Leclerc 1987) and university levels (Tousignant 1989;
Tousignant 1995); Ontario commissioned a similar report (Wesley
1988). The juxtaposition of qualified high school graduates with the
imperative of legal requirements for accommodation convinced most
post-secondary institutions that provision of appropriate services for
these students was necessary.

Legal requirements have had a profound effect on how disability
services operate, and this may make them somewhat distinct from
other post-secondary diversity units. The Canadian human rights
framework, in particular the anti-discrimination clauses of provincial human rights codes, have dictated a particular path of development for disability services. The provision of services and academic
accommodations for students with disabilities has, to a significant
extent, been defined in reaction to fears of legal challenges. The level
of accommodation granted must adhere to the legal requirement to
provide "reasonable accommodation" up to the point of "undue
hardship," and though the term "reasonable" lacks some measure of
precision, as the Alberta Human Right Commission (2004) pointed
out, "The undue hardship standard is a very high standard, and as a
result, in most situations post-secondary institutions will be required
to provide some accommodation" (6). The Ontario Human Rights
Commission (2004) further explained, an appropriate accommodation as one designed to "respect the dignity of the student with a
disability, meet individual needs, best promote inclusion and participation of the person, and maximize confidentiality" (21). Finally, the
Saskatchewan Human Rights Commission (2004) recognized the
constant challenge this situation creates: "If educators are to avoid
discrimination and provide quality of educational benefit to students
with disabilities, they must be familiar with the principles of human

rights law. Educators must also ensure that their understanding of the rights of students with disabilities – an evolving area of law – remains updated" (6).

Two provincial human rights commissions have produced comprehensive and quite prescriptive guidelines on the duty of post-secondary institutions to accommodate students with disabilities (Alberta Human Right Commission 2004; Ontario Human Rights Commission 2003). Many of their recommendations reflect accommodations and approaches developed by service providers in the previous fifteen years. As the Ontario Human Rights Commission (2003) recognized, the "staff in offices for students with disabilities at colleges and universities have expertise in dealing with accommodation issues in the academic environment and, as such, can play a vital role in assisting with the accommodation process" (24). Gradually a number of institutions also developed internal policies, which guaranteed the rights of students within the institution, and defined procedures to be used to determine and provide accommodations and services, as well as to grieve decisions. Hill (1994) recommended that institutions should develop such policies, but she reported that, in 1992, very few had done so. By 1998, twenty-six universities indicated they had policies (Hardy Cox and Walsh 1998). Access advisory committees with members drawn from the wider university community were also established. Killean and Hubka (1999) reported that 40 per cent of institutions responding to their survey had Access Committees. Interestingly, they also reported that larger institutions (10,000–50,000 students) were more likely to have access committees (55.6 per cent) than were institutions with fewer than 2,500 students (29.2 per cent).

Frequent requests for information on legal issues arise at the annual CADSPPE conference (e.g., Roberts 2010). In Ontario, provisions of the Accessibility of Ontarians with Disabilities Act (2005) and subsequent enactment of the Integrated Accessibility Standards Regulation (IASR) (Canadian Mental Health Association 2011) are beginning to create considerable change in many aspects of all Ontario public institutions. Yet this framework produces a sense of disquiet that priority given to a legal approach will hamper service providers from exercising a professional, student-centred model in their work. When a fear of litigation begins to dictate how a service provider interacts with a student, the essence of the service is lost. The service provider has given over their relationship with the student to the dictates of the legal system. Nevertheless it must be acknowledged that concerns about potential litigation, or grievances filed internally within an institution, have become a reality. Many provincial human rights tribunals have some familiarity with adjudicating cases brought against post-secondary institutions by students and their parents, who are unhappy with accommodation decisions. Often in such cases the institution is represented by the disability service provider, who is increasingly defined as a legal gatekeeper for the institution, relegated to monitoring whether the student legally qualifies for support and accommodation. Service providers must be able to balance these sometimes conflicting imperatives, to act on behalf of the student and also the institution.

Despite this potential preoccupation with legal concerns, it would be misleading to imply that the movement towards inclusion of students with disabilities in post-secondary education was simply a response to legal directives or fear of litigation. The changes were also encouraged by a growing understanding on the part of many that it was the right and necessary action to take. The social justice movement that ensured the proclamation of the federal and provincial Human Rights charters led to other profound changes in Canadian society as well. Whether the Charters were a reflection of Canadian values or whether values changed after the Charters were proclaimed is debatable. Nevertheless, it is clear that the Charters have become an integral reference point for Canadians. In a survey on Canadian attitudes towards those with disabilities Environics Research Group (2004) noted:

> Generally, participants felt that all Canadians should have the opportunity to participate in life to the fullest of their ability, that this is part of the Canadian way of doing things ... While they are not quite sure how it will be possible, many feel it is in the best interests of Canada that persons with disabilities are given the assistance that they need to be full participating members of Canadian society. (9–10)

Inclusion of students with disabilities in post-secondary education reflected a much larger movement for change in Canadian society.

Disability services have always been closely connected to social movements beyond the academy. Issues within the disability community have therefore had an impact on the evolution of service provision philosophy and methodology. Changes in terminology are a good example of this. Terms such as "cripple," "the deaf and dumb," and even the more recent "physically challenged" are no longer in general use. Even the apparently subtle change of moving from using "handicapped student" to using "a student with a disability" is profound in terms of the change of perspective it represents. Yet this change has now also come under scrutiny with the disability community, and some disability rights activists prefer the terms "disabled people" and "non-disabled people" (Kroeger 2010).

MEDICAL VERSUS SOCIAL MODEL OF DISABILITY

Such modifications of language reflect a profound social movement resulting in people with disabilities reframing their own perspective of their relationship to society. Prior to the 1980s, disability was seen very much from the perspective of a medical or rehabilitation model, and people with disabilities were treated as having inherent defects and limitations that could not be fixed, as though they were lacking some measure of "normal" humanity. Any problem or limitation created by the disability was seen as intrinsic to the individual. Within such a medical model, providing accommodations and support for people with disabilities often entails assessing what an individual cannot do. For example, in the vignette at the beginning of this chapter, the professor assumed that a student with a vision impairment could not read. Similarly, a student who is hard of hearing might be considered unable to conduct interviews for a doctoral thesis or a student with a mobility impairment might be unable to attend classes in an inaccessible room and therefore told to choose other classes instead. Human rights legislation, funding regulations, and institutional imperatives continue to demand that service providers collect medical and other relevant documentation from students as a condition of service eligibility, and this perpetuates a perspective focused on individual limitations and differences.

A revised concept of disability – the "Social Model" (Oliver 1990) – completely rejects this approach and changes the paradigm to one where disability is seen as a manifestation of the barriers inherent to the environment in which the person lives. A student who has an impairment of vision can function comparably to other students if he or she has access to proper technology and accommodations; a student who is deaf may require a sign language interpreter or an interactive computer system, but will have no problem conducting interviews with such accommodations. A student with the mobility impairment simply needs to have his courses in an accessible room. The "Social Model" and its derivatives (Gabel 2010) thereby remove the emphasis on the limitations inherent in the individual and attribute the creation of disability onto the environmental context imposed by society and its institutions. Concurring with this perspective, Strange (2000) argued for the design of "environments of ability," those capable of accommodating students regardless of their status. Accordingly, campus educational environments, whether beyond or within the classroom, must satisfy a hierarchy of needs, wherein first the inclusion and safety of all participants is assured, followed by provision of flexible structures for involvement or engagement in the learning process, ultimately leading to the fulfilling experience of an integrated learning community. The responsibility for action then is reframed into what the institution needs to change in order for students to function without encountering barriers. A recent example of this approach is found in Suhkai et al. (2014), where the authors reported on the creation of science laboratories for STEM students at Purdue University and McMaster University, designed to enable persons with physical disabilities to access standard laboratory and safety equipment.

This paradigm shift has immediate practical application, but it also challenges service providers to seriously question their attitudes towards those with disabilities. A meeting with a student takes on a different tone when the emphasis is modified to ask what the institution needs to do to ensure that the student can function and be included equally with all other students. This frequently results in the development of solutions that may benefit not only the individual student but also result in broader institutional change (see Burgstahler and Moore 2009).

TOWARD UNIVERSAL DESIGN

This improved perspective on disability and impairment has evolved in conjunction with the rise of the disability studies movement and the promotion of the Principles of Universal Design. The Universal Design movement originated in the field of architecture, and its goal is to promote the construction of facilities accessible and adaptable to the broadest range of people. According to its seven principles, environments and products designed universally: (a) are "useful and marketable to people with diverse abilities" (Equitable Use); (b) "accommodate a wide range of individual preferences and abilities" (Flexibility in Use); (c) are "easy to understand, regardless of the user's experience, knowledge, language skills, or current concentration level" (Simple and Intuitive); (d) "communicate necessary information effectively to the user regardless of ambient conditions or the user's sensory abilities" (Perceptible Information); (e) "minimize hazards and the adverse effects of accidental or unintended actions" (Tolerance for Error); (f) "can be used efficiently, comfortably, and with a minimum of fatigue" (Low Physical Effort); and (g) are environments wherein "appropriate size and space is provided for approach, reach, manipulation, and use regardless of the user's body size, posture, or mobility" (Size and Space for Approach and Use). To these above seven principles are added two more guidelines to complete the picture for Universal Design for Instruction (UDI) (Welch 1995; Shaw, Scott, and McGuire 2001; Scott et al. 2003; Burgstahler and Cory 2008): (h) "the instructional environment promotes interaction and communication among students and between students and faculty" (A Community of Learners); and (i) "instruction is designed to be welcoming and inclusive, and high expectations are espoused for all students" (Instructional Climate).

Application of these principles mitigates the need for special disability-targeted elements. For example, in buildings, a universally designed front entrance has no steps, has easy to operate doors, and is wide enough for many users to enter. The same entrance is therefore accessible to everyone who wishes to enter, including parents with strollers, facilities workers transporting equipment, delivery persons, and people who use a wheelchair. Similar principles can be applied to large individual unisex washrooms, good for travellers with suitcases, parents with babies, trans students, and people with mobility impairments. Thinking within such a framework ensures more accessible and flexible building designs. In terms of curriculum and course designs, faculty are being encouraged to teach and to evaluate students using multimodal delivery models and flexible evaluation methods that support a variety of learning styles and needs. In fact, as one recent study suggested, students with disabilities benefit from the same universal conditions that support other students in their intention to graduate (Fichten et al. 2014). That is,

both personal facilitators (e.g., good financial situation, good family situation, having friends, high level of personal motivation, good study habits, good previous education experiences) as well as school related facilitators (e.g., acceptable course load, good schedule, positive attitudes of professors, nonteaching staff and students, availability of computers on campus, accessibility of building facilities) were related to intention to graduate. (281)

In addition, "students intending to graduate were more likely to have registered for campus disability related services than those who did not intend to graduate" (281).

CADSPPE has taken the lead in promoting principles of universal design and universal instructional design to its members (e.g., Loewen and Wolforth 2005; Thornton 2007). Thornton and Downs (2010) argued that it is now time to apply universal design principles to disability service offices, who need to abandon the medical model and assess how they can change their own practices and image to conform to both the social and universal design models. However this will be a challenge for service providers steeped in working from a reactive framework as the campus experts and deciders on disability accommodation issues. It will require a complete change of perspective for disability service personnel who now must lobby for social model and universal design principles, but do not yet "walk the talk." Roberts's (2010) accommodation decision tree provided an effective illustration of this dichotomy. While the decision tree is an excellent guide for assessing the validity of accommodations, it remains inherently an application of the medical model. Service providers are attracted to it as a tool that provides some certainty in the face of potential litigation. However, if the field is to move forward and retain a role as an ally of the disability movement, it needs to consider how it can embrace a more proactive model of functioning.

Disability studies is an academic discipline that may hold the key to a wider understanding of students and others with disabilities on Canadian campuses. Kraus (2010) suggested that the role of service providers should be expanded to one of a disability culture ambassador, so that the entire campus becomes involved in and knowledgeable about disability culture and disability studies, thereby embracing a collective responsibility for the removal of barriers and for the inclusion of people with disabilities. Clearly this will not be easy. Only a few Canadian institutions have established disability studies programs (e.g., Ryerson University, University of Manitoba, University of Winnipeg, Red River College, York University) and, as Wolforth (2010) detailed, campuses can be astonishingly resistant to such overtures from disability service offices.

Nevertheless it is important to remain optimistic. When the progress of the last twenty years is catalogued, both in terms of material and attitudinal change, it has been significant. Perhaps the same magnitude of change is possible for the future. If widely adopted, Universal Design principles alone could create significant change. Though developed within the disability community, they could have a much wider impact on institutional models of facilities development, problem solving, and curriculum delivery that would produce a more inclusive environment for all students regardless of their backgrounds and learning needs. This makes it a potentially attractive approach for all campuses addressing the needs of a diverse student body. Nonetheless, as Foster-Fishman, Nowell, and Yang suggest in regards to such a goal, it is "only by altering the underlying beliefs and values that direct daily practices and behaviors will significant system change efforts take hold and be sustained over time" (2007, 205). Likewise the "social model" of disability provides a critical framework for significant attitudinal change, which still needs to occur – even in campus disability service offices – if campuses are to become truly inclusive.

CAMPUS DISABILITY SERVICES AND PROGRAMS

In the wake of these significant changes in the broader society and in Canada's post-secondary system, many institutional initiatives are beginning to emerge on various campuses in support of students with disabilities. For example Bow Valley College, Alberta publishes an online "Checklist for Setting up Academic Accommodations and/or Supports for Learners with Disabilities." The checklist is meant to act as a guide in preparation for assisting students who are struggling in class or in the program, with study skills and learning strategies, academic and exam accommodations, assistive technology services and support, sign language interpreting for deaf and hard of hearing students, and education supports, including access to a learning strategist, academic aide, tutor, or note takers. Concordia University of Edmonton, through an Office of Learning Accommodation Services, outlines steps students must take to qualifying in an annual *Individual Service Plan*. At Simon Fraser University, British Columbia, the

Centre for Students with Disabilities has begun an Autism Mentorship Initiative that matches individuals so identified with a specially trained SFU student. This initiative is meant to enhance social experience, support academic success, and connect students to the university community. From a platform of distance learning, in 2014 Athabasca University, Alberta launched the iPad project to explore new technologies and various apps as tools for learning for students with disabilities. Other examples of comprehensive disability services can be found at Memorial University of Newfoundland, McGill University, University of Manitoba, University of Alberta, SAIT Polytechnic, University of Calgary, and University of British Columbia.

Within the context of a bilingual university business school, HEC Montreal addresses concerns of hearing, organic, motor, visual, and language and speech impairments, as well as learning disabilities and attention deficit/hyperactivity, mental health, and pervasive developmental disorders (http://www.hec.ca). Dalhousie University, Nova Scotia created Able@Dal, an orientation program exclusively for students with disabilities. Finally, students themselves have assumed leadership in the matter, for example at Simon Fraser University (SUDS – Students United for Disability Support) and the University of Toronto (SBA – Students for Barrier-Free Access). After much effort, the SBA Centre was established in 2004 as a social and activist space in order to promote ideas of inclusion and accessibility. The facility includes a resource library, a computer lab, a lounge area, and a study room. All of these programs and services are a testament to a society more understanding of its citizens and a post-secondary system increasingly committed to their educational success.

9

Mature Adult Learners

JUDITH POTTER

Soon after visiting Canada several years ago, Sebastian and Paula, a vibrant Argentinian couple in their mid-thirties, knew that they wanted to make this country their home. Both Sebastian and Paula were well educated and had considerable work experience, and although they knew that they would have to improve their language skills, they did not fully appreciate the difficulties they would face in having their credentials and work experience accepted in their adopted home. After many discouraging months of job search, both have returned to a Canadian university for specialized diplomas that will be recognized by employers; they have also taken advantage of advising services and workshops offered by that university to help recent immigrants better understand Canadian workplace culture and ways to effectively make the transition. In addition, the university's scholarship program for motivated adult learners has helped to ease their financial burden and has provided encouraging recognition of their efforts.

Isabelle happily traded her career as a lab technician for that of a stay-at-home mother so that she could provide full-time care for her children, now fourteen, twelve, and nine. During the intervening years, while caring for her family, Isabelle took on leadership roles in several community projects. Now in her late thirties, she needs and wants to return to the workforce but her skills and credentials no longer match the job that she left. And she is looking to explore new avenues that have piqued her interest as a result of her community work. Fortunately, her local university has a Prior Learning Assessment program that can help adults identify and demonstrate the learning that they have achieved through informal, as well as formal, means. She is now enrolled in a program that will build on her skills and passions, and prepare her for a career in communications and marketing. Returning to university as a mature learner has made for many anxious moments, however, and Isabelle has taken advantage of study skills workshops offered by her institution. With a limited family income, she is a good candidate for assistance provided by the Canada Student Loan Program.

Frank spent most of his work life in manufacturing, having taken a factory job immediately following high school graduation. His work provided a living wage for him and his family and a steady occupation, at least until the day management announced the intended closing of the plant facility, having outsourced much of the work to another new site built in Mexico. With only three weeks to vacate his position, he consulted with a friend in similar circumstances who was taking advantage of a career transition program offered at the local community college. Through assessment and advising services, Frank's friend was able to evaluate his skills and interests and enroll in one of the school's programs for mature students. Outside of his work Frank was always an avid reader, mostly about current issues and world events, so learning about new topics was not unusual for him. Since it was quite some time ago that he was last in a formal school environment, Frank wondered about his academic skills and whether he could succeed in college at his age. He did well in high school, but that was then and after so many years away, he had concerns about "rusty brains" and challenges of learning how to write all over again. In spite of real doubts he decided to enroll in college part-time, with the assistance of a provincial grant, and take a course to see how it would go.

Janelle was proud of the family she raised, mostly by herself, having lost her husband to a devastating health crisis early on in their life together. Prior to her years of marriage and children – who were now grown with families of their own – Janelle had always cherished the time spent pursuing her love of art. In the interim though, her busy life of being a partner, a parent, and a provider consumed all but a few rare moments when her interests in the esthetics of things did not have to take a back seat to their practicality. Now time was on her side, with a good fif-teen years remaining until traditional retirement age. Opportu-nities announced for returning adult students at a nearby post-secondary institution caught her eye and her heart one day, fueled by delayed dreams of someday completing a uni-versity degree. Maybe this was a good time to engage in some-thing new, a program that would encourage Janelle to reclaim the interests she put on hold years before.

INTRODUCTION

The four individuals detailed in the above scenarios share in com-mon a desire to learn as well as life circumstances that allowed them to consider a return to formal education. In short, each is a potential adult learner whose moment has come to pursue a diploma, certifi-cate, or degree in one of any number of post-secondary institutions in Canada that offer such programs. Adult learners constitute a sig-nificant demographic in Canadian colleges and universities, perhaps noticeable by their high degree of engagement in the classroom, their single-minded pursuit of select programs, and their calculated bal-ancing of a host of life responsibilities. They do tend to stand out; but they can also pass largely unnoticed as they "blend in" with the crowd. Meanwhile, adult learners face a climbing wall of challenges beyond those associated with traditional post-secondary students. Adult learners are older than direct-from-high-school learners (adult learners are often defined as students twenty-six years of age and above) and usually juggle multiple roles and commitments. They may enroll with hesitation, as some of the adults in the opening sce-narios, in a college or university program, thinking they are "too old" or recalling a less-than-stellar high school career. Once admit-ted, they may slip into the room just as class begins, having rushed to campus from their full-time job. At break times, adult learners may be checking in with babysitters, or touching base with work col-leagues. Traditionally called "mature students," adult learners are typically highly motivated and driven mainly by a desire to improve their employability (Peters 2005). They contribute depth and vitality to classrooms and campuses by bringing the richness of their life experiences to class discussions, and "real world" perspectives to assignments. Adult learners face challenges similar to traditional age students – financial and study skills dilemmas, for example, along

with additional concerns such as work, family, and social responsibilities. Because of this, adult learners need to be apprised of services
for the general student population, as well as about services that cater
to their particular needs.

One key task for student services personnel is identifying adult
learners and steering them towards the services that best meet their
needs. This process should ideally begin with student recruitment,
assist in the transition to studies (including a Prior Learning
Assessment), guidance through programs, and counselling for post-
program employment. Student Services personnel need to provide,
and promote access to, the services adult learners need to access
higher education and to succeed in their studies. As colleges and universities have increasingly recognized the particular challenges facing
these non-traditional students, services for them have expanded
beyond evening and weekend course offerings to include a full menu
of resources to attract and retain these important learners in Canadian
post-secondary campuses.

ADULT LEARNERS IN CANADA

The long view of adult learners in Canada shows a dramatic evolution of formal schooling over the past immediate generations. While
in 1961 less than 10 per cent of Canadian adults, twenty-five to sixty-
four years of age, had completed a post-secondary qualification of
some level (including universities and vocational institutions), that
figure had increased to over 60 per cent by 2006, leaving Canada
among the leaders of OECD (Organization for Economic Co-operation
and Development) countries in metrics of formal adult education.
Furthermore, the proportion of adults aged twenty-five to sixty-four
with tertiary education (college/university completion) increased
from 40 per cent in 2000 to 53 per cent in 2012 – the highest rate
among OECD countries. Whereas it can be argued that Canadian
adults probably have always pursued informal learning, "one of the
most distinctive educational features of recent generations is the
extent to which learning activities have become formally institution-
alized and credentialed" (Livingstone 2012, 53). This intergenerational effect perhaps explains the current uptick in adult student
enrolments in Canadian post-secondary education. One indication of
this trend is found in a Statistics Canada report that in 2002 4.8 million adult workers (aged twenty-five to sixty-four) participated in

formal, job-related training. This is about 35 per cent of all adult Canadian workers, up from 29 per cent in 1997. Perhaps surprisingly, "more than half of students enrolled in universities are adults aged 25 or older" (AUCC 2003, 1). In a recent article on the topic of the so called "silver tsunami," Green (2015) confirmed this growing trend:

> Twenty years ago, in 1995, people holding university degrees in Canada numbered 635,000. Ten years later, that total had grown to 1.3 million, then to 2.1 million by 2015. In 2025, says O'Heron [director of research and policy analysis at Universities Canada] there will be more than 2.5 million degree-holders in Canada. And that year, the cohort of adults aged 50 to 69 with a university degree will be four times larger than it was in 1995: "There is no question the demand for courses outside degree programs is going to grow too," he concludes.

Statistics Canada collects data on this group of learners through the periodic Adult Education and Training Survey (AETS), most recently in 2008. The 2008 AETS relied on the standard OECD definition of "adult education and training," which "generally encompasses the education and training of individuals twenty-five years of age and older who have completed their initial schooling and then returned to further their education" (AETS 2008 User Guide).

The Association of Universities and Colleges of Canada (AUCC), using Statistics Canada data, reports that there are currently about 350,000 adults studying in degree-credit programs at Canadian universities. These are distributed as follows:

- 150,000 in full-time study (half as undergraduate and half as graduate students)
- 200,000 in part-time study (almost three-quarters of the total number of part-time students; about 150,000 undergraduate and 50,000 graduate students)

In addition, there are approximately 400,000 learners (most of whom are working adults) pursuing continuing education opportunities at Canadian universities.

Participation in part-time degree-credit study at Canadian universities has started to regain lost ground after significant declines in the mid-1990s; even so, current levels are about the same as they were in the mid-1980s. A variety of factors, including the rapid rise in tuition fees, have contributed to this decline.

The Colleges and Institutes Canada (CICAN), known previously as the Association of Canadian Community Colleges (ACCC), is Canada's largest provider of post-secondary education and adult education and training, representing 126 publicly supported colleges, institutes, cégeps, and polytechnics in over 3,000 communities coast to coast. Estimates suggest that member institutions serve 1.5 million individuals of all ages and backgrounds. While colleges and institutes vary in size, the average facility serves about 5,000 full-time and 15,000 part-time learners, and the average age of full-time college students is between twenty-six and twenty-eight years.

The Government of Canada aims to increase these participation rates. In *Knowledge Matters: Skills and Learning for Canadians*, prepared by Human Resources Development Canada (HRDC) (2002), the stated goals include: to increase the number of adults who have a post-secondary credential to 50 per cent; to increase the number of adult learners by one million throughout all segments of society; to aim to have businesses increase by one-third their annual investment in training-per-employee. If these goals are met, they will radically increase the number of adult learners making their way onto college and university campuses in Canada.

Beyond the numbers, adult learners are women and men, co-workers, parents, neighbours, and friends. They are people with multiple responsibilities who want to further their education, and support in the form of student services can help them succeed.

ADULT LEARNERS AND LIFE TRANSITIONS

An important backdrop for understanding the context within which adult learners approach the post-secondary experience is found in Goodman, Schlossberg, and Anderson (2006), where the authors examined the dynamics of life transitions, a state that often accompanies the decision for adult learners to return to formal education. Accordingly, life transitions are events (for example, marriage) or non-events (such as an anticipated promotion that never occurs) "resulting in changed relationships, routines, assumptions, and/or roles" (cited in Evans et al. 2010, 218). The meaning of the transition for the individual may vary, depending on whether it was anticipated or not and the degree to which it alters one's life. Timing of the transition is another concern, especially since adult students often find themselves seeking new learning opportunities while anticipating, being in the midst of, or having recently completed a significant life change. This is what Goodman et al. (2006) characterized as "moving in, moving through, and moving out" – a transition the success of which depends on the balance of one's assets and liabilities with respect to four sets of factors: (a) situation; (b) self; (c) support; and (d) strategies. Thus, one copes with a life transition according to the circumstances of the situation, for example, its timing and duration, the control one has over it, one's previous experience with any similar situation, and the degree of personal stress engaged as a result. For some, the unexpected loss of a job (like Frank in the opening vignettes), for example, or sudden illness of a child or spouse might trigger a very stressful and debilitating life moment. Just how disruptive the situation is, according to the model, depends in turn on one's personal and psychological resources, that is, the above second set of factors related to self. Having certain characteristics of socioeconomic status, gender, age, ethnicity, and health might position some to be more capable of coping than others. Likewise, one's ego strength, resilience, outlook, values, and spirituality might predict a more or less successful outcome. Assessing such qualities should be the first order of business of service providers and advisors in supporting adult learners as they begin the process of returning to postsecondary education.

Beyond these personal assets though are the kinds of instrumental supports and strategies one can muster to enhance the experience. Consistent feedback and affirmation from family, friends, and significant others can make all the difference in supporting one's choices during difficult times. So too can the strategies one chooses to cope with the challenges. Some situations can be modified directly, such as electing to change course when it becomes clear that the present one doesn't work. Altering the meaning one attaches to the situation is another possibility, as well as learning techniques to manage the stress caused by the situation. It's in marshaling and guiding these latter two sets of factors that student services personnel can be perhaps most helpful in easing the transition and ultimately success for adult learners as they return to college or university. Regardless, the barriers to such an experience can be formidable.

BARRIERS FOR ADULT LEARNERS

Services for adult learners are perhaps best understood as solutions to barriers facing adult learners. A number of barriers currently exist for adult learners, barriers that are well-documented and present significant impediments to adults achieving their full potential in society and the workplace (Flynn et al. 2011). Cross classified barriers to adult learning in three categories – situational, institutional, and dispositional (1981). Potter and Alderman added barriers to this classification system, using the categories situational, institutional, academic, and attitudinal (1992).

Situational Barriers

Situational barriers consist of broad circumstantial issues that hamper the ability of adult learners to pursue educational opportunities. Examples include balancing multiple responsibilities, lack of time, and financial pressures. The everyday responsibilities of work and family and the multiple roles of parent, spouse, community member, and employee certainly play a part in hindering adults from furthering their education and professional development. The *Report on Adult Education and Training in Canada*, for example, found that lack of time was the most frequently cited barrier by those who wanted to take a course or pursue training, but did not. Location, i.e. distance from an educational institution, also constitutes a situational barrier.

Academic Barriers

The necessity of academic skills for successful learning – for example multiple literacies (e.g., reading, information technology, numeracy), essay writing, and exam writing – can create academic barriers for adult learners. Even though many adults may have acquired such skills through prior academic experiences, significant time lapses in use can diminish their acuity. Nonetheless, data show that adult learners who already have achieved academically are those most likely to pursue further learning. The Statistics Canada Adult Education and Training Survey (2003) showed that of Canadian adults pursuing continuing education in 2002, over half (52 per cent) already had a university degree and about 38 per cent had a college certificate or diploma.

Attitudinal Barriers

Attitudinal barriers entail a general lack of confidence on the part of some adult learners with respect to their academic abilities. They might also include negative previous experiences within the education system, sometimes attributed to negative attitudes – perceived or actual – directed toward them by instructors and feelings of isolation within the academic community. Lastly, such barriers might manifest in difficulty learners experience in being able to concentrate on their work both in class and at home.

Institutional Barriers

Institutional barriers refer to limitations inherent in the institutional framework because it is either biased against, or ignorant of, the needs of adult learners. These include such factors as unwillingness to grant credit for previous learning (formal or informal), inadequate or inappropriate course/program offerings, difficulties of scheduling learning opportunities at times that fit an adult's reality, and lack of appropriate academic or career advising.

The barriers described above seldom exist in isolation and are often interrelated for adult learners. General themes that emerge are lack of time, lack of money, and inadequate offerings that suit the needs and preferences of adult learners.

SERVICES FOR ADULT LEARNERS

The services adult learners require can be grouped according to the point in the process where such services are needed most. An adult contemplating returning to school has different concerns than one who is fitting a study schedule around work and childcare. Student services personnel can help adult learners navigate the myriad obstacles on the path to higher education. While this may appear linear, services adult learners need usually overlap or even "jump" the categories discussed below.

Outreach/Recruitment

Like all students, adult learners need to feel welcome on campus (Strange and Banning 2015). This can be facilitated through orientation or "check us out" workshops or one-on-one tours and discussions. While such services are offered on many Canadian campuses (either formally or informally), there is a particular need to reach out with this information to potential adult learners. Universities and colleges devote time, money, and personnel resources to recruiting each year's new high school graduates, through academic fairs and guidance counselling office visits. Adult learners however are largely out of this information loop (unless they have children at high school) and may therefore miss such opportunities.

Student services personnel can play key roles in reaching out to potential adult learners in several ways. First, it's important to realize that educational institutions can be intimidating for aspiring adult learners – campuses have their own language (e.g., credit hours, tutorials, labs, prerequisites), hierarchy (e.g., presidents, deans, professors, academic advisors, directors), as well as rabbit warrens of buildings and checker boards of categorized parking spots. How easily can potential adult learners find you on campus? Are there ways to improve this path? Solutions may be as simple as providing convenient access to campus maps and routinely intervening when parking tickets are issued for inadvertent violations.

Second, student services personnel can work to develop creative ways of reaching adults who may be interested in returning to school. While websites and other mobile means are certainly available, it's still human contact that can make the difference. Two potential conduits for reaching out to potential adult learners are to actively recruit the parents of new young recruits and to forge partnerships with employers.

Academic Advising

Selecting the right courses or programs from the beginning can greatly enhance the opportunities for success for adult learners. Adult learners should be encouraged to discuss their needs and goals in returning to school in order to find the right academic situation. Those who have been away from formal learning for an extended period may want to start small, with a single course for example, rather than go headlong into a full-time program. Adult learners may also have particular concerns about their study skills and other aspects of being prepared to face academic work.

Study Skills

Most Canadian campuses offer study skills programs, courses, or workshops. Many campuses also have "writing labs" and "math help" centres. Adult learners may likewise lack the necessary information technology skills and need to be directed to the appropriate services. Some schools offer full-scale "bridging year" programs to benefit adult learners, blending academic skills and upgrading courses with traditional first-year offerings. We know that learning begets learning and that the challenges facing under-prepared adults are formidable indeed. Academic guidance through the institutional maze is essential.

Scheduling

When and where courses and programs are available can be of particular concern for adult learners. They may not be aware of new program delivery methods that can make their return to school more manageable. An increasing number of colleges and universities are offering distance education options through a variety of education technologies including e-learning, hybrid courses, and open-schedule online courses. These delivery methods may be especially attractive for mobile learners and students from more remote geographic locations (Advisory Committee for Online Learning 2001).

As accessibility and flexibility improve, availability becomes less important. If adult learners have more access to courses through online delivery mechanisms, and are more readily permitted to transfer credits between institutions, the "when" and the "where" will be less significant – and stressful (CAUCE 2002).

Building on the good foundation laid by Canada's Campus Connection, organized by Industry Canada, consortia that have recently formed to meet needs of flexibility, accessibility, and availability are Campus Canada, Canadian Virtual University (CVU), and Canada's Collaboration for Online Higher Education and Research. Canada's community colleges have also formed the Canadian Virtual College Consortium. Degree completion programs that provide greater opportunity to tailor a program to the individual's needs and interests are examples of good practice in flexibility.

Needs for flexibility refer not to concessions for reduced educational standards, but to the recognition that the realities of adult learners' lives often differ dramatically from more traditional students. Flexibility could, therefore, mean a variety of teaching and learning formats that allow an adult to pursue learning at times and locations more compatible with their lives. Distance education and online learning are key components, as are the required services such as library access to support these formats. Other examples of flexibility include the use of accelerated formats and weekend sessions. Innovations such as night, weekend, and online courses, part-time and accelerated study opportunities, and courses relevant to the demands of adults have helped to better accommodate the complex learning needs of these non-traditional students. The key to making this work for adult learners is getting the information to them when they need it. For example, if adult learners can apply for reduced residency requirements, or alternative assignments, they need to know about these options ahead of time so they can plan accordingly.

Prior Learning Assessment and Recognition

The Canadian Association for Prior Learning Assessment defines Prior Learning Assessment and Recognition (PLAR) as "a systematic process that involves the identification, documentation, assessment, and recognition of learning (i.e. skills, knowledge, and values). This learning may be acquired through formal and informal study, including work and life experience, training, independent study, volunteer work, travel, hobbies, and family experiences" (see www.recognitionforlearning.ca). PLAR may be applied toward the requirements of education and training programs; occupational or professional certification; and labour market entry and organizational and human resource capacity building.

   Although the PLAR process is gaining in national currency, it is far from fully implemented in post-secondary institutions. As a result, adults too frequently experience redundancy of content, excess cost, and waste of previous time. In many cases, potential adult learners are discouraged even before they begin, due to the expectation that their previous learning will be ignored and that they will have to start over if they wish to attain a higher credential.

   PLAR initiatives are moving in the right direction to support lifelong learning in Canada but they nevertheless remain largely fragmented, and institution-based. Even within institutions, the availability of PLAR may vary between faculties and programs. Institutions with PLAR processes in place need to make adult learners aware of these initiatives and encourage participation. Some schools also offer PLAR-connected courses or workshops, for example, portfolio preparation courses in which students build portfolios to submit for PLAR review.

A subset of the recognition of previous learning involves formal transfer of credit and articulation agreements between institutions. Although a growing number of protocols exist, for example, among Canadian universities for transfer of credit for courses at the first- and second-year level – with a similar agreement in place for community colleges – within a nation in which education is largely controlled at the provincial and institutional levels, easy transfer of credit continues to be problematic.

Because of the ongoing changes and developments in both PLAR and transfer credit programs, student services personnel can best assist adult learners by keeping up-to-date on new initiatives and passing along information on these opportunities in a timely fashion. Both PLAR and transfer credits serve two important purposes for adult learners: they validate previous learning, both formal and informal, which can dramatically shorten the time needed to complete a degree or certificate program. This yields financial dividends for students as well, as they don't need to pay for courses they have already taken or material they have already mastered.

Financial Assistance

Financial concerns rank high for adult learners. They may be less likely to seek out on-campus advice for these concerns, either from an assumption that the services are for direct-from-high-school students, or from an expectation that as adults they should "cope." While student services personnel should not be expected to become financial advisors, they can help adult learners address financial challenges by being familiar with financing options available and ensuring that adult learners get the required information.

The need for financial support is frequently a concern for adult learners due to the priorities of adult and family life competing for limited resources. Adult learners are not only less likely to be living at home while they are going to school, but they are also less likely than younger students to use parental assistance as a means of financial support while attending school. Furthermore, those who are unemployed, underemployed, or employed on a part-time basis often face particular challenges. A *Report on Adult Education and Training in Canada* (2001) indicated that finances are a more significant barrier for women than for men. Among non-participants, that is, those who wanted to take a course in the previous year but did not, finances were major barriers for 40 per cent of them. Clearly, improved awareness of financial assistance opportunities is a real need among adult students who, for many different reasons, still perceive that federal and provincial assistance programs are primarily aimed at traditional learners (Potter 1998b).

The Canada Student Loans Programs (CSLP) offer a number of components, including the major loan program that serves approximately 350,000 full-time post-secondary students each year, with loans totaling $1.6 billion in 2003–04 and projected to be $1.9 billion in 2005–06 (Ménard 2005, 8). Additionally, the CSLP for part-time students supports about 3,000 part-time learners annually (CSLP Annual Report 2003). However, awareness among part-time learners of targeted federal assistance (CSLP and Canada Study Grants) is low (Potter 1998a). Along with these loan programs, the CSLP administers several Canada Study Grants for which special groups of adult learners might qualify (e.g., High-need Part-time Students; Students with Dependents; Women in Selected Doctoral Studies; Students with Disabilities).

OTHER ASSISTANCE

While government financial assistance, particularly the CSLP, represents a significant portion of the funding available for adult learners, it is not the only source of financial support for those seeking to enter, or return to, post-secondary opportunities.

Provincial Support   Financial support for full-time adult learners varies considerably across provinces and territories. There are nevertheless a few constants. The CSLP provides up to 60 per cent of full-time students' assessed need, up to a $210 weekly maximum (Ménard 2005) and applicants may be eligible for a provincial/territorial loan in addition to their federal loan. While assessment is based on a single application form, and the requirements for provincial/territorial student loan programs eligibility are the same as for CSLP, assessment criteria and loan amounts for provincial/territorial loans vary across the different regions (CanLearn Interactive 2016). Only the Northwest Territories offers financial support to part-time students, and it does so only in very limited circumstances, such as when the course is only offered on a part-time basis and/or when a student is working full-time. As for the remaining provinces and territories, students are only eligible when enrolled in full-time studies, and taking minimum course loads of 60 per cent, or 40 per cent for students with permanent disabilities ("Compendium" 2003).

Grants, Scholarships, and Bursaries   Grants and bursaries can help offset the need for student loans; they are awarded on the basis of need, do not have to be paid back and so do not add to debt. Among the most familiar granting programs in Canada are the Canada Study Grants (CSGs). In order to be eligible for CSGs, the student must first apply for a loan to the CSLP, either as a full- or part-time student, and then submit a separate application to the same office. Although need is the primary factor determining grant eligibility, there may be additional considerations as well (CanLearn Interactive 2016).

Federal and provincial governments offer various bursaries on the basis of merit and/or financial need. While they do require at least a minimum level of academic competence, whether it is a passing grade or some particular letter-grade average, bursaries are generally made available to those, financially speaking, who need them most. However, with eligibility often limited to full-time enrolment, such resources typically are out of reach for the majority of adult postsecondary learners, who tend to be part-time students (CanLearn Interactive 2016). Bursaries are grants that do not have to be repaid by students, but like scholarships, they are taxable on amounts exceeding $3,000 (CanLearn Interactive 2016).

Institution-based scholarships and bursaries are other financing options available to adult learners. Although many of these are heavily weighted in favour of full-time students, a number of institutions offer awards for part-time learners as well. Most institutions have online databases of internal awards; adult learners may not be familiar with these tools or, as noted above, they may mistakenly believe that all institution-based funding is reserved for straight-from-high-school students.

Work/Study Plans   Work/study plans fall somewhere between bursary programs and jobs. The basic arrangement, as the name suggests, offers students the chance to earn money towards their studies by working for their institution. While in some cases provincial governments provide the funding, the educational institutions themselves usually only administer the programs. Eligibility for these types of programs is based on financial need. Though the intent is to provide work experience in areas related to recipients' areas of study, the jobs often vary – from administrative office duties to research projects, and more. Pay may also vary, according to different jobs and institutions (CanLearn Interactive 2005).

Bank Loans and Lines of Credit   Borrowing mechanisms beyond the CSLP exist for some individuals looking to pursue educational opportunities. Private financial institutions also offer loans to their customers. It should be noted, however, that since these loans are not government supported, interest rates and repayment criteria might vary across the different lending institutions. Other considerations include the fact that non-government loans normally require that interest must begin to be paid immediately, and that these loans may require a guarantor – someone who can co-sign and guarantee loan repayment. Bank loans may take the form of either a standard loan or a line of credit tied to a fixed dollar amount, whereby interest is charged only on the portion that is withdrawn (CanLearn Interactive 2016).

Emergency Loans   Usually administered by financial aid offices at educational institutions, this type of loan is normally awarded on a short-term basis, often limited to ninety days. As its name suggests, such loans are meant to ward off dire situations that students of extremely limited financial means may face. Emergency loans provide food and rent while more lasting financial arrangements can be sought (CanLearn Interactive 2005).

Organizational Support

Some adult learners may be eligible for financial support from their employer. In fact, employers represent one of the two main sources of financial support for adult learners (the other being self-financing). More than 60 per cent of course participants indicate receiving some financial support from their employers. Although extended periods of study, such as what might be required for completion of some programs, are more often self-financed, adult learners with full-time employers should be encouraged to investigate whether or not their employer offers any such benefits. While employer support for adult learners manifests itself in a variety of ways, the most common form is for the organization to pay or subsidize tuition and fees, with

81 per cent reporting this type of benefit. Other types of support include the provision of learning materials, facilities, and organizing training opportunities (Statistics Canada 2001).

Family Responsibilities

For many adult learners, childcare family responsibilities are closely aligned, if not intertwined, with financial concerns about attending school. Lack of available childcare can be a stumbling block for many adult learners, although a growing number of campuses are beginning to offer on-site childcare options. Student services personnel could also keep abreast of the local daycare market in order to provide additional information when appropriate. Beyond these immediate concerns though, adult learners who have children in the home may also find themselves simultaneously caring for their own aging parents. Population projections suggest that increasingly adult learners on Canadian campuses will be part of this "sandwich generation" (Miller 1981), and perhaps require additional personal and family supports (e.g., counselling). Since adult learners are typically undergoing transitions in their own life cycle (Cross 1981) while learning, if these students are to succeed in their educational goals it is paramount that new services be developed to address their concerns.

Career/Employment Counselling

At the culmination of their program of study, adult learners have career and employment counselling needs that differ from those of traditional students. Most likely, some adult learners will be looking for entry-level positions, but others are searching for opportunities to advance in their careers. On-campus career counselling offices provide essential services such as résumé-writing and interview skills workshops. In addition, such services can provide needed focus for adult learners' job searches. Again, these opportunities must be promoted to adult learners, who may assume mistakenly that their special needs might be overlooked in program offerings.

CONTRIBUTION OF STUDENT SERVICES

Student services personnel have a pivotal role to play in recruiting and retaining adult learners on Canadian post-secondary campuses. With their tradition of viewing student needs as paramount, student services personnel are in a unique position to help adult learners address barriers to their academic success. Most effective perhaps is their role of coordinating information and services, acting as advisors as well as advocates for these non-traditional students.

Adult learners typically spend less time on campus than traditional students and may therefore miss the more customary means of advertisement (e.g., posters and brochure blitzes). Student services personnel must think "outside the box" in formulating communications plans for such students. Some institutions find group e-mail notices or texting helpful, others use direct mail effectively; more recently some institutions have begun to capitalize on the proliferation of mobile devices and the multitude of apps designed to navigate resources and opportunities (e.g., Campus Quad). Regardless, it is important to have adult learners identify for themselves their preferred means of contact and communication regarding important opportunities and services.

It is not always enough to point to resources, though; adult learners may appreciate a guide along the way, such as the vast and comprehensive CanLearn Interactive pages. At the same time, the site has its own particular quirks (for instance, "cookies" on this site create defaults that cannot be changed without closing the browser, if one tries first to find information for full-time study Canadian Student Loan Program options and then attempts to change to part-time choices). Adept student services personnel can help adult learners avoid this sort of frustration by knowing how these types of sites function and passing on necessary information.

CHALLENGES

A key challenge for student services personnel intent on benefiting adult learners is to remain up-to-date on services both on and off campus. As Canada's post-secondary institutions embrace emerging technologies, expand use of Prior Learning Assessment and Recognition, improve credit transfer procedures, and take other steps to embrace adult learners, it is up to front-line student services personnel to keep adult learners who are already coping with multiple responsibilities informed of the key services to assist them along the way. Additionally, Student Services can take a lead role in sharing "best practices" among institutions. To name a few exemplars, institutions that have developed comprehensive services for adult/mature students recently include: the University of Winnipeg, which offers advising, prior learning assessment and recognition, and online registration; Brandon University, where outreach focuses on academic skills, career interests, personal counselling needs, disabilities support, and childcare; and York University, which has published on its website a comprehensive list of mature and part-time learner supports in Canadian universities (see http://www.slideshare.net/rossmcmillan/mature-and-part-time-learner-supports-in-canadian-universities-july-11-2012).

Surprisingly, while some limited studies on adult learners in the Canadian post-secondary sector have been published (e.g., Kerr 2011; Livingstone and Raykov 2013) little research has been conducted specifically with regard to student services personnel and the adult learners they serve. There is much knowledge to be gained from current student services practitioners addressing this gap. Benchmark research on learners' perspectives can provide a foundation for longitudinal studies of best practices. Purposeful research can also assist student services personnel with day-to-day projects, planning, and service delivery for improvement of adult learners' experiences on campus. Although service practitioners may be more inclined to focus on immediate program delivery, contributing to an ongoing program of assessment and research can add much in the long run to the quality of campus services for adult learners. In addition to contributing to the body of knowledge on the topic, positive outcomes for adult learners (shared through reports and presentations) also serve as compelling arguments for increased allocation of resources to support the success of such students.

10

First-Generation Students

TIM RAHILLY AND LISA BUCKLEY

Marcel sat alone in the high school library and thought, "Ugh! What should I do?" Earlier in the day he had met with his guidance counsellor, who had encouraged him to apply to the history program at a nearby university. Marcel really liked studying history but wondered how much it cost to go to university and what kind of job he could get once he finished in four years. Neither of Marcel's parents had attended a post-secondary institution, but they have done well for themselves and have provided a comfortable lifestyle for their family. Marcel's parents encouraged him to take a year, get a job, and think about what he wants to do. His uncle runs a paint store and offered Marcel a job mixing paint, and said maybe he could move up to be store manager some day. A few of Marcel's friends were planning to be accountants or work in the IT industry; others were planning on going to the local college to learn a trade. They would be studying for a shorter period of time and seemed to think they'd land good jobs. Marcel imagined that he might be good at teaching history. He wasn't sure if he was strong enough academically, though. His parents were willing to support part of his studies, but he knew he'd have to work part-time to pay his tuition. He didn't want to borrow money and his parents feared he'd go into debt and wouldn't have a good job at the end of his studies. Eventually Marcel took the plunge and applied to study history. Before arriving on campus, though, he was quite anxious and hoped that he'd find friends at university. He also worried about whether or not he'd be up for the academic challenge. He heard from his guidance counsellor about a program for new students, where he could meet others like himself and learn about support services. He thought he would sign up.

INTRODUCTION

There is considerable evidence to suggest that parental education and income levels have a strong influence on whether Canadian students pursue post-secondary education (Auclair and Bélanger et al. 2008; Bouchard and Zhao 2000; Frempong, Mia, and Mensah, 2012; Knighton and Mirza 2002), the timing of their decision to do so (Finnie, Childs, and Wismer 2010), and on the likelihood they will persist to graduation once begun (Hottinger and Rose 2006; Ishitani 2003; Pascarella and Terenzini 2005). Furthermore, deficits of cultural and educational capital, in addition to limited resources, also render first-generation students less engaged and academically successful than other groups (Grayson 2010; Kamazi et al. 2010; Turcotte 2011). Student service professionals generally acknowledge the challenges for first-generation students but sometimes lack a deeper appreciation of the social, academic, and financial barriers these students encounter. Although colleges and universities offer general support services, until recently there were few Canadian schools that directly address the specific needs of this unique group. Extant literature indicates and student affairs professionals understand intuitively that these students have a clear need for guidance in setting and achieving their educational goals (Folger and Carter et al. 2004; Pascarella and Pierson et al. 2004), in addition to basic tools and skills for academic success (Filkins and Doyle 2002). Furthermore, they need social support to remain motivated while studying alongside students benefiting from parents educated at the post-secondary level (Pike and Kuh 2005).

The literature on first-generation students is often confounded by related variables such as financial capacity, racial identity, and ancestry. The same can be said for services to support these students. Indeed, a quick survey of college and university administrative structures and programs in Canada indicates little overt outreach to or support of this important group of students; many support services do exist, but embedded in other campus offices. Services offered in transition programming, First Nations support programs, financial assistance, women's centres, and many others include elements of first-generation support, but may fall short if not coordinated to meet these students' needs. It is hoped that as more Canadian colleges and universities develop strategic enrolment and retention strategies, services and programs will begin to more specifically target the needs of this student sub-population, rather than assume they are accounted for in the offerings of general programs and services.

In this chapter we first examine the characteristics of first-generation students and provide a historical overview of their entry into the Canadian post-secondary system in pursuit of the benefits it provides. Next we examine the prevalence of first-generation students in our colleges and universities and discuss some of the key issues they face. Last we suggest ways student affairs and services can support the success of these students in achieving their learning goals.

BENEFITS OF A POST-SECONDARY EDUCATION

People who work in the post-secondary sector may have a certain bias toward pursuing higher education, but such a path is not appropriate for everyone. Although by no means the sole measure of personal achievement or happiness, post-secondary education has been shown to have a positive impact on many aspects of people's lives. For example, life expectancy increases and the rate of unemployment decreases with higher education (Statistics Canada 1999). For people in midlife and for seniors, education level is strongly correlated with good health, even more so than income level, and for all Canadians, socio-economic status increases as one's level of education increases (Martel and Bélanger et al. 2005). Data from the 2006 Canadian Census indicate a clear increase in personal income for Canadian-born earners who have completed a university degree. Although women do not see the same percentage gain, in real dollars, as men, their increase represents the difference between being perilously close to a low-income threshold and something much higher (Statistics Canada 2008c).

In addition to individual benefits, there are gains to be had for the economy and society at large from advanced learning. Many jobs of the future will require higher education, and given the new emphasis on attracting knowledge workers across all industries, workers will need the kind of intellectual skills that enable them to function at a high level of effectiveness (Association of American Colleges and Universities 2007; Association of Universities and Colleges of Canada

2002). The losses to individuals and the economy are inevitable in the absence of better preparation for all (Outcomes Working Group and British Columbia Ministry of Advanced Education 2006). One can also argue that Canadian society as a whole benefits from investing in post-secondary education. Completion of a college or university education is strongly and positively correlated to no fewer than four significant measures of civic engagement – volunteering, membership in an organization, political activity (in addition to voting), and attending public meetings (Rothwell and Turcotte 2006). Canadian post-secondary graduates are more likely to contribute a greater number of volunteer hours and to make charitable donations (Hall and Lasby et al. 2006). Others have suggested that higher learning also promotes greater societal cohesion, acceptance of difference, and even lower crime rates (Canadian Council on Learning 2006).

Innovative recruitment efforts are important if Canadian higher education is to contribute to building a skilled workforce from this potential first-generation population. Since the population of traditional-aged students is expected to decline (Statistics Canada 2002; Usher and Dunn 2009), it is critical to reach out to such groups who are still underrepresented within the system. A wealth of new knowledge supports the recruitment and retention of these students, and makes their participation in post-secondary education more likely – and more successful. In sum, the choice to further one's education need not be inhibited by income level or status as a first-generation student. But if Canadian student services professionals are to support the efforts of this cohort group, they need to improve their own collective understanding of the needs and potential of these students.

FIRST-GENERATION STUDENTS IN CANADA

The term "first-generation" student generally refers to those who come from families where neither parent completed a college or university credential (Billson and Terry 1982), although this definition is not consistent in the literature (Auclair and Belanger et al. 2008). Neither are first-generation students a homogeneous group. Some identified as such may come from families where no one in the family has pursued any post-secondary education; others have grandparents or aunts and uncles, but not parents, with post-secondary degrees. Parents of first-generation students reflect a variety of backgrounds, from working-class families in both rural and urban Canada and

Aboriginal people in northern communities, to recent immigrants in major urban centres. While this potential heterogeneity implicates very different sets of needs, relatively few Canadian institutions identify such students as requiring any special considerations.

Our understanding of first-generation students is complicated by the general practice of Canadian colleges and universities not to seek – out of privacy concerns or for some other reason – relevant identifying information as part of the admissions process. Educational institutions also fail to use what demographic data are collected (e.g., aboriginal status, address, financial assistance data) to target various support programs (Friesen 2009). Consequently, first-generation students often remain an invisible sector of the student population, whose support is a matter of individual initiative. Failure to account for these students further diminishes educators' understanding of how programs might affect their success.

Regardless of institutional practices, it is clear from other data sources that first-generation students constitute a significant portion of the post-secondary population in Canada, and their numbers are increasing (Parkin and Baldwin 2009). A recent survey of first-year students (direct-entry from high school) found that on average about one in four university students are from families where neither parent has completed any post-secondary education (Canadian Undergraduate Survey Consortium 2013). This proportion parallels that of the general Canadian population, about 24 per cent of which reports having no post-secondary educational experience. The extent to which the adult learner population and first-generation students intersect in Canada is less clear. In US studies, 21 per cent of first-generation students entering college and universities were over twenty-five years of age, while the majority were twenty-four years or younger (Hottinger and Rose 2006). Age is an important factor in the success of first-generation students, with some research indicating that older first-generation students are more certain of their career goals and have higher rates of success in post-secondary education (Dietsche 2005). However they are defined, all first-generation students share, as noted above, two significant common concerns: (a) they are less likely to attend university than students whose parents completed college or university (Bouchard and Zhao 2000; Knighton and Mirza 2002); and (b) if they do attend, they are less likely to persist and succeed (Hottinger and Rose 2006; Pascarella and Terenzini 2005).

SOCIAL TRENDS IN CANADIAN HIGHER EDUCATION

Historically, unless one's parents were of a certain higher social class, one did not generally pursue higher education. A diverse post-secondary population from various socio-economic and educational strata is a relatively recent development in Canada. Whereas in the late nineteenth century only 2 per cent of Canadians between the ages of twenty and twenty-four went to university – mostly to pursue careers as clergy, lawyers, or doctors – that proportion had only increased to 4 per cent by the early 1940s (Canadian Council on Learning 2006). Today, that picture has changed in both the scale and the variety of enrolments.

At least five major trends have contributed to dramatic changes in the class demographics of Canadian post-secondary education, increasing the participation rates of students from a wider variety of backgrounds. First, in the 1947–48 academic year, over 32,000 World War II ex-service personnel received government assistance for university training (Clark 2000); the Canadian War Museum calculates this post-war figure to be as many as 50,000 (Canadian War Museum, no date). Many of these men and women were the first in their families to pursue post-secondary opportunities; many would not have been able to do so without government assistance in the form of guaranteed admission, tuition, housing, and living allowances. Second, in 1951 the Massey Royal Commission recommended that the federal government make direct and unrestricted grants to universities, shifting the responsibility for post-secondary education from a mostly private model to one that is more public (Clark 2000). This had a clear impact on the expansion and accessibility of post-secondary opportunities.

Third, in 1964 the federal government introduced the Canada Student Loan (CSL) program to supplement the resources of students in financial need wishing to pursue full-time post-secondary studies. As has been documented the CSL program was an important step in improving access for students, especially those from first-generation families (Hemingway and McMullen 2004; Junor and Usher 2004; Usher 2005). Fourth, reflecting their changing role in Canadian society, more women began attending university. At first, they pursued more traditional fields, like education and nursing, but more and more women are now studying science, engineering, law, and medicine (Statistics Canada 2006). In 1960, only one-quarter of university students were women; by 1988 the balance had tipped, with more eighteen-to-twenty-one-year-old women than men enrolled full-time in Canadian undergraduate programs (Andres 2004). Increasing female enrolment accounted for three-quarters of the growth in university enrolments in the 1980s and 1990s (Junor and Usher 2004). Recent assessment indicated that women now account for almost 57 per cent of the national enrolment in Canadian public post-secondary institutions.

Finally, increases in immigration and ethnic diversity have also changed the composition of the post-secondary population in Canada. Although data in the US clearly indicate that race is a factor limiting post-secondary access, limited analysis on such questions has been done in Canada. However, sufficient data do indicate that racial minorities and new immigrants to Canada have lower income levels and are more likely to be underemployed, even among those with a post-secondary credential obtained in their country of origin (Statistics Canada 2008c). While an abundance of research indicates that lower-income families encounter limited access to post-secondary opportunities (Swail 2004; Usher and Junor 2004), more study needs to be done on first-generation students from immigrant families, and on those students who may be the first in their family to attend a Canadian college or university. Overall, these five trends contributed to a larger percentage of Canadian youth from more diverse family and socio-economic backgrounds now attending colleges and universities. By 1992, there were 885,000 students enrolled in Canadian universities; by 2002 enrolment surpassed one million (Junor and Usher 2004), and it has now nearly doubled (Statistics Canada 2012).

FIRST-GENERATION STUDENTS' ACCESS TO HIGHER EDUCATION

In spite of these increases in diversity and scale, evidence suggests that first-generation students are still not gaining admittance to colleges and universities as often as other students. Recent Canadian research has found that parental education level plays a significant role in determining if a person pursues any post-secondary education, and the level they pursue, even after accounting for other factors (Finnie and Lascelles et al. 2005; Foley 2001). Further, parental education is also linked to student persistence (Martinello 2007).

Knighton and Mirza (2002) found that 88 per cent of young adults with university-educated parents pursued post-secondary education, compared to 68 per cent of those with college-educated parents or 52 per cent with a high school diploma or less. Young adults whose parents were university-educated were almost three times more likely to pursue a university education than those whose parents had a high school diploma or less. Young adults whose parents had a high school diploma or less were also more likely to choose a college over a university (49 per cent versus 17 per cent).

Several explanations for such disparity between first-generation and other students have been posited, including:

- family income levels impact the likelihood children will attend post-secondary education;
- the lack of good information and role models results in students self-selecting out of the applicant pool;
- the intergenerational outcomes of post-secondary education favour students who have college and university educated parents; and
- recent trends in Canadian post-secondary education (including tuition increases, changes in focus of recruitment, etc.) do not encourage such students to participate.

We discuss each of these claims to suggest types of service interventions that might best support first-generation students. At the outset we acknowledge that, in addition to each of these individual factors, there are interactional effects that researchers and practitioners continue to explore. While many student services personnel can cite, within this student population, inspirational stories of personal resilience that seem to defy the effects of group differences, these are usually atypical cases that diverge from the general patterns observed. The present discussion is limited to group differences for purposes of framing and understanding such distinctions.

Family Income and Socio-Economic Status

First-generation students are more likely to come from low-income families, and in spite of programs like Canada Student Loans, lower-income Canadians are still less likely to pursue a post-secondary education. Corak, Lipps, and Zhao (2003) reviewed post-secondary education participation rates across several decades and found that by the late 1990s, students from higher income families were still significantly more likely to access a university education than students from low-income families (although it had less influence on their likelihood of pursuing a college education). An earlier study by Bouchard and Zhao (2000) had already put forward this finding. While, in 1986, university participation rates for those from lower- and middle-income families were similar, by 1994 there was a significant gap, with participation rates at 18.3 per cent for lower-income families and 25.3 per cent for middle. It is noteworthy that tuition rates started to rise significantly in Canada in 1989, contributing to a cycle where those who could most benefit from a post-secondary education were least likely to pursue it.

Lack of Good Information and Role Models

Parents, regardless of educational background, often hope that their children will attend post-secondary education (Canadian Council on Learning 2006). However, Canadian Millennium Scholarship Foundation research has found that parents of first-generation students may have less information about such opportunities than parents who have attended post-secondary education themselves. Also, parents with lower incomes and education levels are less likely to talk to their children about financial planning for post-secondary education (Canada Millennium Scholarship Foundation 2003). Further, lower-income families tend to overestimate considerably the cost of tuition and underestimate the future financial benefits of attending post-secondary education (Baldwin and Motte 2007; Junor and Usher 2004). In many cases, they are simply not as familiar with the post-secondary system as those parents who experienced it, making it even that much more difficult to act as mentors and coaches in certain contexts.

In *The Price of Knowledge 2004*, Junor and Usher concluded that students from first-generation and low-income families may be self-selecting out of the university pool because of lack of perceived benefits. Their analysis controlled for income and academic barriers and found that motivation was one of the key challenges for students from low-income families. Simply stated, why pursue higher grades if post-secondary education is not seen as a realistic possibility? Why save for education if one does not believe it is of benefit to do so? First-generation students often take themselves out of the running for post-secondary education before they apply – even if they might have previously articulated a desire for a career path that requires post-secondary education.

Encouragement and positive role models are important for all students, but particularly for first-generation students. For students with strong identities of class and race, moving from the familiar to the new can cause conflict. Family and friends who have not pursued post-secondary education may be effectively unsupportive or even obstructionist (Gold 1995; Hsiao 1992; York-Anderson and Bowman 1991). It can be difficult to contemplate going to college or university, perhaps leaving home, family, and friends behind, especially when no family member or peer cohort has done so before. For some, this personal risk is simply higher than any perceived benefit.

Intergenerational Impacts of Post-Secondary Education

Completion of a post-secondary credential is one of the few educational attainments with well-documented multigenerational impact. Studies in the US have long shown that parents' levels of formal education are positively linked with good prenatal care, parental involvement in the child's school, the likelihood of reading to the child and helping with homework, and access to computer resources (Pascarella and Terenzini 2005). Canadian studies further corroborate that children of parents with lower levels of education are more likely to experience poorer health and are less likely to enjoy unbroken good health (Statistics Canada 1999).

Much of the effect here can be attributed to what sociologists term *cultural capital* (Bourdieu and Passeron 1990) – that is, forms of knowledge, skill, and education that give a person higher status in a society. In this case, cultural capital would function to make college or university a more comfortable or familiar place for some, a place where one felt welcome. And this feeling would contribute to success. Further, various forms of cultural capital are used to judge the suitability for entrance to post-secondary education. Parents gain knowledge and access to cultural resources and pass these benefits to their children (Marjoribanks 2005). Pascarella and Terenzini (2005) reviewed numerous studies that demonstrate how parents pass on cultural capital to their children, for example by modeling civic involvement, by using public libraries, and by attending cultural events – as well as by interacting with more people who have also attended post-secondary education. Such a family environment "fosters capacity for life-long learning and crystallizes a general personal disposition for life-long learning and intellectual development" (585). It is this type of cultural capital that post-secondary education recognizes and rewards in its admission process, and it is presumed to advantage such students with the knowledge and tools needed to succeed at all levels of the education system. Lacking this benefit, many first-generation students are at a distinct disadvantage when competing for limited seats in Canadian post-secondary institutions. However such an effect can be mitigated somewhat through parental involvement in, and support of, a student's school life (Auclair and Bélanger et al. 2008; Frenette 2007).

Institutional Trends

Although first-generation students constitute a significant cohort of potential recruits for many institutions – albeit a challenging one for all the reasons noted above – there are several trends that might further impinge on the success of such efforts. First, as a result of declining government funding, Canadian post-secondary education has implemented significant tuition increases since 1989. While costs to pursue programs like business, commerce, pharmacy, dentistry, medicine or law, are considerably greater than those in arts or sciences, claims of their being a "good return on investment" may be insufficient to overcome financial barriers perceived by first-generation students or their sense of belonging in such programs. This, combined with the perceived erosion of support from Canada Student Loans and similar programs – that is, fewer grants, increased loan amounts required to cover rising tuition costs, and reluctance to recognize some essential costs associated with attending post-secondary education (e.g., equipment, supplies, and computers) (Hemingway and McMullen 2004) – suggests that prospects of enrolment for this group are dwindling further. All of this is further exacerbated by the vagaries of economic cycles, which may have a greater impact on first-generation students and, in turn, influence the composition of the post-secondary education cohort at any given time.

Adding to these dynamics of cost and affordability is a second trend of the changing demographics of post-secondary education, resulting in colleges and universities having to compete increasingly for qualified students. One way institutions have done this is to brand their schools and programs, most often promoting their historic reputations, exemplary research, or distinguished alumni (Kaufman 2007). Such marketing, though, is unlikely to resonate with first-generation students – especially given the information deficits of these students and their families. If this group is targeted successfully such information gaps might be closed, which in turn could potentially mitigate some of these declines in general enrolment (Berger 2008).

A third trend in this mix is the increasing governmental and community pressure on institutions to meet the needs of their local and provincial populations (Plant 2007). In some areas of the country this has resulted in schools targeting a particular sub-group of first-generation students. Thus, while one school may be looking to increase rural students, another is looking to increase participation for Aboriginal students. Both strategies should be commended, although it is evident that the Canadian system could greatly benefit from a coordinated recruitment and retention effort to relay a more consistent message to potential students. Recruiting first-generation students is a formidable task for many institutions, given the above forces at work, but retaining these students once they do enroll is another significant challenge.

Persistence of First-Generation Students

A number of studies have established that first-generation students are at greater risk for attrition, especially in their first and second year of post-secondary education (Ishitani 2003; Lohfink and Paulsen 2005). Although a paucity of Canadian research has addressed such questions, challenges for these students are well documented in research from the US. Auclair and Bélanger et al. (2008) reviewed Canadian research in some depth and documented numerous differences between first-generation and other students that do not hold across all groups if the non-first-generation group is further subdivided and examined in light of other factors. However, they affirm that there are real differences between the two groups with respect to persistence and student success.

Before examining specific components that contribute to student attrition, it is important to understand that the interaction between students and institutions is not easily explained by reference to any given single influence. As Andres (2004) pointed out, post-secondary researchers lack a robust understanding of the influence and interaction among individual (e.g., psychological, psychosocial), institutional (e.g., program), and extra-institutional factors (e.g., society, family, and community support). Nonetheless, there are several well-supported predictors for student persistence and attrition: a) academic factors; b) social factors; and c) institutional factors (Swail 1995). Applying these to first-generation students, they include: their academic preparation and aspirations; their engagement in the campus community and academic and social integration; and their financial constraints.

Academic Preparation and Aspiration

Several factors influence academic achievement for students, including personal aspirations and motivation. Pike and Kuh (2005) found that first-generation students have lower educational aspirations than their peers, tend to be slower in identifying a major upon entering post-secondary study, and complete fewer credit hours (Chen and Carroll 2005). In order to be motivated, first-generation students need to be able to see themselves as capable of fulfilling their academic responsibilities and need to perceive academic tasks as useful and interesting (Naumann and Bandalos et al. 2003; Pintrich 1995). Those who articulate clear educational aspirations are more likely to persist (Lohfink and Paulsen 2005; Somers and Woodhouse et al. 2000) and experience positive educational outcomes (Carter 2001; Strayhorn 2006).

A number of studies suggest that first-generation students come to college and university with less academic preparation than traditional students. They also have lower scores on pre-college reading and math skills (Terenzini and Springer et al. 1996), are less likely to take high school math and language courses that predict academic achievement (DiMaria 2006; Friesen 2009; Harrell and Forney 2003), have lower high school GPAs and entrance-test scores (Grayson 1997; Hahs-Vaughn 2004), and are more likely to need remedial help at university (Chen and Carroll 2005). Earning low test scores in high school decreases the likelihood of earning a bachelor's degree and increases the likelihood of leaving college without a degree (Chen and Carroll 2005). Thus, some first-generation students begin the post-secondary experience with less than desirable measures of academic achievement up to that point.

Engagement and Integration in Campus Community

According to Tinto, "the more students are academically and socially involved, the more likely they are to persist and graduate" (2003, 4–5). Tinto's 1987 model of attrition argues that students who are not engaged in the university community are less likely to achieve academic and social integration, and are therefore at greater risk for attrition. Pascarella and Pierson et al. (2004) found that first-generation students, by their second and third year of university, completed fewer credit hours, worked more hours, and were less likely to live on campus; they also exhibit lower levels of extra-curricular involvement, athletic participation, and volunteer work than their academic peers. This research underlined an important problem, as generally it is first-generation students who derive strongest developmental benefits from extracurricular activities and non-course related interactions with peers.

Student engagement in the post-secondary community is a complex and difficult concept to measure. However, scholars have an increasing appreciation for the fact that campus populations are becoming much more diverse, and in the case of first-generation students, much more varied in terms of their intersecting identities. Andres (2004) has used the term "fit" to describe the influence of one's characteristics and identities (e.g., sex, ethnicity, family, community of origin, skills, values, prior schooling) on the formulation of intentions and commitments to a goal. Such commitments, in turn, influence a myriad of experiences within a post-secondary institution. Committed and integrated students engage in the institution, and "the higher one's level of institutional and goal commitment, the more likely one is to persist" (Andres 2004, 2).

How students perceive the campus environment is an important part of their institutional commitment, inasmuch as it is difficult for them to engage unless they see themselves as "fitting in" and being welcomed on campus (Strange and Banning 2001; 2015). Filkins and Doyle (2002) found that students' perceptions of the campus environment being supportive of their academic and non-academic efforts had the greatest impact on the outcomes they experienced in general education, personal and social development, and vocational and workplace skills. However, first-generation students report significantly lower levels of academic and social integration, and their perceptions of the college environment are also less favourable (Pike and Kuh 2005). How students perceive their own role or status within the campus community also strongly affects the likelihood that they will engage in it and succeed. Yet, Orbe (2004) found that first-generation students, even in institutions where they enrolled in significant numbers, tended to place less salience on such an identity. Similarly, Grayson (1997) also posited that perhaps the large number of first-generation students at some institutions lessen the potential impact of first-generation student status on various academic outcomes.

Finally, research suggests that classroom engagement also has a beneficial impact on first-generation students. In particular, low-income first-generation students usually benefit more from educational practices that involve active learning, such as class presentations, discussions, and collaborative learning processes (Filkins and Doyle 2002). In addition, their persistence is improved by small group interventions that encourage connections to peers, staff, and faculty (Folger and Carter et al. 2004). Consistent with this, both the frequency and quality of student-faculty interactions are other strong predictors of persistence for these students (Dietsche 1995).

Financial Challenges

Recent research indicates that Canadian post-secondary students in general are working more than ever, both to supplement student financial assistance and to avoid further borrowing (Motte and Schwartz 2009). Unfortunately, because of financial constraints, first-generation students in particular are more likely to have to work (some full-time) than their traditional counterparts. A potential negative effect of this is that they are less likely to persist when working full-time while attending school (Somers and Woodhouse et al. 2004), since longer work hours have been shown to contribute significantly to involuntary withdrawals (Grayson 1997). It is no surprise then to learn from the research that first-generation students work longer hours and their work experiences negatively impact their development during college, including achievement of lower GPAs (Pascarella and Pierson et al. 2004). Further related to this effect is the fact that Canadian parents with a university education are four times more likely to be saving for their child's education than parents who have only a high school education or less (Junor and Usher 2004).

Completing this picture is the finding that family income has a very direct impact on persistence for first-generation students, that is, for each $10,000 increase in family income, a first-generation student is 2 per cent more likely to persist (Lohfink and Paulsen 2005). In the end, in spite of such barriers, the effects of being first generation are reduced for these students as they self-select and progress through post-secondary studies (Auclair and Bélanger et al. 2008). In the meantime though a number of steps can be taken to increase the potential for success among members of this group.

SUPPORTING SUCCESS FOR FIRST-GENERATION STUDENTS

Due to factors noted above – increased competition among schools, demographic shifts, and a fluctuating economy – Canadian post-secondary institutions are embracing strategic enrolment management or "an institution-wide, systematic, comprehensive, research-driven system designed to locate, attract, and retain the students the institution wishes to serve" (Hossler 1986). Many institutions are also turning their attention to retaining students rather than simply replacing those who leave. Doing so has resulted in Canadian colleges and universities paying greater attention to the needs of underserved populations like first-generation students. Supporting this trend has been the emergence of a new body of literature addressing the specific identities and developmental needs of previously disenfranchised groups in society, especially around issues of race, ethnicity, age, and sexual orientation, to name a few (see chapter 2). These are the very same identifiers that define the mix of first-generation students coming to campus. Because this is an emerging area of post-secondary education, many of the programs to support first-generation students specifically are new, and it may be some time before researchers can measure their full impact. However, a body of evidence in the US demonstrates that student services can have an impact on the persistence and success of these students.

Programs that provide the best support to first-generation students take a comprehensive approach to student success by addressing the multiplicity of needs noted here. Most institutions already have the knowledge, skills, and programs that could help first-generation students, but it is not sufficient to simply "offer" such services.

Successful programs are proactive and they identify first-generation students and their needs explicitly. They also create partnerships between student services, academic programs, staff, and faculty. Finally, they utilize comprehensive measures of the in- and out-of-classroom student experience, such as the National Survey of Student Engagement (nsse.indiana.edu) or Community College Survey of Student Engagement (ccsse.org) to evaluate their impact.

Successful programs for first-generation students in addition reject the misguided notion that underserved and underrepresented students have a "deficit" that must be overcome if they are to access higher education. In many ways such an approach is based in class bias (Green 2006) and does not acknowledge the many skills and abilities these students bring to the learning environment. Further, the deficit approach underestimates the significant role that other non-academic factors play, such as self-confidence and social affiliation (Lotkowski and Robbins et al. 2004). Yosso also argued that North American institutions, in particular, typically value the cultural capital of white, upper-class culture, and devalue the knowledge, experiences, and skills of persons of other races and classes (2005). Finding ways to restructure "social institutions around the knowledge, skills abilities and networks – the community cultural wealth – possessed by People of Color" could broaden understanding of many first-generation students (82).

BEST PRACTICES IN SERVING
FIRST-GENERATION STUDENTS

Preparation and Entry

From the start, first-generation students often experience challenges that might make it less likely they will pursue post-secondary education in the first place. Comprehensive bridging programs can go a long way in helping such students define a pathway into an institution. For example, Handel and Herrera (2003) detailed the University of California's (uc) efforts to recruit and retain underrepresented students. uc is working with partner community colleges to ensure that students have adequate preparation and are encouraged to transfer to university; it is expanding outreach, providing advising and academic preparation beginning in kindergarten through grade twelve; it is increasing outreach programs to students, families, teachers, and counsellors to ensure these first-generation students have good information; and it is researching and evaluating underlying causes of educational disparities to help shape future programming. Since 1997, U C has seen an increase in overall transfer rates of 7 per cent per year and an increase in underrepresented student groups of 38.5 per cent (transfers from traditional students grew 26.7 per cent in the same period).

These kinds of college and university partnerships have a great deal of potential for supporting first-generation students who often find community colleges more financially and geographically accessible at first but later wish to transfer to university. Project C O N N E C T in Texas supports low-income first-generation students, including those with disabilities, in a partnership between Sam Houston State University and two junior colleges (Edmonson and Fisher et al. 2003). The program provides good information (e.g., advising, career counselling, internships), mentoring from peers and faculty, academic preparation and access to research resources like books and computers, and it encourages college students to aspire to attend university, and to engage in it actively when they get there. Though only in its first few years of operation, it has increased retention, graduation, and transfer rates among these targeted students.

Effectively engaging parents is another important strategy for encouraging first-generation students to pursue post-secondary education. The US-based Futures & Families project reviewed by Auerbach (2004) is an example of a small pilot program that successfully engaged parents of Latino high school students. It provided important factual information about college and its academic requirements. However, participants found that the greatest help came from the mentorship of Latino parents whose first-generation students had already gone on to college: the connections they formed with other parents in the program, the fact that it was offered in both English and Spanish, and that it built meaningful relationships between the parents, high school staff, and college admission staff.

Similar bridging programs have been launched in Canada with promise, although there are few published outcomes. For instance, the Toronto District School Board and York University's Advanced Credit Experience targets at-risk students by giving high school students from the Jane-Finch area (an economically depressed, crime-ridden neighborhood in Toronto) a chance to experience university, with in-class experiences, work experiences on the university campus, and alumni and peer mentorship (Coward 2004).

Retention and Persistence

Helping first-generation students persist is not unlike helping other students persist; first-generation students may differ, though, in terms of the amount and timing of the support required. Arguably the most critical factor in retaining first-generation students – after meeting their academic needs – is engaging them in the campus community. According to Astin (1999), engaged students are those who spend time on campus both studying and participating in student activities and organizations; such students also have frequent interactions with faculty, staff, and peers.

In Salinas, California, Hartnell College uses a multi-pronged approach to encourage first-generation students to persist and succeed (Kane and Beals et al. 2004). Their population is 82 per cent first generation, and 67 per cent identify as ethnic minorities. The program encourages first-generation students to enter academically rigorous fields of study. It uses a combination of targeted student services (e.g., educational planning, academic counselling, priority registration and transfer, career counselling, and college orientation); academic support (e.g., workshops, peer and faculty tutorials, study centre, tutoring, and study groups); mentorship (e.g., industry field trips and leadership retreats); and financial aid. It also features outreach and advising programs to local high schools. This program has resulted in increased enrolment of first-generation students in math and science programs, increased GPAs, and 90 per cent of the students transferring from junior college to four-year programs persisted in math, engineering, and technology programs.

One Canadian study indicated that retention of students requires a combination of supports and incentives (Angrist and Lang et al. 2006). Accordingly, the researchers provided financial incentives for students who used student services and who attained satisfactory grades; additional incentives were provided if students achieved higher-than-average grades. Interestingly, the strategy worked better for women than for men, but overall it affirmed the value of multiple initiatives to support first-generation students.

Another way to engage students is through use of cohort-based programs. For example, Bloom and Sommo (2005) found that placing first-generation students in small cohorts of twenty-five as part of a learning community encouraged their persistence, suggesting that a human scale design (Strange and Banning 2015) best supports first-generation success. While institutions might not always offer such academic programs, use of cohort-based student programming remains a possibility. Such an approach offers an ideal opportunity to involve academic staff as role models in motivating students, particularly during critical times like the first year of study. This may be challenging to do since first-generation students are more likely to "stop out" – they are more likely to temporarily suspend their studies and return a semester or two later.

Cohorts, peers, and mentors are all potentially critical sources of information and support for first-generation students. Rodriguez (2003) found that many first-generation students are discouraged by interactions with counsellors, teachers, and other professionals who could not look beyond stereotypes (for example those of race and class) to see their potential. As the data suggested further it is often a personal mentor who initially encourages first-generation students to aspire to post-secondary education, and gives them the information they needed to get there. Institutions would be well advised to ensure equitable academic counselling for all students and utilize mentors for effective outreach, in addition to developing a diverse staff and being vigilant against sources of bias.

RECOMMENDATIONS FOR PRACTICE

In Canada, a number of institutions are using new federal and provincial funding to pilot or enhance existing programs, including targeted first-generation orientation, mentorship, academic preparation, and financial aid (e.g., University of Toronto, Brock University, University of Western Ontario, Queen's University, McMaster University, Lakehead Universtiy, Concordia University, and Mohawk College). Recognizing the intersection of identity and demographic, in 2005 the University of Victoria and the Canadian Millennium Scholarship Foundation partnered on the LENONET Project, which aims to develop strategies promoting Aboriginal student retention and success, and to assess the effectiveness of strategies used (The

Canadian Millennium Scholarship Foundation 2008). Similarly, in August 2006, the University of Regina announced a new mentorship program for Aboriginal Students, focusing on the fact that many are also first-generation students.

Based on the literature, and as suggested by the programs referenced above, there appear to be some clear actions and steps that Canadian student services professionals can take to encourage first-generation students to choose post-secondary education:

- Advocate for programs targeted to the specific needs of first-generation students and the demographic groups where these students are over-represented. Particular attention needs to be given to attaining the approval of the community, families, faculty, staff, and senior administrators.
- Advocate for early intervention (e.g., middle school and high school) and provide accurate information for students and families so they may make choices that will better support post-secondary aspirations.
- Promote role models early in students' lives and assist them by providing mentorship programs. For example, offer programming that features community members from similar backgrounds who have chosen to pursue post-secondary education.
- Offer first-generation cohort orientation programs to promote strong bonds and a sense of connection among students, between students and faculty, and between students and staff members (e.g., student affairs staff).
- Offer parent orientation programs as early as middle school to partner with them to help bolster student motivation. Engage parents in a manner that respects their existing cultural capital (i.e., welcomes and supports knowledge from multiple backgrounds), builds meaningful relationships, and uses multiple languages. Include appropriate information about post-secondary education to help them coach and support their student.
- Offer financial aid and financial planning information for parents and students with special focus on understanding the true costs and benefits of a post-secondary education. Highlight schools that have made an ongoing commitment to access to education (e.g., University of British Columbia and the University of Toronto) which guarantees that academically suitable students will receive an education, regardless of their financial means.

- Create and feature programs that help young parents and single parents attend school.
- Highlight programs that support distinct populations, such as Aboriginal and First Nations students, older students, students with disabilities, women, as well as gay, lesbian, bisexual, trans, and queer students.
- Highlight alternative paths to post-secondary education, including the transfer system that allows students to attend colleges and transfer to university. Indicate multiple entry and exit points.
- Implement admissions processes that recognize the diversity of skills, knowledge, and life experiences of students, rather than simply emphasizing secondary school GPAs.

The literature discussed and the programs outlined above also suggest some clear principles for programs and services that may help first-generation students persist:

- Increase their comfort, sense of fit, and knowledge about their chosen institution, through programs such as orientation, welcome programs, and peer mentorship.
- Create an inclusive environment with programming, initiatives, and policies that support students from multiple backgrounds and identities, thereby ensuring that first-generation students are not singled out as a minority.
- Ensure that first-generation students have opportunities to make connections with faculty members outside the classroom environment, such as in faculty mentorship programs.
- Foster learning environments that capitalize on the strengths of first-generation students and utilize teaching methods proven to support their intellectual engagement.
- Provide appropriate academic support, such as Learning Commons programs, to help support those students who have lower reading and mathematical skills on entrance to post-secondary education.
- Offer culturally appropriate support and engagement programs for First Nations students, as this group has a disproportionately large number of first-generation students.
- Make it easier for students to persist, especially those who may need to take time away from school for family or financial obligations, by building in multiple points of exit and entry.

- Advocate for and offer financial aid programs that focus more on grants and scholarships, rather than loans (which are more burdensome to financially disadvantaged students).
- Create opportunities for work through on-campus employment and co-op programs. Such programs provide a source of income and also encourage transformational learning and community engagement.
- Ensure that students from low-income families have access to the full post-secondary experience. Targeted scholarships and grants can ensure that international exchange programs and unpaid internships, for example, are within reach of all students.

FUTURE CHALLENGES FOR POLICY AND PRACTICE

A number of new initiatives have been launched by governments to encourage first-generation students to enter and persist in college and university:

- Ontario is investing $5 million in programs to encourage first-generation students to access post-secondary education. This includes outreach centres and targeted bursaries (Government of Ontario 2006).
- British Columbia introduced Achieve BC to address the information deficit, making information about post-secondary education, career counselling, and financial aid more accessible to all potential students (Achieve BC 2006). The province has also launched Advancement Via Individual Determination (AVID) to assist students who are either "academically in the middle" or first-generation, and help them prepare for post-secondary studies (Ministry of Education 2006).
- Manitoba is encouraging students to attend post-secondary education and stay in the province upon completing their training by allowing graduates to deduct 60 per cent of their tuition from future income taxes for six years following their graduation – provided that these graduates remain in the province (Birchard 2007).
- The Canadian Millennium Scholarship Foundation has partnered with the University of Victoria on a program to encourage First Nations students to choose to attend university, most of whom are first-generation students.

With this new awareness and understanding, new funding, and new government priorities, colleges and universities in Canada are better equipped than ever before to support first-generation students. Student services professionals must challenge themselves to work with government, senior administration, and academic programs to ensure that programs are compatible with these broader initiatives.

Further research into the needs of first-generation students in Canada is also warranted in order to design effective initiatives that will have a real and lasting impact on the access gap in this country. In addition, it is important for institutions to explicitly identify first-generation students as a cohort with unique needs, and to track their admission, progress, and persistence. Coordination of such initiatives across student services units, much like what is done for other cohorts (e.g., mature students and first-year students), would further support such efforts. Finally, learning from programs shown to have a significant benefit for first-generation students, such as coordinating early interventions across educational levels (i.e., from elementary through post-secondary), would add to an understanding of what works. Above and beyond this, more programs are required to address the significant financial barriers these students encounter, including the rising costs of college and university education, particularly in fields of study with differential tuition rates. Likewise greater attention needs to be given to the needs of First Nations and Aboriginal students in particular as they intersect with first-generation concerns (See Chapter 3).

CONCLUSION

In the end, equal access to higher education for first-generation students is fundamentally an issue of social justice. Given the chance, not everyone would choose to pursue a post-secondary degree, as it is only one of many appropriate life paths. For too many, however, access to education is not a matter of ability or choice, especially in the face of ethnic, family, and socio-economic barriers that limit their educational opportunities. If one's passion and life's work require a post-secondary degree, one should have the opportunity to pursue these dreams. Canadian colleges and universities in general, and student services professionals in particular, have an important role to play – indeed, an obligation – in facilitating fair access to education and success for all who desire it.

11

Navigating Group Rights in Diverse Campus Communities

JIM DELANEY

INTRODUCTION

In a community that is diverse not only in ethnicity and culture, but also with a multitude of faiths, sexualities, and other differences, the question arises as to how an institution can balance the right to free speech with individuals' needs to not feel hurt or be offended. Political activist Noam Chomsky once said: "If we don't believe in free-dom of expression for people we despise, we don't believe in it at all" (quoted in Berk and Carluccio 2000, 228). But the very question of what speech should be tolerated on campus has been an emerging debate across Canada. What free expression, and in particular, whose free expression is at the heart of this discussion? Is free expres-sion an absolute right on a post-secondary campus? To what degree should student affairs administrators intervene to contain free speech, if at all, in order to balance the rights of various campus community members?

As Canadian campuses continue to evolve in diversity, and univer-sities and colleges learn to better serve diverse populations, a new conflict is emerging. It manifests at the intersection of institutional and personal values and identity. While this conflict is by no means an articulation of the "clash of civilizations" as suggested by Huntington (1993), it is nonetheless reflective of differences in his-tory, language, culture, tradition, and religion as they manifest in campus communities. Such conflict challenges administrators and student affairs professionals to address institutional values in new

and innovative ways while also supporting student success and learning. For example, in 2006, a series of events sponsored by a Zionist
organization, Betar-Tagar, at the University of Toronto entitled
"Know Radical Islam Week" (see Betar-Tagar 2006; Farrar 2006;
Harpham 2006) included events that the organizers believed were
relevant to the theme of the week – that is, life in the Middle East and
domestic and international terrorism. Even prior to the events,
controversy arose over the name and stated intent of the week
(Kuitenbrouwer 2006). Following this the university received a number of complaints from Muslim campus groups objecting to the content of the events and describing them as "Islamophobic." Although
judged by university administrators to be within the boundaries of
legal free speech, students reported that they found the events to be
offensive and hurtful (Naylor 2006).

Campus administrators are sometimes accused of applying double
standards in supporting institutional values of freedom of expression and civil discourse (See Chase 2010; Cravatts 2009; The Global
Free Press 2010; Yaffe 2010). Boston University professor Richard
Cravatts (2010) described this double standard as follows:

> Either because they are feckless or want to coddle perceived
> protected student minority groups in the name of diversity, uni-
> versity administrations are morally inconsistent when taking a
> stand against what they consider "hate speech," believing, mis-
> takenly, that only harsh expression against victim groups needs
> to be moderated. When other groups – whites, Christians,
> Republicans, heterosexuals, Jews, for example – are the object
> of offensive speech, no protection is deemed to be necessary. So,
> while campus free speech is enshrined as one of the university's
> chief principles, experience shows us that it rarely occurs as free
> speech for everyone, only for a few.

While such accusations appear to be leveled more often by so-called
"conservative" voices, "liberal" and so-called "progressive" com-
mentators also accuse universities of applying double standards
(Schofield 2009). Other organizations, such as the Canadian Civil
Liberties Association (CCLA), have entered the debate by arguing for
the protection of the rights of anti-abortion groups on campus –
despite identifying as a "pro-choice" organization.

But post-secondary institutions devote significant resources to
addressing and managing such issues. In 2009 and 2010, presidents

and other representatives of a number of schools described various
approaches to addressing issues related to campus events, anti-
Semitism, racism, hate speech, freedom of speech, and civil discourse
to the Canadian Parliamentary Coalition to Combat Antisemitism
(Canadian Parliamentary Inquiry into Antisemitism 2009; Canadian
Parliamentary Coalition to Combat Antisemitism 2010). In her
address to the Parliamentary Coalition, Professor Bonnie Patterson,
president and chief executive officer of the Council of Ontario Universities acknowledged the challenge in addressing these concerns.

> Fostering respect on our campuses is a continuing challenge
> and a continuing mission of our institutions. Our universities
> have in place procedures. They have codes of conduct. They
> have protocols. They have policies that address human rights,
> equity, discrimination, and harassment, and reinforce these
> policies and codes when issues arise. They promote respect-
> ful and constructive dialogue and debate on campus, but
> debate there is, on many varying issues that are difficult in
> society. (Canadian Parliamentary Coalition to Combat
> Antisemitism 2010)

By and large, modern higher education institutions in Canada
espouse core values of free expression and academic freedom (Horn
1999). Universities promote a central value associated with the protection of freedom of speech. For example at Concordia University
"all members have the freedom of conscience and religion; freedom
of thought, belief, opinion and expression; freedom of peaceful
assembly, and freedom of association" (Concordia University 2010).
The University of Toronto similarly holds that "all members of the
University must have as a prerequisite freedom of speech and expression" (University of Toronto 1992b). York University also affirms a
commitment to "provide an environment conducive to freedom of
enquiry and expression" (York University 2001). Arguably, the freedom to explore all ideas – including those considered repugnant by
some – is at the core of a university's raison d'être.

However, universities and colleges also promote values of civility
and respect. The University of British Columbia strives to provide
"a climate in which students, faculty, and staff are provided with
the best possible conditions for learning, researching and working,
including an environment that is dedicated to excellence, equity, and
mutual respect" (University of British Columbia 2008). Similarly, the

University of Calgary "seeks to create and maintain a positive and productive learning and working environment" and has stated further that the "privilege of academic freedom is accompanied by the responsibility to respect the right of every person to work and study in an environment free of prohibited discrimination and harassment" (University of Calgary n.d.).

Providing a safe learning environment is also an important principle for universities. Failure to do so jeopardizes the basic condition conducive to student engagement and learning in community (Strange and Banning 2015). This is reflected not only in how various codes of conduct are articulated, but also in the provision of campus services, such as safe walk programs, community safety offices, and campus security and police. The challenge is that legal free expression includes many forms of advocacy in addition to academic discourse – and advocacy on college and university campuses is a time-honoured tradition, if not a protected right. Advocacy on many world issues can nevertheless place one group at odds with another, who may argue that their own rights have been breached or – for one reason or another – may have legitimate claims to feeling targeted or hurt as a result of another's freedom to express oneself.

In summary, addressing civility and respect and freedom of expression, in the context of a diverse campus community, is a significant challenge. How such values and other institutional values are balanced in a cultural mosaic is among the most pressing concerns of student affairs professionals and policy makers in Canadian postsecondary education. This chapter offers a summary of some relevant incidents from across the country and provides an outline of several emerging approaches to address such issues.

THE INSTITUTIONAL CONTEXT

Campus organizations engage in a number of activities (e.g., lectures, displays, debates, theatre, and dissemination of printed materials) designed to advocate for a particular position on a variety of issues. The disruption of campus activities associated with some forms of advocacy has become a growing concern of institutional constituents. Such concerns arise from a need to preserve students' rights to explore all ideas within legal parameters and while maintaining a safe and secure environment. When controversial events occur, and particularly when there is a complaint about an event or a disruption of an activity, there can be considerable pressure on the institution.

There is acceptance that controversial events will occur on campus and that there may be considerable conflict associated with these events. The question for administrators is how to address this conflict in a manner that reflects institutional values, while also protecting the rights of community members. Fish (1994) suggested that since a university "is informed by a core rationale, an administrator faced with complaints about offensive speech should ask whether damage to the core would be greater if the speech were tolerated or regulated" (108). But universities are also viewed as the very place where difficult questions must be examined. Horn suggested that universities "are not repositories of approved ideas and attitudes: they do not exist primarily to make people feel intellectually or emotionally 'at home'" (1999, 332).

In response to calls for policy to address campus speech, Carnegie Foundation for the Advancement of Teaching (1990) argued against the establishment of restrictive speech codes because, in their view, such policies would not provide an adequate response. Instead, they suggested that universities establish "high standards of civility and condemn, in the strongest possible terms, any violation of such standards" (Campus Life 1990, 20). Downs (2005) attempted to strike a balance, arguing that it is important for administrators, faculty, and students to reinforce individual rights while also articulating "moral intolerance" when acts of speech make people feel excluded:

> such obligations should be promoted not by coercive codes that affect a wide range of speech but rather through exhortation, setting positive examples, and demonstrating moral support for individuals who are in need of such support. If speech acts cross the line that separates offensiveness and rudeness from threats and intimidation, then actual legal intolerance is called for. (2005, 273)

There is a long history of student dissent and activism on Canadian university campuses that began well before the so-called student movement of the 1960s. Horn (1999) provided an overview of Canadian student engagement in protest and dissent since the nineteenth century through the latter part of the twentieth century; he offered numerous examples of student engagement in activities that sought to establish or enhance student rights. Interestingly, at the beginning of the twenty-first century, there appears to be an increasing prevalence of students concerned about other students' freedom of expression as illustrated by the examples provided in the next section. According to Holton (1998) the interference of others and incompatible goals are among the three key sources of conflict in campus settings (limited resources being the third source). Similarly Barsky (2002) found that incongruent beliefs, values, norms, and conduct are among the sources of conflict in universities. More generally, differences in social power, resources, values, and other incongruities, form the real differences between groups, which help create the conditions for conflict. In addition, groups in conflict are known to pressure members to conform to group norms (Fisher 2000). In combination, it is not surprising that one group's freedom of expression might be perceived as "hate" by another group, even if it does not fulfill the legal definition of hate speech.

What is the relationship between the advocacy activities of campus groups and the attitudes about institutional values such as free expression and civil discourse? From a systemic perspective, there may not be widely disparate attitudes about such values inasmuch as they may also be in-favour or out-of-favour values, depending on the circumstances as suggested in several of the forthcoming examples. To what extent do differences in attitudes exist when comparing student affairs leaders and the students engaged in campus activities that are potentially controversial? There are some indications in these case examples that the values of civil discourse and free expression are seen subjectively in a cultural context.

In this chapter, "free speech" or "free expression" is defined as the right to explore and express all ideas, including those considered offensive to some, but excluding those considered hate or incitement to hatred, which is illegal pursuant to Canadian law (Criminal Code 2005). Civil discourse is generally referenced here as Isaacs' (1999) concept of dialogue, as a discourse in which people communicate and think together in a mutually beneficial relationship. Civil discourse is not an activity that necessarily results in agreement. It is a process whereby participants exchange ideas and attempt to understand each other.

THE LEGAL CONTEXT

The Canadian Charter of Rights and Freedoms (1982) provides that freedom of religion, thought, belief, and expression are among the fundamental freedoms in Canada. However, the charter applies to the legislatures and governments of Canada, as well as the provinces, in relation to all matters within the authority of these bodies. The question of the applicability of the Charter to post-secondary institutions has been explored on a number of occasions since its establishment. Generally, in order to be considered part of a government, an entity must either comprise or serve as an extension of the government's administration. In effect, the entity must be under the control of the government. The application of the Charter to colleges and universities then depends upon the degree to which the institutions are autonomous from the government (Hannah 1998).

By and large, universities in Canada are not subject to the provisions of the Charter. However, in a recent decision a Calgary judge ruled on a case involving the free speech rights of two students who posted comments online, which ultimately led to sanctions imposed pursuant to the University of Calgary's Statement of Principles of Conduct and its provisions for non-academic misconduct (Pridgen v. University of Calgary 2010). After appealing the university's decision within the institution, the students then sought judicial review of that decision and sought to quash the sanctions, arguing that their rights to free expression under the Canadian Charter of Rights And Freedoms (1982) were infringed. The court concluded that the Charter did indeed apply to the university in this case, and that the students' rights were in fact being breached (Lederman 2010; Sarna 2010).

Whether this case could have broader implications to other situations is a matter of speculation. For example, to what extent might groups that believe their rights to free expression have been prohibited or restricted by universities also seek judicial relief? John Carpay, a Calgary lawyer and columnist, wrote: "This court ruling makes it clear that when a university tries to use its legitimate disciplinary proceedings for an illegitimate purpose, such as censorship, the Charter protects the students' right to free speech" (Carpay 2010). In late November 2010 it was reported that the University of Calgary subsequently filed a notice to appeal the decision and the degree to which colleges and universities fall under the provisions of the Charter (Canadian Press 2010; Slade 2010b). Another relevant case occurred in the fall of 2010, when two former students announced the commencement of litigation against the University of Toronto, a number of administrators, and Toronto police arising from a March

2008 sit-in and various institutional, police, and court proceedings since the initial incident (Morrow 2010). This case is notable in the context of this section because of the plaintiffs' claim, among other things, that their Charter rights and freedoms were breached by the university.

Provincial human rights legislation, which protects various individual rights and which, generally speaking, protect individuals from discrimination, also apply to post-secondary institutions in various degrees (Hannah 1998). However, there are some legal limits to free expression in Canada. Sections 318 and 319 of the Criminal Code of Canada prohibit advocating genocide, the public incitement of hatred against identifiable groups (where such incitement is likely to lead to a breach of the peace), and the willful promotion of hatred against identifiable groups (2005). While a fulsome discussion of the law, its interpretation, and its application are beyond the scope of this chapter, it is clear that not all speech in Canada is protected. See Moon (2000) for a more comprehensive discussion of the constitutional protection of free speech.

An obvious challenge emerges then, when one attempts to balance rights and values. Sumner provided an in-depth analysis of freedom of expression and its relationship to equality values, and noted that "hate propaganda is a difficult issue for liberals because it seems to reveal a conflict between their two most cherished values" (2004, 52). On the one hand there is a need to protect individuals from discrimination, while on the other there is a need to protect the expression of opinions. The intersection of the rights articulated in the Charter of Rights and Freedoms (1982) (e.g., "freedom of thought, belief, opinion and expression," section 2 (b); and the right to "the equal protection and equal benefit of the law," section 15) and the prohibition of willful promotion of hatred against identifiable groups under the Criminal Code (2005) circumscribes a complex legal context and setting for this discussion. More importantly, in a campus context there are also different understandings of the concepts of hate and hatred. The Oxford English Dictionary defines hate as: "An emotion of extreme dislike or aversion; detestation, abhorrence." However, an emotion is a far cry from actions that might rise to the level of criminal incitement of hatred or willful promotion of hatred against identifiable groups. In addition, "identifiable group" is defined in the Criminal Code (2005) as "any section of the public

distinguished by colour, race, religion, ethnic origin or sexual orientation." This point is critical when attempting to distinguish some
forms of political advocacy from hate speech.

RELEVANT RECENT HISTORY

The following accounts provide a variety of illustrations on value-
laden conflicts in relation to institutional values of free expression
and civil discourse. These examples are by no means an exhaustive
sampling of these types of conflicts in Canadian higher education.
Rather, they have been selected because of the unique features each
provides for the purposes of this discussion. In addition, no conclusions should be drawn from the inclusion of these examples with
regard to the actions taken by any of the proponents in each case.

Case 1: University of British Columbia – The Genocide Awareness Project

The Genocide Awareness Project (GAP) is a display of abortion-
related images juxtaposed with images of historically recognized
instances of genocide and other crimes. GAP is an initiative of the
Center for Bio-Ethical Reform, a United States – based organization
which seeks to "establish prenatal justice and the right to life for the
unborn, the disabled, the infirm, the aged and all vulnerable peoples
through education and the development of cutting edge educational
resources" (Center for Bio-Ethical Reform n.d.). After considerable
discussion, debate, negotiation, and legal challenges involving various campus organizations – including a campus anti-abortion group,
Lifeline/Students for Life, a student government, the Alma Mater
Society, a campus pro-choice group, Students for Choice, and the
university – GAP images were ultimately displayed on campus in the
fall of 1999. Several students tore down the display in protest and
were ultimately disciplined under the university's procedures for
non-academic conduct (Bradley 1999; Bradley 2000; Bradley and
Merzaban 1999; Dimison 2000). The incident marked the first in a
series of controversies over the mounting of the display across
Canada and sparked a debate over balancing a campus group's right
to free expression against the rights of others to not view the potentially offensive materials, as illustrated in the next case.

Case 2: University of Calgary and Other Canadian Universities – Anti-Abortion Activities and Groups on Campus

In 2008, after several years of controversy over the display of the Genocide Awareness Project at the University of Calgary, and following the university's insistence that the Campus Pro-Life group display GAP images in a manner that allows passers-by the option of viewing the display, the organization instead chose to display the images openly. The university responded by issuing warnings to the group. Ultimately, a number of students were charged with trespassing (Azuelos 2008; Carpay 2008; McGinnis 2009). Although the charges were later stayed (Urback 2009), the case marks a shift in approaches to balancing free expression with the rights of others. Subsequent displays of materials were also met with action by the university (Dormer 2010). In a similar set of circumstances during the fall of 2010, several students were arrested for trespassing after mounting an anti-abortion display at Carleton University in Ottawa (Lewis 2010; Pearson 2010). A number of other universities have faced similar dilemmas when addressing the issue of how to manage the display of potentially offensive materials (Martell 2008).

More broadly, the recognition and funding of anti-abortion groups by student governments has emerged as a challenging issue for a number of institutions (CBC News 2009; Kaufman 2010; *National Post* 2008; Robson 2008; Spears 2010). The conflict emerges in some cases as a disconnect between student associations' stated "pro-choice" policies and positions and the campus groups' objectives to limit abortion (*National Post* 2010). In some cases, moves by student associations have resulted in university administrations taking action to protect free speech. For example, in 2008, when the York University Federation of Students refused a booking for an anti-abortion event on campus, the administration made arrangements instead to hold the event in university-controlled space (Coleman 2008; Macleans.ca 2008).

The conflict over anti-abortion groups' rights on campus is symbolic of the struggle between the rights to free expression and the values of other groups, as well as the rights of others to choose not to be exposed to images or speech they find offensive. Like other campus conflicts on various issues, it may also intersect with values that are influenced by faith and ethno-cultural values, as well as differing individual worldviews. This may certainly become the case as increasing numbers of students from underrepresented or disenfranchised groups are accommodated on college and university campuses.

Case 3: University of Waterloo – Address by Christie Blatchford

As part of a book promotion tour for *Helpless: Caledonia's Nightmare of Anarchy and How the Law Failed All of Us* (Blatchford 2010), Christie Blatchford, a Canadian newspaper columnist and broadcaster, was scheduled to address an audience at the University of Waterloo in the fall of 2010. In protest of the book's perceived failure to acknowledge European settlement on Aboriginal lands, and also because of Ms Blatchford's previous writings, a number of protestors chained themselves together on the stage in an effort to prevent the speech. At the urging of the university and insistence of Ms Blatchford's publicist, the talk was cancelled and rescheduled for later in the fall (Blatchford 2010; Brean 2010; D'Amato 2010). The case is one of a number of situations in Canadian institutions where apparently unwelcome voices have allegedly been silenced. Ms Blatchford herself stated: "I'm just unnerved to be in the company of people who are more genuinely controversial than me, but I long ago gave up any hope that universities were the defenders of free expression" (quoted in Brean 2010). The next three cases speak to this concern.

Case 4: Concordia University – Address by Benjamin Netanyahu

In the fall of 2002, Palestinian advocates staged a significant protest in response to a planned speech at Concordia University by former Israeli Prime Minister Benjamin Netanyahu. As a result of safety concerns in the face of public protest that some deemed violent, the speech was cancelled (Grohsgal and Anber 2002). The university later accepted responsibility for the melee, admitting that it had failed to provide proper security, but it also criticized a student group for its purported effort to prevent the speech. Following the riot the university imposed a moratorium on all Middle East–related events, but later lifted the ban (Canadian Press 2003). *Confrontation at*

Concordia (Himel 2003), a film about the actions of various protagonists in the affair, was broadcast on CanWest media in 2003. The film gave rise to complaints to the Canadian Radio-television and Telecommunications Commission and the Canadian Broadcast Standards Council about the depiction of pro-Palestine activists as "'thugs' bent on 'persecuting' Jewish students" (Zerbisias 2003). Another film, *Discordia* (Addelman and Mallal 2004), documented the life of three campus activists as they responded to the planned Netanyahu address and its aftermath.

Some years later, David Bernans provided a fictional narrative with factual historical background and an account of the events at Concordia in *North at 9/11* (Bernans 2006). This publication is significant because the author accused Concordia University of blocking him from conducting a reading of it, due to the book's claim that the administration had failed to act appropriately in the Netanyahu event. Reportedly, after receiving an initial approval for the public reading, a subsequent communication indicated that the request was declined (Canwest News Service 2006). The event was later permitted because there was a reported administrative error in the consideration of the request (Meloche-Holubowski 2006).

Overall, the events at Concordia are significant for the reference point they create in how administrators view such issues in the twenty-first century. Few discussions about students' freedom of speech on campus in contemporary discourse occur without reference to the incidents at Concordia in 2002. For example, the University of Toronto acknowledged that there were lessons learned coming out of the Concordia conflict (Fairbairn 2006). Such is also the case in the next example.

Case 5: York University – Address by Daniel Pipes

Considerable controversy emerged in 2003 over a planned speech at York University by Daniel Pipes, American writer and critic of Islamic extremism. After initial plans for Pipes to speak in a student-organization-operated facility were dropped, following criticism from campus organizations – including a Middle-Eastern student association – the university administration reportedly worked out detailed plans for the event in other university space with the Canadian Jewish Congress, which also bore part of the costs of security. The planning of this event was haunted by fear of a repeat of the

Concordia riot (Gladstone 2003; Porter 2003). While the protest itself was an issue of concern at the time, the planning for this event also confirmed that memories of the events at Concordia University would continue to influence Canadian campuses in the modern era. In particular, questions concerning the perceived need for security and police at campus events would be among the most critical and contentious thereafter.

Case 6: University of Ottawa – Address by Ann Coulter

In the spring of 2010, a speech by American conservative Ann Coulter was cancelled following a risk assessment suggesting the potential for violence around the event. Ezra Levant, a lawyer and conservative activist, described the cancellation as emblematic of the state of Canadian freedom of expression: "When you start to intimidate and pose a security threat, there is no longer free speech" (quoted in Chase 2010). A day later, Ms Coulter's speech at the University of Calgary went off without incident (Church and Walton 2010). The case is significant because of criticism of the University of Ottawa's warning to Ms Coulter in advance of the planned address. The university wrote to Ms Coulter advising her to use caution in her address in order to avoid facing criminal charges for promoting hatred (Chase 2010). This case raises questions relating to the degree to which institutions might attempt to head off criminal speech in advance rather than address such speech in complaint-driven processes after the fact. After all, is it even possible (let alone desirable) for an institution to accurately anticipate or predict the content of speech before an event?

Case 7: George Galloway's Cancelled Visit to Canada and Canadian Campuses

Outspoken British politician and Palestine advocate George Galloway was scheduled to visit Canada and a number of Canadian campuses in the spring of 2009. While Mr Galloway had previously visited Canada and addressed student audiences (Campbell 2005), the Canadian government moved to ban Galloway's entry into Canada on the basis that he provided support to Hamas, an alleged terrorist organization which is listed as a group associated with terrorism by the Government of Canada (Brennan 2009; Public Safety Canada n.d.). In light of the denial of entry to Canada, Galloway spoke to audiences via an Internet broadcast (rabble.ca 2009). Galloway and supporters challenged the Canadian Border Services' decision to deny him entry into Canada in court, and the ban on his travel was then lifted. Subsequently Galloway spoke at York University in November 2010 to the protest of Israel advocates and politicians (Carlson 2010; Kim 2010). This case is significant for the reaction to reports that the university criticized a Toronto rabbi who encouraged opponents to stage a protest. An editorial in the *National Post* stated:

> Something is very wrong with Canadian campuses these days. Left-wing students and outside agitators get away with shouting down speakers they disagree with, smashing windows to prevent lecturers they don't want to hear, even chaining themselves to a stage and screaming "racist, racist, racist" at the University of Waterloo to prevent Christie Blatchford from talking about her new book. Student unions routinely decertify pro-life clubs, and administrators frequently cater to the demands of a handful of vocal socialist anarchists. But when right-of-centre student groups attempt to protest the censorship they face, or demonstrate against leftist speakers and those they believe are hateful, they are met with threats of lawsuits or expulsion by administrators or student unions ... The reason for all this is ideological bias: Definitions of free speech, equality and political rights all have been reworked to show favouritism to those espousing leftist ideology. It's a sad development for institutions that are supposed to be bastions of free inquiry into controversial and diverse ideas. (Editorial Board 2010)

Ironically there was no mention in the editorial of the Canadian government's previous actions to deny Galloway's entry to Canada, thereby preventing his freedom of expression.

Case 8: University of Toronto – Israeli Apartheid Week and the Winter and Spring of 2006

In the spring of 2006, a series of events and incidents at the University of Toronto created controversy and conflict among students and non-students alike. In addition to the event referenced above, entitled Know Radical Islam Week (KRIW), the Arab Students' Collective held its second Israeli Apartheid Week (IAW). IAW is a series of Palestine advocacy events aimed at developing support for the cause of Palestinian identity and statehood, and which promote the concept of boycotts, divestments, and sanctions against Israel (History of Israeli Apartheid Week n.d.). This event is significant at the University of Toronto because it originated there in 2005 and now is held at many institutions and in many cities around the globe (History of Israeli Apartheid Week n.d.; Weinryb 2008). The juxtaposition of the scheduling of the two weeks created considerable discussion on campus and in the external media (Farrar 2006; Harpham 2006; Kuitenbrouwer 2006; Spurr 2006a; Spurr 2006b) and followed from significant debate about the events held in the first Israeli Apartheid Week the year prior (Siddiqui 2005). The previous year's events were marked by complaints from external organizations and coverage on the American cable news network, CNN. The reaction to IAW and to KRIW was complicated by the self-identity of many of the protagonists on the Israel advocacy side, which Aiken-Klar addressed in 2009:

> What is clear from this brief overview is that through the efforts of the [organized Jewish community], and as a response to fears of increased assimilation and antisemitism, the approach to strengthening Jewish identity on campus has become highly focused on Israel advocacy. As a result of this blurring of Jewish and Zionist interests, the perceived threat to Israel (both in the Middle East and on campus) is experienced by the Jewish community as a direct assault against the primary means by which it has chosen to identify itself. (Aiken-Klar 2009, 111)

Following these two awareness weeks in 2006, on the University of Toronto's St George campus a number of incidents occurred that were described as "Islamophobic" (Bovee-Begun 2006; Canadian Federation of Students 2008). Additionally, in the shadow of the publication of the now-infamous *Danish Mohammed* cartoons, a campus newspaper at the University of Toronto published an original cartoon depicting Mohammed in an embrace with Jesus Christ (Canadian Press 2006; O'Hare 2006).

Overall, the winter and spring incidents of 2006 were described as particular moments of strain for the University of Toronto community and were documented in an address by the president to the university's Governing Council on 23 March, 2006:

> Clearly, these incidents take place in a setting of growing ethnic and religious tensions in Western society. That a university such

as ours, which pursues diversity as a central tenet, should find itself a venue for the ugliest displays of that tension is perhaps inevitable.

It is most certainly regrettable, and it is without question intolerable.

Other Canadian universities have faced similar tensions in recent years. We, like they, can only respond to racism by confronting it directly, prosecuting it whenever warranted, protecting the safety of our members, and promoting diversity with unwavering commitment. This University has long been and remains opposed to Islamophobia, anti-Semitism, and every conceivable form of discrimination based on race, religion or faith, or ethno-cultural identity. Combating these myriad forms of racism and discrimination is the daily work for many members of your administration, and it is a daily commitment made by countless members of the wider U of T community.

There will be offensive expressions that we cannot suppress or censor because of our respect for the core value of free speech on our campus and in our society. But I want to serve notice that this administration will not hesitate to communicate its concerns to those who seek not to promote a dialogue, but to posture as demagogues.

The University of Toronto will continue to uphold the principle of free expression – even, at times, to a degree that may be uncomfortable in broader society – because it is the cornerstone of our daily work. In so doing, we expect all members of this community to be mindful of the fine line between discourse that is provocatively reasonable and that which is unreasonably provocative because it targets individuals on the basis of their identity. Racism and discrimination on the basis of religion or ethno-cultural identity are unacceptable on our three campuses. (Naylor 2006)

These events of the winter and spring of 2006 formed the foundation for an articulation of the institution's approach to these issues as summarized in the following section.

An Evolving Conceptual Model

Higher education institutions play a unique role by acting as guardians of important principles of freedom of speech and freedom of inquiry. Academic freedom is perhaps the most cherished value in academia. Without giving licence to prejudice, there must be a freedom to explore, examine, debate, and criticize issues, which are potentially controversial. At the same time, hate speech and incitement to hatred are prohibited by the Criminal Code of Canada (2005), and institutions have a responsibility to expose hate and address it for what it is – a crime. There are times when legal commentary and advocacy on various world issues will undoubtedly make some feel uncomfortable, angry, or hurt. On such occasions, we call upon our values of civility and respect and show tolerance for the rights and freedoms of the members of various campus communities. Ideally, freedom of expression co-exists with respect for human rights – and indeed thrives because of it. In this context, the University of Toronto developed a conceptual model for understanding potentially controversial activities. This "spectrum of discourse" provides a lens for decision makers to help gauge a response to various types of campus activities. The model is illustrated in Figure 11.1.

Academic Discussions (Level 1) include some of the more traditional academic and campus activities such as colloquia, symposia, and conferences. Generally, such activities are designed to advance scholarship and knowledge, and welcome opportunities for discourse, disagreement, and different points of view. Such events also are characterized by respectful, constructive, and collegial interactions and, as such, are consistent with institutional values. Activities characterized as *Debate* (Level 2) generally aim to advance a discourse and are not always devised to expand knowledge. Often polarized and sometimes confrontational, such debates may be intended to move, ultimately, towards a winning perspective and a losing perspective. While not always "academic" in nature, such debates are a traditional part of campus life. Those interested in advancing a particular position or worldview engage in *Advocacy* (Level 3) activities. Events in this category may be a means to rally supporters and explore an issue from a defined perspective. Those representing opposing views may feel unwelcome at these types of events and may feel targeted for action. However, opponents and opposing views are not necessarily delegitimized. While universities are often sites of advocacy carried out by students and student groups, the institution itself is rarely a sponsor or supporter of such activities.

At Level 4, special scrutiny is required. Activities such as these advocate for specific positions and challenge the personal legitimacy

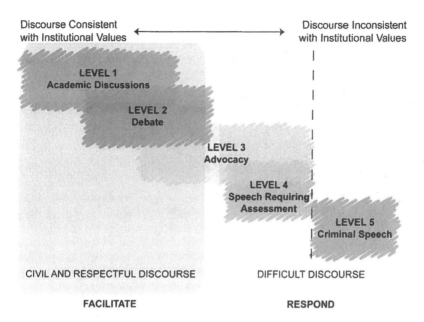

Figure 11.1 Spectrum of discourse (University of Toronto)

of other individuals or groups who do not agree. As with advocacy the intent may include the rallying of supporters and the exposition of an issue from a single perspective. However, opponents and opposing views are not welcome and may be generally targeted for attack. Events may be provocative and may be named or designed to generate external media attention. Although such speech may be considered to exceed the protected boundaries of academic freedom, an institution should nonetheless weigh its principles and policies carefully, prior to a response. Depending upon the college or university's policy framework as well the degree to which freedom of expression and civil discourse are prioritized, a variety of institutional responses are possible. In many cases, the approach may be to protect free speech while also openly commenting that an activity is not consistent with institutional values of civility and respect for others. For example, while the University of Toronto's Policy on the Disruption of Meetings (University of Toronto 1992c) reinforces the right of free expression, as well as freedom from physical intimidation and harassment, it also goes on to require the administration to set a standard of conduct that does not conflict with individuals' rights and also allows for "the maximum opportunity for dissent and debate." At the same time, the university's Statement on Freedom of Speech (University of Toronto 1992b) includes a helpful provision articulating the limitations and cautions for those exercising their right to free expression:

> Of necessity, there are limits to the right of free speech, for example, when members of the University use speech as a direct attack that has the effect of preventing the lawful exercise of speech by members or invited guests, or interfering with the conduct of authorized University business, the University may intervene. Similarly, although no member of the University should use language or indulge in behaviour intended to demean others on the basis of their race, ancestry, place of origin, colour, ethnic origin, citizenship, creed, sex, sexual orientation, handicap, age, marital status, family status, the receipt of public assistance or record of offence, *the values of mutual respect and civility may, on occasion, be superseded by the need to protect lawful freedom of speech. However, members should not weigh lightly the shock, hurt, anger or even the silencing effect that may be caused by use of such speech.* [Emphasis added] (University of Toronto 1992b)

On occasions when the institution has an obligation to protect speech at Level 4 in the spectrum, it may also be necessary to explain to students why it is important to do so because the potential hurt that might be caused by such events may challenge an individual's notion of the role of the institution in providing an environment conducive to learning. In addition, it may be advisable to outreach to specific groups and communities, which may be impacted by others' free expression.

When it is alleged that events and activities exceeding the limits of Level 4 constitute hate speech or incitement to hatred as defined by the Criminal Code (2005), administrators may consider referring the matter to external police for investigation or to other relevant experts for review. *Criminal Speech* (Level 5) may be characterized as racist, homophobic, sexist, anti-Semitic, Islamophobic, or other otherwise discriminatory and/or demonstrative of intolerance – not just of the other's opinion, but of the other's rights. For the purposes of this discussion, criminal speech is activity that is contrary to the law (see sections 318 and 319 of Criminal Code 2005) and which is designated as prohibited on the grounds of discrimination in the relevant provincial human rights code. There may be expressions of hatred for other groups or incitement to hatred against groups' beliefs and/or ideology. Such attacks are often framed as advocacy, but can be distinguished because they attack other people, rather than attacking an idea. As hate speech and incitement to hatred are criminal activities, institutions have an opportunity to articulate the principles behind freedom of speech and academic freedom and may clearly indicate that such freedoms are not designed to protect hatred. As above, institutions may choose to reach out to affected groups in order to reinforce institutional values and provide support to individuals.

The University of Toronto's general approach was outlined at the Canadian Parliamentary Coalition to Combat Anti-Semitism (2009). Its methodology is set out in four core elements: a) outreach to vulnerable groups; b) aggressive education; c) monitoring; and d) follow-up.

Outreach to Vulnerable Groups. Student affairs professionals and equity officers maintain close relationships with groups on campus, which may feel the impact of others' free expression. At times, this outreach simply involves ensuring that various groups are aware of various activities on campus and the important principles the university draws upon in order to support freedom of speech. On other occasions, outreach involves intentional programming designed to address particular issues or the direct impact that campus activities might be having on members of other groups. A key feature of this element is the identification of appropriate contacts within the administration who are available to address various issues.

Aggressive Education. Proactively and in response to provocative and potentially controversial campus events, the administration reaches out to organizers in order to remind them of the responsibilities that accompany free speech and of their obligations under university policies and law. In particular, expectations concerning the participation and tolerance of those with opposing views are articulated in order to encourage a civil and respectful dialogue, free from harassment. In addition, organizers are provided with information and advice regarding the management of disruptive situations and other event planning considerations.

Monitoring. Many potentially controversial events are attended by senior student affairs professionals and equity officers. Attendance is a physical reminder of the institution's policies and expectations, but more practical considerations can come into play. For example, should an event experience disruption, university representatives can offer advice about strategies that can assist organizers in managing the event, thereby helping to protect free expression. Should there be a complaint about an event, individuals present at events can act as witnesses.

Follow-up. On occasion, this may take the form of further intervention and support by a relevant student affairs or equity officer to an individual or group that has been impacted by another group's free speech, in order to address the offense or hurt that might have been experienced. On other occasions, it is a follow-up with event organizers in relation to compliance with policy or with respect to planning for future events in light of incidents or experiences that might suggest a change in the manner in which future events are staged. When the university receives complaints about events, further inquiry occurs and matters are referred for appropriate disposition. If a complaint is received alleging that an activity or an event constitutes illegal conduct – such as a violation under the Criminal Code (2005) provisions for hate and incitement to hatred – the matter may be referred to police for investigation.

The university's representative at the inquiry conducted by the Canadian Parliamentary Coalition to Combat Anti-Semitism (2009), Robert Steiner, emphasized that the approach does not sanitize the university environment. Rather, the approach is rooted in institutional values. The university's role is not to insulate students from opposing views or the tensions arising from them. Instead, it should maximize opportunities for debate and dissent in a manner that is inclusive, civil, and respectful.

In recognition of the role that academic freedom and free expression play in an institution of higher learning, and in democratic societies themselves, the approach is based on the principle that legal expressions of belief and advocacy cannot be banned. The approach also recognizes that members of the campus community should be prepared to experience – and when deemed appropriate, confront – opinions that may be repugnant. The challenge is to protect free speech while also encouraging collegiality and discouraging intolerance. Perhaps the best remedy to poor speech is more and better speech. In 2008 president of the University of Toronto David Naylor discussed his institutional strategy:

U of T's approach works. Year after year, events on our campuses have been far quieter than the storm surrounding them outside our community. Why does U of T's approach succeed? It succeeds because we work to help student organizers understand the difference between free speech and hate speech and monitor events very closely if there is any chance they will cross the line. It succeeds because we have the resources to respond to complaints of racism promptly and thoroughly and because our policies prioritize safety and are based in Canadian and Ontario law. Our approach also works because we do not, in fact, simply refuse controversial bookings. Cancelling events because of anticipated controversy rapidly changes the nature of the debate. Instead of public attention focusing on the actual position of the speaker or sponsoring group (sometimes extreme and therefore lacking broad appeal), the focus shifts to the abrogated free speech rights of the affected groups and can create publicity and even sympathy for an extreme view. (Naylor 2008)

The University of Toronto's approach, embedded in the policy framework and campus culture of the institution is, of course, only one approach. Other institutions employ other strategies and tools to address these issues, and it may be the case that no one approach may be easily adapted to another institutional context. The example is provided here as one illustration of how an institution conceptualizes and operates, and is suggestive of the need to develop a multifaceted lens through which to explore these issues at a systemic level, as well as a comprehensive plan to respond to complex issues.

Any institutional approach, however, must work in concert with other strategies to address other related matters. For example, in 2009, the Ontario component of the Canadian Federation of Students issued its *Final Report of the Task Force on Campus Racism* (Canadian Federation of Students 2011). It followed an earlier report that focused on issues related to the needs of Muslim students on Ontario campuses (Canadian Federation of Students 2008). The Task Force on Campus Racism was created to provide opportunities for campus community members to articulate concerns about racism and racial discrimination; it also sought to raise awareness of and education about racism and racial discrimination, and to gather anecdotal evidence of students' experiences. The recommendations of the Task Force covered a wide variety of issues relevant to post-secondary institutions, including addressing racism in the classroom, student engagement and representation, orientation activities, residence life, student support services, campus media, and various aspects of institutional policies and practices.

In relation to the issues addressed in the present chapter, the recommendations include suggestions that students be encouraged to speak out about incidents of perceived racism at campus events and appropriate mechanisms be provided for students to report such incidents. The Task Force also recommended provision of a diversity of options for events and activities and the promotion of events in a manner that encourages wide participation. Some recommendations emphasize the importance of quick responses to incidents of racism on campus and, like the approach outlined above, the need to work closely with those experiencing perceived racism to provide support.

The Task Force operationalized "racism" as "an ideology that either explicitly or implicitly asserts that one group is inherently superior to others, based on race" (Canadian Federation of Students – Ontario 2009). The challenge emerges when events, activities, or other incidents occur that are perceived by some groups and individuals as offensive, hurtful, or hateful. A person might experience the content of a campus event to be highly offensive without necessarily constituting racism. For example, while one person might perceive a Palestinian advocacy activity as political activism, another might perceive it as anti-Semitism, because the event included criticism of Israel. These issues will continue to be difficult to address because they are interwoven with issues of identity, ideology, and cultural belief systems – which are beyond the scope of this chapter. However, in addressing such issues with students and campus groups, care should be exercised in clarifying definitions and terminology, while helping people understand other worldviews.

PRACTICAL ISSUES

The following questions are designed to assist student affairs administrators in addressing the need to balance individual rights and institutional values in relation to campus activities that some might find controversial or offensive. This is by no means an exhaustive list and the questions themselves are not devised in order to bring about particular responses. Instead, they are points of discussion and prompts for further exploration.

- To what extent is the activity an academic discussion or advocacy of a particular point of view?

- What institutional values are relevant to planning in relation to the activity?
- In what ways might members of the campus community react to, respond to, or be affected by the activity?
- In what ways might external organizations react to, respond to, or be affected by the activity?
- To what degree will campus and external media take an interest in the activity? What might impact that interest or lack thereof?
- What are the objectives of the organizers? How might potential controversy about the activity impact or support these objectives?
- To what extent does the activity constitute an impediment to individuals in their normal daily activities?
- What is the relationship between the activity and other campus events?
- To what extent is there a risk that the event will be disrupted? How likely is protest about the activity?
- To what extent is security or campus police required in order to protect safety or property? When should the cost of security or campus police be passed along to event organizers? To what extent might these costs inhibit free speech?
- What are the beliefs, influences, and forces that may impact the activity and its relationship to the campus as a whole as well as to the external community?
- To what degree do organizers understand relevant institutional values, policies, and procedures? How might these be communicated?
- To what extent do activity participants, including those from the external community when applicable, understand relevant institutional values, policies, and procedures? How might these be communicated?
- What roles will various staff play in relation to the activity? How will media interest, if any, be handled?

CONCLUSION

In this chapter, I have attempted to document the issues facing twenty-first-century student-affairs administrators in addressing seemingly conflicting values of freedom of expression and civility in a complex post-secondary campus context. As the nature of campus communities change in demographics and ethno-cultural makeup, new challenges emerge in protecting primal institutional values associated with free speech. In this century, instead of focusing on students' rights and dissent against institutional decision-making, there are a growing number of instances of conflict over decisions to allow or disallow certain forms of speech. Such conflicts play out in court and in the court of public opinion.

Advocacy in all its forms plays out on campuses across the country, resulting in some students and others feeling offended, hurt, or otherwise unrepresented. However, the question of the nature of advocacy is also an emerging concern. When issues seem to have a public face of two extreme viewpoints, what happens to the middle ground where civil discourse might be facilitated and where the debate might be more closely aligned with institutional values? While addressing the emergence of a campus group with a goal of creating constructive dialogue, one commentator noted that "it is a sad day when the tone surrounding discussions of an issue at university campuses descends to such a point that individuals feel they have to form an organized group to promote such reasonable ideas as listening to the other side and recognizing that 'none of the principal parties is absolutely right and none is absolutely wrong'" (Serebrin 2010). This remains, and will continue to remain, the challenge.

Section Three

12

Serving Diverse Students: A Conclusion

C. CARNEY STRANGE AND DONNA HARDY COX

The clarion call-to-change for Canadian post-secondary education is sounding loud and clear as non-traditional constituents are finding their way into its traditional halls. The above chapters demonstrate that select groups of students now entering Canadian higher education differ significantly from those it previously served. Whether of another ethnic origin, of an older age, differently abled, speaking a different language and living a different culture, of a different sexual orientation and expression, or the first in a family to pursue advanced learning, a full 25 per cent of students in the Canadian post-secondary system now bring with them characteristics and experiences that both enrich but also isolate them on its campuses.

What has functioned to serve students well in the past may no longer suffice while enrolment compositions continue to evolve in Canadian colleges and universities. The lessons absorbed from each of these overviews is that student success is not solely a matter of individual student effort, but also a function of how well the institution adapts to the needs of each student. In the parlance of researchers, this insight recognizes the importance of "conditional effects" (Pascarella and Terenzini 2005) in the mix of post-secondary outcomes; that is, educational interventions of any sort exert their effects differentially, depending on the target demographic. Thus an orientation program operating on the assumption, for example, that students come fully primed with clear expectations about their impending educational experience, might be understood very differently by and potentially result in further confusion for incoming first-generation students, for instance, for whom this is a completely novel situation. Even among those who are relatively prepared for the mechanics of higher learning, the reality of fending for one's identity in a world that seems less than welcoming – perhaps even hostile – is a daunting task that often siphons off energy much needed otherwise to achieve overall success.

Accommodating non-traditional student groups on campus is a matter of both individual and institutional success. While students can succeed only by accomplishing the tasks that lead to their goals, institutions have an equal responsibility to understand and respond to changing needs so that student success is more probable. In order to assist students in their success, colleges and universities must themselves be successful. This involves the resolution of several critical steps in a hierarchy of institutional designs (Strange and Banning 2015) (see Figure 12.1). Researchers and observers of higher education have argued that powerful learning, and ultimately student success, is achieved best under conditions of community. Palmer (1987) averred a similar claim: "Community must become a central concept in ways we teach and learn" (160). Building a community of learners requires that institutional "goals, structures, values, people, and resources come together in a seamless experience for purposes of self-actualization and fulfillment" (Strange and Banning 2015, 141). Thus community-building and its associated tasks have become a major focus in recent years in how we think about the goals of higher education and the means to achieve them.

Nevertheless, achieving conditions of community entails several pre-requisites: first, students must feel like they belong in our institutions, and that who they are does not place them at undo risk in these settings. This first crucial step is about achieving a sense of inclusion and security among students. If either of these conditions is in doubt, for whatever reasons, it is not long before students tend to check out psychologically, and soon thereafter physically as well – that is, they leave the institution. Colleges and universities must understand what it takes to welcome to campus students of all groups, especially those who differ from the dominant enrolment profile. Furthermore, members of non-dominant groups overviewed above might inherently experience a sense of risk in such places, if for no other reason than little is familiar to them and at practically every turn the presumed

Figure 12.1 A hierarchy of learning environment purposes

Strange, C., and J. Banning (2015). *Designing for Learning: Creating Campus Environments for Student Success*. San Francisco: Jossey-Bass Publishers.

potential for failure lurks. For example, for students of non-dominant ethnic origins (e.g., Aboriginal), the absence of like mentors among faculty and staff might inadvertently discourage them at a time when they are questioning their own choice to pursue such a goal as higher learning in the first place. Similarly, students with various disabilities inevitably encounter hurdles while sensitizing the campus to the basic requirements for their success. With every pioneer, so to speak, comes an additional burden to create new and more accessible pathways for those to follow.

While feeling welcomed and secure are necessary first steps toward the ultimate experience of learning in community, they are insufficient to achieve such an end. Satisfaction and comfort alone do little to advance students toward their educational goals. There is an additional critical step in the process: becoming an engaged student. Engagement or involvement in active learning is a critical mechanism for educational success. Students who become engaged in learning take on a degree of responsibility that challenges their capacities to achieve beyond theirs and others' expectations. Well established in the literature some time ago, this theory of involvement is based on the claim that:

> A highly involved student is one who, for example, devotes considerable energy to studying, spending a lot of time on campus, participates actively in student organizations, and interacts frequently with faculty members and other students. Conversely, an uninvolved student may neglect studies, spend little time on campus, abstain from extracurricular activities, and have little contact with faculty members or other students. (Astin 1985, 134)

Thus, involvement is most clearly manifested in actions such as joining, participating, attaching, committing, immersing, and volunteering.

Although a person's motivation is a potentially important dimension of involvement, Astin also contended that "it is not so much what an individual thinks or feels but what he or she *does* that defines and identifies involvement" (ibid., 135). Similarly, Pace suggested that "what counts most is not who they [students] are or where they are but what they do" (1984, 1). Since this basic tenet was first articulated, however, a wealth of new understandings has appeared in the higher education literature to suggest that a revision of such a claim is in order. Who a student is *does* matter, and the various sub-group attributes examined in this volume offer a starting point for exploring how such differences may "count" in the matter of student engagement. Regardless, the experience of learning in full community remains out of reach if conditions for student engagement are not in place. For mature adult learners this may mean the institution's recognition and accrediting of their prior experiences; for Francophone students it may mean the accommodation of their first language in course materials and assignments; and for students of marginalized sexual orientations or expressions it may mean extending a sense of legitimacy to their status through readings and observations inclusive of authors so identified. Students who are engaged in learning see themselves as integral to the setting, whether a classroom, student club or society, residence hall, or advocacy organization, such that without their participation the setting's goals and outcomes are jeopardized. Active involvement or engagement is the engine of learning.

Over time, as included, secured, and engaged students actively carry out the activities of learning, something very special happens. Individual efforts soon give way to a collective sense of achievement in creating a powerful and memorable experience. Some students might consider this to be the experience of an especially powerful class; some may associate this with their organization and implementation of a significant event, e.g., institution-wide festival or campaign; and others might recognize this as the outcome of having lived together with a special group of peers, e.g., residential learning community. Whatever the case, the standard rises to that of an experience of community, where "unifying purposes and values, traditions and symbols of belonging and involvement, and mutuality of care, support, and responsibility encourage a synergy of participation and worth, checking and cross-checking, to create a positive learning environment" (Strange and Banning 2015, 214). The ultimate test of having achieved such a quality of experience is that, when students leave it, they are missed. The community of learning no longer exists without them, at least in the form it once did when they were part of it. In an age driven by economies of scale, especially in the beginning years of post-secondary education (e.g., large lecture classes), experiences of community are becoming rarer in our colleges and universities, but nonetheless remain critical for assuring maximum impact of what educators have to offer. The experience of community is the capstone of post-secondary learning, one that capitalizes on students having felt like they belonged and were secure on our campuses, were motivated to embrace engaging possibilities, and sustained their efforts to the point where some level of synergy and achievement was apparent for all. Students who look back on their post-secondary years with fond memories and a deep sense of accomplishment are those most likely to have been included, secured, engaged, and invited into the community of higher learning.

PRINCIPLES OF GOOD PRACTICE
FOR DIVERSE STUDENT SUCCESS

Within the context of institutional design outlined above, the following are principles or points we offer for reflection that we contend are critical for developing the kind of responsiveness required to succeed with serving diverse students in Canadian post-secondary education (or any educational setting for that matter). These tenets represent understandings or assumptions we sometimes overlook in our policies and practices, too often resulting in unnecessary barriers to the success of these non-traditional groups on campus. Essentially these are ways of thinking about the problem; operationalizing such principles on campus is an important step for becoming an institution more supportive of diverse students. Many of these ideas are extensions of the general principles first outlined in Hardy Cox and Strange (2010) for good practice in student services, but are discussed further here in the context of the above diverse student groups.

While not an exhaustive listing, there is certainly enough evidence and obvious examples in the preceding chapters to suggest that these are important operational ideas. In an order that is not meant to reflect any sort of hierarchy, we address each, exploring its essence and considering its potential effect through examples imbedded in the services and programs they illustrate. Some are quite obvious and apply universally across any attempt to organize and manage resources responsive to different students' needs. Some are worth restating because in the push for expediency and efficiency we sometimes overlook – or frankly, forget – them. Finally, others extend from our core mission as educators, as human resource providers, and as student service professionals committed to the success of all students, especially those who bring diverse backgrounds and experiences to our campuses.

Differences Matter. The hierarchical dynamic of design proposed above as a universal framework for institutional planning of any response to student groups on campus implicates the importance of differences. All of the above chapters collectively suggest the significance of varying identities that place some student groups outside the standard assumptions and expectations that characterize our thinking about who attends college and university. While the end goals of institutions remain the same – inclusion, security, engagement, and community – how they achieve those goals depends much on the backgrounds and characteristics of the students they serve. This "differential interactionist" (Hunt and Sullivan, 1974) perspective (a behavioural-science iteration of "different strokes for different folks") recognizes that what works for one group may not work for another – for that matter, what works for the intended target group might not work for an individual member of that group. The paradox of educational practice is that each student is, paradoxically and simultaneously: like every other student, like only some other students, like no other student. Effective practice requires the capac-ity for holding these three perspectives at once – so that Aboriginal students, for example, who aim at success (like any other student) will pursue their dream within the context of a defined people and culture (as some other students do), and in doing so will honour their own individual history and experience within that group (as no other student does).

In the process of engaging the endless variety of human experi-ences, as we do in higher education and student services, we are not at all surprised that individual differences manifest themselves in a myriad of ways. Some students arrive seemingly already fully formed to "take on the world," as it were. We are amazed at their indepen-dence and bravado such that we are tempted to just turn them loose and let them chart their own paths. In the best of times we point to them as archetypes of success for others to admire and emulate. Our fears are that, if not careful, we might get in their way or burden their momentum. More often than not, though, students come to us in various earlier stages of growth and development; our task then becomes facilitating their basic sense of personal agency so that self-direction will prevail in their lives. This may be the case in particular with members of the student sub-groups discussed in the above chapters. For example, to the extent that first-generation students also often belong to more than a few other sub-groups overviewed here (e.g., Aboriginal and international students), the lack of prior socialization to the tasks of higher learning may prove more than daunting for some at a time when their personal understandings and motives are most fragile. Good educational practice begins with the recognition of individual differences and careful assessment of how they manifest in students' lives.

An important correlate of this principle is the intersectionality of human identities (see chapter 2). While the general characteristics of group membership are emphasized in the above analyses, caution must be observed in applying these distinctions to students whose individual identities extend from multiple intersecting sources and for whom the salience of any given distinction depends greatly on context, timing, and values. Rather than fixed, identity is more fluid. For example, an African-Canadian male who identifies as gay and first-generation may place greater emphasis on one aspect of his iden-tity during an immersive stage of development. Over time or given different circumstances, the importance of being first-generation may take precedence, and so on. Intersectionality recognizes the importance of both idiographic (i.e., unique and individual) and nomothetic (i.e., attributed to the group) differences. One of the foundational tenets of student affairs work is to meet students where they are. In the case of students' personal identities, this correlate suggests that the best starting point is to ask students how they identify themselves as a prerequisite for engaging in their success. Presumptions of group differences must be approached contingently while encouraging individual differences to present themselves. What is manifest in particular students must be informed by exploring meaning they attach to their expressions of self. Only then can we hope to accompany students on their developmental journey with integrity and authenticity.

Fairness above Uniformity. Engaging individual differences becomes a critical standard in the metrics of success when considering how students come from so many different circumstances and with so many different expectations and preferences. The inclination is to "treat them all the same," letting the chips fall where they may. Although less labour intensive, such an approach deems our typical way of doing things "sufficient," and relegates failures to "experimental error" or lack of effort on the students' part.

"One size fits all" is a misguided fiction of practice that serves no one well. Illusions of fairness at times are also reinforced by an over-reliance on aggregate reports and group stereotypes, which fail to consider students' unique circumstances. On the other hand, responding to individual differences is demanding and comes at the price of additional staff time and resources. Given that success ultimately depends on recognizing such differences, individualization – when possible – is the more effective approach. Responsiveness accounts for differences; uniformity ignores them. Thus, to "be fair" often entails doing more, or less, for some students than others, depending on who they are and what assets they bring to their learning. Knowing that a student comes from a family background with no prior post-secondary experience, every effort must be made – especially early on – to anticipate his or her concerns and to create compensatory structures or systems that will eventually enable self-direction and success. To ignore such differences in the name of "fairness" places the student at a certain disadvantage, potentially leading to undue discouragement and failure. While seemingly efficient and clear, uniformity does little to assure a more level playing field for all. Fairness, on the other hand, seeks to contextualize differences and expectations so that the inter-mix of challenges and opportunities is such that the greatest potential for success, however defined, is made possible for all. A fair outcome is both relative and standardized – relative in the sense that while particulars might differ, the overall result is acceptable within a range of standard possibilities.

The Paradox of Community. The challenge of building communities of learners on campus is complicated in many ways by the need to accommodate, at the same time, both differences and commonalties among students. Spitzberg and Thorndike characterized this as a paradox of sorts, wherein the "community of the whole" often competes with the "community of the parts" (1992). As discussed in Strange and Banning (2015), "that which contributes to strong sub-communities usually detracts from the community of the whole, and that which sustains the whole community often does so at the expense of various sub-communities" (224). In terms of the many sub-group concerns noted in the above chapters this dilemma often plays out in the design and allocation of campus resources to meet such challenges. The debate is often between those who contend that focused diversity initiatives (e.g., Aboriginal Cultural Center, LGBTQQ Office) are unnecessary and in fact fragment the overall campus community into isolated pockets of participation, and those who underscore the importance of such initiatives for providing "safe spaces" and visible concentrations where diverse students can connect with each other and be empowered through peer culture. Connection to both the community of the whole and the community of the parts is important in the end. This requires a balance between the two sources of support, where appropriate timing must also be considered. For example, focused diversity initiatives are critical as members of diverse campus sub-groups negotiate the initial transition into unfamiliar settings. The visibility of relevant centres (e.g., disability or LGBTQQ) sends important signals and serves to include and secure students who so identify at a time when their participation may be most fragile. They also typically offer an integration of "one-stop shop" services for students, further facilitating institutional access. Perhaps later then, as their sense of self emerges, these students can branch out with more confidence into the community of the whole. Regardless, the absence of such initiatives could potentially jeopardize the matriculation of such students at a time when initial barriers might seem insurmountable to them. In the balance of challenge and support (Sanford and Adelson 1962), affirmation is the more important strategy for students just beginning their post-secondary journey. This is especially true for students who differ from the normative and dominant culture on campus.

Student-Centred Practice. If ever there was a first principle that frames both what and why we do what we do as educators and student service professionals, this principle would certainly rise to the top of the list. We exist to serve students; we are defined by students. So our practices must begin with two fundamental questions: first, how do students learn, develop, and grow? And second, how do the policies, programs, and practices we fashion enhance that transformative process? Our work is essentially student-centred. Reflections of this principle in action are apparent, for example, in the holistic indigenous framework proffered by Michelle Pidgeon (chapter 3), the first-year initiatives for international students outlined by Leary, Hotchkiss, and Robb (chapter 7), and the design of the Dalhousie Black Student Advising Centre described through an Africentric values framework by McIntyre and Hamilton-Hinch (chapter 4). All of these efforts arise from the active participation of students themselves as program components are implemented in response to different needs. Student-centred practices begin and end with student perspectives and input – not to suggest that ignoring other concerns (e.g., costs, legality, institutional traditions) is appropriate, but that students themselves are (and must be) a critical source of information when it comes to creating effective educational design.

Flexibility of Approach. Extending from the above principles is the wisdom of offering a range of flexible service options that cater to a variety of needs and possibilities. This tenet affirms that just as students differ, one from another, so too should our approaches and practices to serve them. Individual differences dictate that flexible alternatives increase the potential of any service or program to respond to the unique circumstances and changes in the lives of students. Rules, standards, and systems are important for consistency and accountability, but adaptability is equally important in tailoring opportunities to support the needs of students seeking them. Thus, engaging students representative of the non-traditional groups overviewed above entails a level of creative flexibility that offers a variety of means for meeting the same goal.

Maintaining a flexible approach requires a careful listening to students' presenting needs or situations and responding in an empathic and timely manner. It might also suggest that questions such as "What options do you see for doing this?" or "How will that work for you?" should be considered prior to invoking a rule or concluding "That's the way it is." Even though such an end might be inevitable, the discussion of alternatives can serve as an important source of ideas for future policies and practices. Such an exchange affirms the agency of the student while also providing a learning moment for the institution to consider how best to respond to students who differ from the traditional profile.

Another aspect of this principle involves anticipating student needs. Flexibility of approach must be rooted in an understanding of how student needs differ by circumstance and change over time during the post-secondary experience. By examining trends and looking forward, while drawing from the knowledge base that informs the growth and development of these student sub-groups, educators and student service professionals can increase their capacity to accommodate needs for certain programs and services at predictable intervals throughout the academic year. In doing so the potential for the institution to continue to grow as a diverse community is enhanced and the record of success over time for diverse students will likely increase.

Oriented to Results. The ultimate questions any service provider must satisfy are: did this program, intervention, or assistance work? Did it lead to the desired effect, either (or both) from the perspective of the provider and/or the consumer? We can hardly afford to stop at reporting on input efforts for a particular service or program, without also accounting for outcome. Ultimately, the effectiveness of a service is a measure of its contribution to the overall learning mission of the institution. There are a number of measures that have been developed in response to questions of the effectiveness of student services. Some focus on the specific services appropriate to a particular unit (e.g., CAS Standards), while others (e.g., National Survey of Student Engagement, Canadian University Survey Consortium – CUSC) examine the outcomes of broader institutional purposes to which some areas of student services might contribute (e.g., student leadership and involvement programs).

Reciprocity of Effect. Serving diverse students on campus is not simply a matter of "doing something well for them." Obviously, being responsive makes a difference, but not just for the students being served. The time and effort put into considering how to accommodate various non-traditional student groups also benefits the service itself. Rather than offering a singular approach based on one uniform set of assumptions, it becomes capable of several approaches based on a variety of assumptions. That is inherently more effective and thus more efficient. To begin the processes of adaptation to and accommodation for diverse students, colleges and universities could benefit from a systematic examination of the following categories of questions and concerns:

Questions for Institutional Improvement

Student Information: What is known about the student groups identified above at your institution? What are their numbers and what are their needs? How available are data on these students and who is responsible for assembling and reporting on this information? What additional groups not discussed above warrant a similar level of attention on your campus?

Available Services: What services to these student groups currently exist on your campus? What services or programs are yet to be developed? How are such services and programs coordinated or integrated to more effectively focus your institution's response to these diverse students?

Professional Development: What training or professional development opportunities, with regard to these student groups, are available to academic and student services staff on your campus? How are new understandings and insights about these groups shared across your institution? Who is responsible for including this emerging knowledge base on diverse student groups in ongoing staff meetings and discussion opportunities?

Student Guidance: What pathways of success have been charted to guide members of these non-traditional student groups toward their educational goals? What models of student achievement exist and how are such stories communicated to students just beginning their post-secondary journey? How are students representative of these diverse groups incorporated into the planning and implementation of student services on campus?

Outcomes Assessment: How are the achievements and learning outcomes of these student groups monitored and evaluated on your campus? Who is responsible for assessing the results of their efforts? How is such information cycled back through the institution to evaluate its status as a diverse educational community responsive to all students' needs?

Developing an inclusive institution entails both intention and information. Colleges and universities intent on serving diverse students well must become active consumers of the theories and research that inform the qualities of these emerging student groups on campus. Revisiting questions such as those above on a regular basis can go a long way in advancing an institution's capacity for responsiveness and effect in serving students from diverse populations.

CONCLUSION

For much of its history Canadian post-secondary education, like most traditional systems of higher learning, has focused on "selecting winners" as its principal strategy for institutional success. That is, those who have already achieved the most will continue to do so as they advance through the system. Having the "best students" is the most effective way of increasing an institution's profile. Indeed there is some evidence that students best prepared traditionally are those most likely to achieve in our colleges and universities. However, higher learning is not just about channeling and certifying talents and abilities or increasing institutional prestige; more so, it's about opportunities for success, regardless of who comes in the door. Today it's clear that marginalized and/or non-dominant groups of students are beginning to avail themselves of these opportunities in increasing numbers. Assumptions about students that once served to guide our policies and practices must now be questioned and some changed. However, as Kirby (2009) cautioned: "Re-orienting the post-secondary education system to accommodate new types of learners will not be an easy task ... since academic systems, especially at the university level, are steeped in tradition and are highly resistant to change" (4). Nevertheless, change is imperative if Canadian post-secondary education is to become a positive and transformative opportunity for students of diverse backgrounds.

References

Abel, C.F. 2002. "Academic Success and the International Student: Research and Recommendations." *New Directions for Higher Education* 117:.13–20.

Abes, E.S., S.R. Jones, and M.K. McEwen. 2007. "Reconceptualizing the Model of Multiple Dimensions of Identity: The Role of Meaning-making Capacity in the Construction of Multiple Identities." *Journal of College Student Development* 48: 1–22.

Abes, E.S., and D. Kasch. 2007. "Using Queer Theory to Explore Lesbian College Students' Multiple Dimensions of Identity." *Journal of College Student Development* 48: 619–36.

Aboriginal Affairs and Northern Development Canada. 2012. "Summative Evaluation of the Post-secondary Education Program." *Evaluation, Performance Measurement, and Review Branch, Audit and Evaluation Sector*, Project number: 1570-7/09058. http://www.aadnc-aandc.gc.ca/eng/1365456454696/1365456526014. Accessed 24 January 2016.

Addelman, B., and S. Mallal. 2004. *Discordia* [Motion Picture].

Aiken-Klar, E.J. 2009. "The Fear Factor: Assimilation, Antisemitism and the Relationship between Zionism and the Jewish Diasporic Identity." *Vis-à-Vis: Explorations in Anthropology* 9, no. 1: 106–14.

Alberta Human Rights Commission. 2004. "Duty to Accommodate Students with Disabilities in Post-secondary Educational Institutions." http://www.albertahumanrights.ab.ca/publications/bulletins_sheets_booklets/bulletins/duty_to_accommodate_students.asp. Accessed 24 January 2016.

Alboim, N., and K.A. Cohl. 2012. *Shaping the Future: Canada's Rapidly Changing Immigration Policies*. Maytree Foundation.

Allen, W. 1985. "Black Student, White Campus: Structural, Interpersonal, and Psychological Correlates of Success." *Journal of Negro Education* 54, no. 2: 134–47.

Althen, G. 1995. *The Handbook of Foreign Student Advising*, revised ed. Yarmouth: Intercultural Press.

Anderson, K.A., P.T. Shattuck, B.P. Cooper, A.M. Roux, and M. Wagner. 2014. "Prevalence and Correlates of Postsecondary Residential Status Among Young Adults with an Autism Spectrum Disorder." *Autism* 18: 562–70.

Anderson, S. 2002. "Orientation and Support for International Students." In *International Educator's Toolbox*, edited by M. Kane, 64–6. Ottawa: Canadian Bureau of International Education.

Andres, L. 2004. "Today's Post-secondary Students – Adding Faces to Numbers." In *Student Affairs: Experiencing Higher Education*, edited by Lesley Andres and Fiona Finlay, 1–13. Vancouver: UBC Press.

Angrist, J., D. Lang, and P. Oreopoulos. 2006. "Lead Them to Water and Pay Them to Drink: An Experiment with Services and Incentives for College Achievement." National Bureau of Economic Research working paper no. 12790. http://www.nber.org/papers/w12790. Accessed 24 January 2016.

AQICESH. 2010. "Association Québécoise Interuniversitaire des Conseillers aux Étudiants Ayant des Besoins Spéciaux." http://www.aqicesh.ca/association-aqicesh/statistiques-et-rapports. Accessed 2 February 2016.

Archibald, J., S.S. Bowman, F. Pepper, C. Urion, G. Mirenhouse, and R. Shortt. 1995. "Honoring What They Say: Post-secondary Experiences of First Nations Graduates." *Canadian Journal of Native Education* 21, no. 1: 1–247.

Armstrong, N. 2015. "Second African Canadian Summit to Discuss Critical Issues." *PRIDE News*, 22 April.

Asante, M.K. 1988. *Afrocentricity: The Theory of Social Change*. Trenton: Africa World Press.

Association Française des Municipalités de l'Ontario. 2009. Profile of the Francophone Communities – Trillium. http://www.afmo.on.ca/en/statistics/profile-of-ontarios-francophone-communities-trillium-2009/. Accessed 3 February 2016.

Association of American Colleges and Universities. 2007. "College Learning for the New Global Century: A Report from the National Leadership Council for Liberal Education and America's Promise." https://www.aacu.org/sites/default/files/files/LEAP/GlobalCentury_final.pdf. Accessed 24 January 2016.

Association of Canadian Community Colleges (ACCC). 2002. Brief Submitted to Government Caucus on Post-Secondary Education and Research: Roundtable Discussion. Ottawa: ACCC.

Association of Universities and Colleges of Canada (AUCC). 2003. *Reality Check: Myth: Adults Don't Go to University to Acquire and Upgrade their Skills.* Ottawa: AUCC.

– 2010. *Moving Forward: National Working Summit on Aboriginal Postsecondary Education.* Ottawa: AUCC.

– 2011. "Trends in Higher Education." http://www.cais.ca/uploaded/trends-2011-vol1-enrolment-e.pdf. Accessed 24 January 2016.

Astin, A.W. 1985. *Achieving Educational Excellence. A Critical Assessment of Priorities and Practices in Higher Education.* San Francisco: Jossey-Bass.

– 1999. "Student Involvement: A Developmental Theory for Higher Education." *Journal of College Student Development* 40, no. 5: 518–29.

Atkins, M.P. 2012. "Black Students' Perspectives on Academic Success." Master's thesis, Western University.

Auclair, R., P. Bélanger, P. Doray, M. Gallien, A. Groleau, L. Mason, and P. Mercier. 2008. *Transitions – First-Generation Students: A Promising Concept?* Ottawa: The Canadian Millennium Scholarship Foundation.

Auerbach, S. 2004. "Engaging Latino Parents in Supporting College Pathways: Lessons from a College Access Program." *Journal of Hispanic Higher Education* 3, no. 2: 125–45.

Azuelos, S. 2008. "Pro-lifers Face Fines and Misconduct." *Gauntlet* (Calgary, AB), 27 November. http://www.archive.thegauntlet.ca/story/pro-lifers-face-fines-and-misconduct. Accessed 24 January 2016.

Barsky, A.E. 2002. "Structural Sources of Conflict in a University Context." *Conflict Resolution Quarterly* 20, no. 2: 161–76.

Bartram, B. 2007. "The Sociocultural Needs of International Students in Higher Education: A Comparison of Staff and Student Views." *Journal of Studies in International Education* 11, no. 2: 205–14.

Battiste, M. 1998. "Enabling the Autumn Seed: Toward a Decolonized Approach to Aboriginal Knowledge, Language, and Education." *Canadian Journal of Native Education* 22, no. 1: 16–27.

– 2002. *Indigenous Knowledge and Pedagogy in First Nations Education: A Literature Review with Recommendations.* http://www.afn.ca/uploads/files/education/24._2002_oct_marie_battiste_indigenousknowledgeandpedagogy_lit_review_for_min_working_group.pdf. Accessed 27 January 2016.

– ed. 2000. *Reclaiming Indigenous Voice and Vision.* Vancouver: UBC Press.

Battiste, M., and J. Barman, eds. 1995. *First Nations Education in Canada: The Circle Unfolds*. Vancouver: UBC Press.

Battiste, M., L. Bell, and L.M. Findlay. 2002. "Decolonizing Education in Canadian Universities: An Interdisciplinary, International, Indigenous Research Project." *Canadian Journal of Native Education* 26, no. 2: 82–95.

Battiste, M., and J. Youngblood Henderson. 2000. *Protecting Indigenous Knowledge and Heritage: A Global Challenge, Purich's Aboriginal Issues Series*. Saskatoon: Purich Publishing Ltd.

Baxter-Magolda, M. 1992. *Knowing and Reasoning in College: Gender-Related Patterns in Students' Intellectual Development*. San Francisco: Jossey-Bass.

Beemyn, B. 2003. "Serving the Needs of Transgender College Students." *Journal of Gay & Lesbian Issues in Education* 1, no. 1: 33–50.

Benlolo, A., and L. Adler. 2008. "Open Letter Regarding Israel Apartheid Week at U of T." Advertisement in the *National Post* (Toronto, ON), 5 February.

Bennett, M.J. 1993. "Towards Ethnorelativism: A Developmental Model of Intercultural Sensitivity." In *Education for the Intercultural Experience*, edited by R.M. Paige, 21–71. Yarmouth: Intercultural Press.

Berger, J. 2008. *"Why Access Matters" Revisited: A Review of the Latest Research*. Ottawa: The Canadian Millennium Scholarship Foundation, Millennium Research Note no. 6.

Berger, J., and A. Motte. 2007. "Mind the Access Gap: Breaking Down Barriers to Post-secondary Education." *Policy Options*, November 2007. http://policyoptions.irpp.org/issues/ontario-2007-dalton-mcguinty/mind-the-access-gap-breaking-down-barriers-to-post-secondary-education/. Accessed 24 January 2016.

Berk, S.A., and M. Carluccio. 2000. *The Big Little Book of Jewish Wit & Wisdom*. New York: Black Dog & Leventhal Publishers.

Bernans, D. 2006. *North of 9/11*. Montreal: Cumulus Press.

Betar-Tagar. 2006. "Know Radical-Islam Week at the University of Toronto." *The Varsity*. http://www.tagarnet.com/getDoc.do?name=KRIprogram.pdf. Accessed 15 October 2010.

Beykont, Z.F., and C. Daiute. 2002. "Inclusiveness in Higher Education Courses: International Student Perspectives." *Equity and Excellence in Education* 35, no. 1: 35–42.

Billson, J. M., and M. Brooks Terry. 1982. "In Search of the Silken Purse: Factors in Attrition among First-generation Students." *College and University* 58, no. 1: 57–75.

Bilodeau, B.L. 2009. *Genderism: Transgender Students, Binary Systems and Higher Education*. East Lansing: VDM Verlag.

Bilodeau, B.L., and K.A. Renn. 2005. "Analysis of LGBTQ Identity Development Models and Implications for Practice." In *Gender Identity and Sexual Orientation: Research, Policy and Personal Perspectives: New Directions for Student Services* 111, 25–39. San Francisco: Jossey Bass.

Blatchford, C. 2010a. *Helpless: Caledonia's Nightmare of Fear and Anarchy, and How the Law Failed All of Us*. Toronto: Doubleday Canada.

– 2010b. "Three Protesters Shut Me Down Once; They Won't Do It Again." *Globe and Mail*. http://www.theglobeandmail.com/news/national/christie-blatchford/three-protesters-shut-me-down-once-they-wont-do-it-again/article1806961/. Accessed 24 January 2016.

Bloom, D., and C. Sommo. 2005. *Building Learning Communities: Early Results from the Opening Doors Demonstration at Kingsborough Community College*. New York: MDRC Report. http://www.mdrc.org/publications/410/overview.html. Accessed 24 January 2016.

Bochenek, M., and A.W. Brown. 2001. *Hatred in the Hallways: Violence and Discrimination against Lesbian, Gay, Bisexual and Transgender Students in U.S. Schools*. New York: Human Rights Watch.

Bouchard, B., and J. Zhao. 2000. "University Education: Recent Trends in Participating, Accessibility and Returns." *Education Quarterly Review* 6, no. 4: 24–32.

Bourdieu, P., and J.C. Passeron. 1990. *Reproduction in Education, Society, and Culture*. London: SAGE Publications.

Bovee-Begun, A. 2006. "Students Hold Forum against Islamophobia." *Varsity*, 30 November 2010. http://thevarsity.ca/2006/07/24/students-hold-forum-against-islamophobia/. Accessed 24 January 2016.

Bowleg, L. 2008. "When Black + Lesbian + Woman ≠ Black Lesbian Woman: The Methodological Challenges of Qualitative and Quantitative Intersectionality Research." *Sex Roles* 59, nos 5–6: 312–25.

Boyd-Franklin, N. 2003. *Black Families in Therapy: Understanding the African American Experience*. 2nd ed. New York: The Guilford Press.

Bradley, N. 1999. "University's Stop-GAP Measures Work." *Ubyssey*, 28 September. http://ubcpubs.library.ubc.ca/?db=ubyssey. Accessed 27 January 2016.

– 2000. "GAP Coming to UBC Tomorrow." *Ubyssey*, 22 February. http://ubcpubs.library.ubc.ca/?db=ubyssey. Accessed 27 January 2016.

Bradley, N., and D. Merzaban. 1999. "Anti-abortionists to Sue UBC." *Ubyssey*, 1 October. http://ubcpubs.library.ubc.ca/?db=ubyssey. Accessed 27 January 2016.

Brant Castellano, M. 2000. "Updating Aboriginal Traditions of Knowledge." In *Indigenous Knowledges in Global Contexts: Multiple Readings of Our World*, edited by G.J. Sefa Dei, B.L. Hall, and D. Goldin Rosenberg, 21–36. Toronto: OISE/University of Toronto Press.

Brean, J. 2010. "Latest Tool in War on Free Speech: Bike Locks." *National Post*. http://www.nationalpost.com/news/Blatchford+questions+giving+bikelock+blockade/3832811/story.html. Accessed 30 November 2010.

Brennan, R.J. 2009. "Canada Blocks Outspoken British MP." *Toronto Star*. http://www.thestar.com/News/Canada/article/605682. Accessed 11 February 2016.

Briguglio, C. 2000. "Language and Cultural Issues for English-as-a-Second/Foreign Language Students in Transnational Educational Settings." *Higher Education in Europe* 25, no. 3: 425–34.

Brislin, R.W., and T. Yoshida. 2004. "The Content of Cross-cultural Training: An Introduction." In *Improving Intercultural Interactions*, edited by R.W. Brislin and T. Yoshida, 1–14. Thousand Oaks: Sage.

Brown, L., and I. Holloway. 2008. "The Initial Stage of the International Sojourn: Excitement or Culture Shock?" *British Journal of Guidance and Counselling* 36, no. 1: 33–49.

Brown, T., and L. Ward. 2007. "Preparing Service Providers to Foster Student Success." In *Fostering Student Success in the Campus Community*, edited by G.L. Kramer and Associates, 302–17. San Francisco: Jossey Bass.

Browning, C., and P. Walsh. 2002. "LGBTQ Peer Counselors." In *Our Place on Campus: Lesbian, Gay, Bisexual, Transgender Services and Programs in Higher Education*, edited by R. Sanlo, S. Rankin, and R. Schoenberg, 148–57. Westport: Greenwood Press.

Burgstahler, S.E., and R.C. Cory, eds. 2009. *Universal Design in Higher Education*. Cambridge: Higher Education Press.

Burgstahler, S.E., and E. Moore. 2009. "Making Student Services Welcoming and Accessible through Accommodations and Universal Design." *Journal of Post-secondary Education and Disability* 21: 155–74.

Butler, J. 1993. *Bodies That Matter: On the Discursive Limits of "Sex."* New York: Routledge.

Campbell, T. 2005. "George Galloway Wants Real Change." *Varsity*. http://thevarsity.ca/2005/09/15/george-galloway-wants-real-change/. Accessed 24 January 2016.

Canadian Association for University Continuing Education (CAUCE). 2002. *Response to Knowledge Matters: Skills and Learning for Canadians and the National Summit on Innovation and Learning.* Kanata: CAUCE.

Canada Advisory Committee for Online Learning. 2001. *The E-Learning E-Volution in Colleges and Universities.* Ottawa: Government of Canada.

Canada's International Education Strategy. 2014. Her Majesty the Queen in Right of Canada.

Canadian Bureau for International Education (CBIE). 1981. *The Right Mix: The Report of the Commission on Foreign Student Policy in Canada.* Ottawa: Canadian Bureau of International Education.

– 2004. "Canada First, The 2004 Survey of International Students Ottawa: Canadian Bureau of International Education."

– 2014. *A World of Learning: Canada's Performance and Potential in International Education.* Ottawa. http://net.cbie.ca/download/ CBIE%20Flagship%202014%20E%20-%20WEB%20RES%20final. pdf. Accessed 4 February 2016.

Canadian Charter of Rights and Freedoms (Part I of the Constitution Act). 1982. https://www.canlii.org/en/ca/laws/stat/schedule-b-to-the-canada-act-1982-uk-1982-c-11/latest/schedule-b-to-the-canada-act-1982-uk-1982-c-11.html. Accessed 24 January 2016.

Canadian Council on Learning. 2006. *Canadian Post-Secondary Education: A Positive Record – An Uncertain Future.* Ottawa: Canadian Council on Learning, Report on Learning in Canada 2006.

Canadian Federation of Students. 2008. *The Final Report of the Task Force on Needs of Muslim Students.* Toronto: Canadian Federation of Students.

– 2011. *The Final Report of the Task Force on Campus Racism.* Toronto: Canadian Federation of Students.

Canadian Mental Health Association. 2004. "Your Education, Your Future." http://www.cmha.ca/youreducation/. Accessed 24 January 2016.

Canadian Parliamentary Coalition to Combat Anti-Semitism. 2009. "Transcript: Tuesday, November 24, 2009." http://www.cpcca.ca/09.11.24transcript-E.pdf. Accessed 1 October 2010.

– 2010. "Transcript: Monday, January 25, 2010." http://www.cpcca.ca/10.01.25transcript-E.pdf. Accessed 1 October 2010.

Canadian Press. 2003. "Concordia U. Regrets Anti-Netanyahu Riot." CTV News. http://www.ctv.ca/CTVNews/Canada/20030115/concordia030115/. Accessed 30 November 2010.

– 2006. "Storm at U of T after Student Newspaper Publishes Muhammad Cartoon." *Canadian Press.* http://www.freerepublic.com/focus/f-news/1581236/posts. Accessed 24 January 2016.

– 2010. "University of Calgary Appeals Facebook Ruling." *Globe and Mail.* http://www.theglobeandmail.com/news/technology/university-of-calgary-appeals-facebook-ruling/article1815596/?cmpid=rss1. Accessed 24 January 2016.

Canadian Race Relations Foundation. 2000. "Racism in Our Schools: What to Know About It: How to Fight It." http://www.crr.ca/diversfiles/en/pub/faSh/ePubFaShRacScho.pdf. Accessed 8 February 2016.

Canadian Undergraduate Survey Consortium. 2004. "2004 CUSC Survey of Undergraduate Students: Master Report." http://www.cusc-ccreu.ca/publications.htm. Accessed 15 March 2009.

Canadian War Museum. n.d. "Life on the Homefront: Veterans and Veterans' Programmes." http://www.civilization.ca/cwm/newspapers/canadawar/veterans_e.html. Accessed 1 May 2006.

CanLearn. 2016. Student Financial Assistance. http://www.esdc.gc.ca/en/student_financial_aid/index.page. Accessed 11 February 2016.

Canwest News Service. 2006. "Writer Barred from Reading 9/11 Novel at Concordia." http://www.canada.com/montrealgazette/news/story.html?id=a157daf3-f000-4602-bfeb-7bc2932676aa&k=73073. Accessed 24 January 2016.

Carlson, K.B. 2010. "University Threatens to Sue Rabbi Over Anti-Galloway Email." *National Post.* http://www.nationalpost.com/story.html?id=3845066. Accessed 30 November 2010.

Carnegie Foundation for the Advancement of Teaching. 1990. *Campus Life: In Search of Community.* Foreword by Ernest L. Boyer. Princeton: Carnegie Foundation for the Advancement of Teaching.

Carpay, J. 2010. "Charter Defends Free Speech Rights of University Students." *Calgary Herald.* http://www.calgaryherald.com/Charter+defends+free+speech+rights+university+students/3675695/story.html. Accessed 28 November 2010.

Carpay, J.V. 2008. "Fury over Free Speech, Not Dead Fetuses: An Open Letter to Advanced Education and Technology Minister Doug Horner." *Gauntlet,* 27 November. http://thegauntlet.ca. Accessed 30 November 2010.

Carter, D.F. 2001. *A Dream Deferred? Examining the Degree Aspirations of African American and White College Students.* New York: RoutledgeFalmer.

Cass, V.C. 1979. "Homosexual Identity Formation: A Theoretical Model." *Journal of Homosexuality* 4: 219–35.

CBC News. 2009. "McGill Anti-abortion Student Club Suspended." http://www.cbc.ca/news/canada/montreal/mcgill-anti-abortion-student-club-suspended-1.792454. Accessed 24 January 2016.

Center for Bio-Ethical Reform. n.d. *About Us*. http://cbrinfo.org/. Accessed 24 January 2016.

Chapdelaine, R.F., and L.R. Alexitch. 2004. "Social Skills: Model of Culture Shock for International Graduate Students." *Journal of College Student Development* 45, no. 2: 167–84.

Chase, S. 2010. "Ann Coulter's Speech in Ottawa Cancelled." *Globe and Mail*. http://www.theglobeandmail.com/news/politics/ann-coulters-speech-in-ottawa-cancelled/article1509793/. Accessed 24 January 2016.

Chen, X., and C.D. Carroll. 2005. "First-generation Students in Postsecondary Education: A Look at Their College Transcripts: Postsecondary Education Descriptive Analysis Report." National Center for Education Statistics (NCES) 2005–171. http://nces.ed.gov/pubs2005/2005171.pdf. Accessed 24 January 2016.

Chiang, C. 2010. "Racist Graffiti Mars U of C Students' Election." *Calgary Herald*. http://www.calgaryherald.com/news/Racist+graffiti+mars+students+election/2653092/story.html. Accessed 10 September 2015.

Chickering, A.W. 1969. *Education and Identity*. San Francisco: Jossey-Bass.

Chickering, A.W., and L. Reisser. 1993. *Education and Identity*. 2nd ed. San Francisco: Jossey-Bass.

Church, E., and D. Walton. 2010. "Spurned in Ottawa, Ann Coulter Gets a Big Welcome in Calgary." *Globe and Mail*. http://www.theglobeandmail.com/news/politics/spurned-in-ottawa-ann-coulter-gets-a-big-welcome-from-calgary/article1511247/. Accessed 24 January 2016.

Clark, W. 2000. "100 Years of Education." *Canadian Social Trends* 59 (Winter): 3–12. http://publications.gc.ca/Collection-R/Statcan/11-008-XIE/0030011-008-XIE.pdf. Accessed 24 January 2016.

Coleman, J. 2008. "York Gets It." http://www.joeycoleman.ca/2008/03/york-gets-it. Accessed 24 January 2016.

Colleges and Institutes Canada (CICAN). 2014. *Annual Report (2014–2015)*. Ottawa: CICAN.

Collins, P.H. 1990. *Black Feminist Thought: Knowledge, Consciousness, and the Politics of Empowerment*. New York: Routledge.

– 2000. *Black Feminist Thought: Knowledge, Consciousness, and the Politics of Empowerment (Perspectives on Gender)*. New York: Routledge.

Concordia University. 2010. *Code of Rights and Responsibilities*. http://
vpexternalsecgen.concordia.ca/documents/policies/BD-3.pdf. Accessed
24 January 2016.

Consortium of LGBTQ Resource Professionals in Higher Education 2016.
"Find a LGBTQ Center." http://www.lgbtcampus.org/find-a-lgbt-center.
Accessed 7 February 2016.

Corak, M., G. Lipps, and J. Zhao. 2003. *Family Income and Participation
in Post-Secondary Education*. Ottawa: Statistics Canada, 11F0019MIE
No. 210. http://www.statcan.gc.ca/pub/11f0019m/11f0019m2003210-
eng.pdf. Accessed 24 January 2016.

Council of Ministers of Education (CMEC) and Statistics Canada. 2010.
*A Literature Review of Factors That Support Successful Transitions
by Aboriginal Peoples from K–12 to Postsecondary Education*. Toronto:
CMEC.

Council of Ontario Universities (COU). 2010. *Ministry of Energy and
Infrastructure Consultations On the 10-Year Infrastructure Plan*. Toronto:
COU. http://www.cou.on.ca/publications/reports. 24 January 2016.

Coward, A. 2004. "Local High School Students Experience Life at York."
YFile. 16 June. http://www.yorku.ca/yfile/archive/index.asp?Article=2952.
Accessed 24 January 2016.

Cravatts, R.L. 2009. "Double Standard for Campus Free Speech."
National Post. http://network.nationalpost.com/np/blogs/fullcomment/
archive/2009/02/20/richard-l-cravatts-double-standard-for-campus-free-
speech.aspx. Accessed 25 November 2010.

– 2010. "Free Speech on Campus, Depending On Who's Speaking."
Canada Free Press. http://canadafreepress.com/index.php/article/20981.
24 January 2016.

Crenshaw, K.W. 1991. "Mapping the Margins: Intersectionality, Identity
Politics, and Violence against Women of Color." *Stanford Law Review*
43, no. 6: 1241–9.

Criminal Code (R.S.C., 1985, c. C-46). 2005. Department of Justice
Canada. http://laws-lois.justice.gc.ca/eng/acts/C-46/. Accessed
24 January 2016.

Crosby, A. 2010. "The International Student Experience in Canadian Post
Secondary Education: Democratic Racism, Anti Racism, Education and
Internationalization at Home." In *Our Schools/Ourselves* 19, no. 3:
399–41.

Cross, K.P. 1981. *Adults as Learners: Increasing Participation and
Facilitating Learning*. San Francisco: Jossey-Bass.

Cross, W.E., Jr. 1995. "The Psychology of Nigrescence: Revising the
Cross Model." In *Handbook of Multicultural Counseling*, edited by

J.G. Ponterotto, J.M. Casas, L.A. Suzuki, and C.M. Alexander, 93–122. Thousand Oaks: Sage.

Cross, W.E., Jr, and P. Fhagen-Smith. 2001. "Patterns in African American Identity Development: A Life Span Perspective." In *New Perspectives on Racial Identity Development: A Theoretical and Practical Anthology*, edited by C.L. Wijeyesinghe and B.W. Jackson III, 243–70. New York: New York University Press.

Cuseo, J. 2004. "'Decided,' 'Undecided,' and 'In Transition': Implications for Academic Advisement, Career Counseling and Student Retention." In *Improving the First Year of College: Research and Practice*, edited by R.S. Feldman, 26–48. Mahwah: Erlbaum Associates.

Dalhousie University Presidential Task Force. 1989. "Breaking Barriers: Summary and Recommendations of the University Task Force on Access for Black and Native Students." MacKay Task Force Report. Halifax: Dalhousie University.

Dalton, J. C., and Diana Imanuel Gardner. 2002. "Managing Change in Student Affairs Leadership Roles." *New Directions for Student Services* 98: 37–48. San Francisco: Jossey-Bass.

D'Amato, L. 2010. "Dec. 7 Date Set for Blatchford's return to UW." *The Record*. http://news.therecord.com/news/article/818406. Accessed 30 November 2010.

Danziger, E. J., Jr. 1996. "Taking Hold of the Tools: Post-secondary Education for Canada's Walpole Island First Nations, 1965–1994." *The Canadian Journal of Native Studies* 16, no. 2: 229–46.

Dao, T., D. Lee, and H.L. Chang. 2007. "Acculturation Level, Perceived Social Support Level, and Depression Among Taiwanese International Students." *College Student Journal* 41, no. 2: 287–95.

D'Augelli, A.R. 1994. "Identity Development and Sexual Orientation: Toward a Model of Lesbian, Gay, and Bisexual Identity Development." In *Human Diversity: Perspectives of People in Context*, edited by E.J. Trickett, R.J. Watts, and D. Birman, 312–33. San Francisco: Jossey Bass.

Deer, F. 2011. "Aboriginal Identity: A Perspective on Hegemony and the Implications for Canadian Citizenship." *In Education* 17, no. 3 (Autumn). http://ineducation.ca/ineducation/article/view/69/555. Accessed 1 February 2016.

Dei, G.J.S., B.L. Hall, and D.G. Rosenberg, eds. 2000. *Indigenous Knowledges in Global Contexts: Multiple Readings of Our World*. Toronto: OISE/University of Toronto Press.

Dei, G.J.S., L. Holmes, J. Mazzuca, E. McIssaac, and R. Campbell. 1995. *Drop Out or Push Out: The Dynamics of Black Students'*

Disengagement from School. Toronto: Institute for Studies in Department of Sociology.

Dei, G.J.S., and G.S. Johal, eds. 2005. *Critical Issues in Anti-Racist Research Methodologies*. New York: Peter Lang Publishing Inc.

Department of Justice Canada. *Official Languages Act*. 1985. Current to 5 May 2011. http://laws-lois.justice.gc.ca/PDF/O-3.01.pdf. 24 January 2016.

Dietsche, P.H.J. 2005. *Project Brief: The Pan-Canadian Study of College Students, the College Experience and Determinants of First Year Outcomes*. Ottawa: Association of Canadian Community Colleges.

– 2010. "Perspectives des étudiants sur les obstacles à la réussite dans les collèges de l'Ontario." Paper presented at L'accès des francophones aux études postsecondaires en Toronto, Ontario.

DiMaria, F. 2006. "Keeping Our Engaged, At-risk Kids in College." *Education Digest: Essential Readings Condensed for Quick Review* 72, no. 2: 52–7.

Dimison, A. 2000. "GAP Decision Made." *The Ubyssey*, 12 September. http://ubcpubs.library.ubc.ca/?db=ubyssey. Accessed 27 January 2016.

Dodd, J.M., F.M. Garcia, C. Meccage, and J.R. Nelson. 1995. "American Indian Student Retention." *NASPA Journal* 33, no. 1: 72–8.

Dormer, D. 2010. "Anti-abortion Group Awaits Fate." *Calgary Sun*. http://www.calgarysun.com/news/alberta/2010/04/28/13756161.html. Accessed 24 January 2016.

Downs, D.A. 2005. *Restoring Free Speech and Liberty on Campus*. Cambridge: Cambridge University Press.

Ebersold, S. 2008. "Disability in Higher Education: A Key Factor for Improving Quality and Achievement." Paper presented at OECD conference, Paris, France, 8–9 December. http://www.oecd.org/site/eduhe30/41887103.ppt. Accessed 24 January 2016.

Edgeworth, K., and J. Eiseman. 2007. "Going Bush: International Student Perspectives on Living and Studying at an Australian Rural University Campus." *Journal of Research in Rural Education* 22, no. 9: 1–13.

Editorial Board. 2010. "*National Post* Editorial Board: Canada's Universities, Bastions of Censorship." *National Post*. http://fullcomment.nationalpost.com/2010/11/18/national-post-editorial-board-canadas-universities-bastions-of-censorship/. Accessed 24 January 2016.

Edmonson, S., A. Fisher, and J. Christensen. 2003. "Project CONNECT: A University's Effort to Close the Gaps." Paper presented at the Annual Meeting of the American Educational Research Association, Chicago, Illinois, 21–25 April.

Edwards, P. 1981. "Race, Residence, and Leisure Style: Some Policy Implications." *Leisure Sciences* 4, no. 2: 95–111.

Ellis, L. 1996. "Theories of Homosexuality." In *The Lives of Lesbians, Gays, and Bisexuals: Children to Adults*, edited by Ritch C. Savin-Williams and Kenneth M. Cohen, 11–34. Fort Worth: Harcourt Brace.

Engstrom, C., and V. Tinto. 2008. "Access without Support Is Not Opportunity." *Change: The Magazine of Higher Learning* 40, no. 1: 46–50.

Environics Research Group Limited. 2004. "Canadian Attitudes Towards Disability Issues: A Qualitative Study." http://environicsresearch.com/. 24 January 2016.

Erikson, E.H. 1950. *Childhood and Society*. New York: W.W. Norton.

Evans, N., and A. D'Augelli. 1996. "Lesbians, Gay Men, and Bisexual People in College." In *The Lives of Lesbians, Gays, and Bisexuals: Children to Adults*, edited by Ritch C. Savin-Williams and Kenneth M. Cohen, 201–26. Fort Worth: Harcourt Brace.

Evans, N., D. Forney, F. Guido-DiBrito. 1998. *Student Development in College: Theory, Research, and Practice*. San Francisco: Jossey-Bass.

Evans, N., D. Forney, F. Guido, L. Patton, and K. Renn. 2010. *Student Development in College: Theory, Research, and Practice*. 2nd ed. San Francisco: Jossey-Bass.

Evans, N.J., and T.K. Herriott. 2004. "Freshmen Impressions: How Investigating the Campus Climate for LGBT Students Affected Four Freshman Students." *Journal of College Student Development* 45, no. 3: 316–32.

Eyermann, T., and R. Sanlo. 2002. "Documenting Their Existence: Lesbian, Gay, Bisexual and Transgender Students on Campus." In *Our Place on Campus: Lesbian, Gay, Bisexual, Transgender Services and Programs in Higher Education*, edited by R. Sanlo, S. Rankin, and R. Schoenberg, 33–40. Westport: Greenwood Press.

Fairbairn, S. 2006. "University of Toronto Allows Controversial Student-led Debates on Middle East." *Canadian Press*. 10 February.

Farmer, D. 2001. "Francophone Immigrants in Ontario: Invisible Reality, Challenges for Research." Paper presented at Fifth National Conference of Metropolis, Ottawa, Ontario.

Farr, M. 2005. "Then & Now: Revisiting Diversity on Campus." *University Affairs*, 26–29 September.

Farrar, D. 2006. "Freedom of Speech and Events Organized by Campus Organizations." University of Toronto. http://www.provost.utoronto.ca/public/pdadc/0506/79.htm. Accessed 24 January 2016.

Fassinger, R.E. 1998. "Lesbian, Gay, and Bisexual Identity and Student Development Theory." In *Working with Lesbian, Gay, Bisexual, and Transgender College Students: A Handbook for Faculty and Administrators*, edited by R.L. Sanlo, 13–22. Westport: Greenwood Press.

Feinberg, L. 1998. *Trans Liberation: Beyond Pink or Blue*. Boston: Beacon Press.

Feldman, R.S., ed. 2004. *Improving the First Year of College: Research and Practice*. Mahwah: Lawrence Erlbaum Associates.

Ferdman, B.M., and P.I. Gallegos. 2001. "Racial Identity Development and Latinos in the United States." In *New Perspectives on Racial Identity Development: A Theoretical and Practical Anthology*, edited by C.L. Wijeyesinghe and B.W. Jackson, 32–66. New York: New York University Press.

Fichten, C., J. Asuncion, M. Barile, C. Robillard, M. Fossey, and D. Lamb. 2003. "Canadian Post-secondary Students with Disabilities: Where Are They?" *Canadian Journal of Higher Education* 33: 71–114.

Filkins, J.W., and S.K. Doyle. 2002. "First Generation and Low Income Students: Using the NSSE Data to Study Effective Educational Practices and Students. Self-reported Gains." Paper presented at the Annual Forum for the Association for Institutional Research, Toronto, Ontario, 2–5 June. http://cpr.indiana.edu/uploads/Filkins,%20Doyle%20% 282002%29%20-%20first%20gen%20and%20low%20income.pdf. Accessed 24 January 2016.

Finnie, R., E. Lascelles, and A. Sweetman. 2005. "Who Goes? The Direct and Indirect Effects of Family Background on Access to Post-secondary Education. Analytical Studies Branch Research Paper Series." *Statistics Canada Catalogue* 11F0019MIE-237(no. 237). http://www.statcan. gc.ca/pub/11f0019m/11f0019m2005237-eng.pdf. Accessed 24 January 2016.

Finnie, R., S. Childs, and A. Wismer. 2010. "When Did You Decide?" In *Higher Education Strategy Associates*. http://higheredstrategy.com/mesa/ pub/pdf/MESA-WDYD_02_24_10.pdf. Accessed 24 January 2016.

Fish, S. 1994. *There's No Such Thing as Free Speech*. New York: Oxford University Press.

Fisher, R.J. 2000. "Intergroup Conflict." In *The Handbook of Conflict Resolution: Theory and Practice*, edited by M. Deutsch and P.T. Coleman, 166–84. San Francisco: Jossey-Bass.

Flaitz, J., ed. 2003. *Understanding Your International Students: An Educational, Cultural, and Linguistic Guide*. Ann Arbor: The University of Michigan Press.

Floyd, M.F., F. McGuire, K. Shinew, and F. Noe. 1994. "Race, Class, and Leisure Activity Preferences: Marginality and Ethnicity Revisited." *Journal of Leisure Research* 26, no. 2: 158–73.

Foley, K. 2001. *Why Stop after High School? A Descriptive Analysis of the Most Important Reasons that High School Graduates Do Not Continue to PSE.* Montreal: Canada Millennium Scholarship Foundation. https://qspace.library.queensu.ca/bitstream/1974/5812/1/foley_en.pdf. Accessed 11 February 2016.

Folger, W.A., J.A. Carter, and P.B. Chase. 2004. "Supporting First Generation College Freshmen with Small Group Intervention." *College Student Journal* 38, no. 3: 472.

Foster-Fishman, P.G., B. Nowell, and H. Yang. 2007. "Putting the System Back into Systems Change: A Framework for Understanding and Changing Organizational and Community Systems." *American Journal of Community Psychology* 39, nos 3–4: 197–215.

Fowler, J.W. 1981. *Stages of Faith: The Psychology of Human Development and the Quest for Meaning.* New York: Harper Collins.

Frempong, G., X. Mia, and J. Mensah. 2012. "Access to Postsecondary Education: Can Schools Compensate for Socioeconomic Disadvantage? *Higher Education* 63, no. 1: 19–32.

Frenette, M. 2007. "Why Are Youth from Lower-income Families Less Likely to Attend University? Evidence from Academic Abilities, Parental Influences, and Financial Constraints." *Statistics Canada Analytical Studies Branch Research Paper Series Catalogue* n11F0019MIE (no. 295).

Friesen, H.S. 2009. "Participation and Persistence of First Year Students in a British Columbia University: Towards a Predictive Model." PhD thesis, Simon Fraser University.

Gardner, J. 2007. "An Interview with John Gardner." *The Educational Policy Institute's Student Success: The Newsletter for Higher Education Professionals*, 6–8. November.

Garigue, P. 1985. "Bilingual University Education in Ontario." *The Canadian Modern Language Review* 41, no. 5: 941–6.

Gatfield, T., M. Barker, and P. Graham. 1999. "Measuring Student Quality Variables and the Implications for Management Practices in Higher Education Institutions: An Australian and International Student Perspective." *Journal of Higher Education Policy and Management* 21, no. 2: 239–55.

Gilligan, C. 1982. *In a Different Voice: Psychological Theory and Women's Development.* Cambridge: Harvard University Press.

Gingras, F. 2005. "Appartenance linguistique et identité plurielle chez les jeunes universitaires au Canada, en France et en Belgique." In

La gouvernance linguistique: le Canada en perspective, edited by Jean-Pierre Wallot, 237–55. Ottawa: University of Ottawa Press.

Gladstone, B. 2003. (January 2). "After Threats and Postponements, Pro-Israel Scholar Allowed to Speak." *Jewish Telegraphic Agency.* http://www.jta.org/2003/02/03/archive/after-threats-and-postponements-pro-israel-scholar-allowed-to-speak. 11 February 2016.

Global Free Press. 2010. "B'Nai Brith Canada Condemns Free Speech Double Standard on Campus as Coulter Talk is Cancelled in Ottawa." http://www.globalfreepress.org/sections/free-speech/2397. Accessed 9 February 2016.

Gochenour, T., and A. Janeway. 1993. "Seven Concepts in Cross-cultural Interaction: A Training Design." In *Beyond Experience: the Experiential Approach to Cross-Cultural Education,* 2nd ed., edited by D. Batchelder and E.G. Warner, 1–9. Washington: Library of Congress.

Gold, J.M. 1995. "An Intergenerational Approach to Student Retention." *Journal of College Student Development* 36, no. 2: 182–7.

Goodman, J., N. Schlossberg, and M. Anderson. 2006. *Counseling Adults in Transition: Linking Theory to Practice.* 3rd ed. New York: Springer Publications.

Graham, K., C. Dittburner, and F. Abele. 1996. *Soliloquy and Dialogue: Overview of Major Trends in Public Policy Relating to Aboriginal Peoples.* Vol. 1, *Public Policy and Aboriginal Peoples 1965–1992.* Ottawa: Royal Commission on Aboriginal Peoples.

Grayson, P. 1994. *Attitudes to Gay and Lesbian Students at York.* Toronto: York University, President's Task Force on Homophobia and Heterosexism.

Grayson, J.P. 2008. "The Experiences and Outcomes of Domestic and International Students at Four Canadian Universities." *Higher Education Research & Development* 27, no. 3: 215–30.

– 2011. "Cultural Capital and Academic Achievement of First Generation Domestic and International Students in Canadian Universities." *British Educational Research Journal* 37, no. 4: 605–30.

Green, D. 2006. "Historically Underserved Students: What We Know, What We Still Need to Know." *New Directions for Community Colleges* 135: 21–8.

Green, J. August 5, 2015. "The Boomers Are Coming." *University Affairs.* http://www.universityaffairs.ca/features/feature-article/the-boomers-are-coming/. Accessed 24 January 2016.

Grohsgal, J., and D. Anber. 2002. "Violence Silences Netanyahu." *McGill Tribune.* http://www.mcgilltribune.com/2.12363/violence-silences-netanyahu-1.1636678. Accessed 30 November 2010.

Guo, S., and M. Chase. 2011. "Internationalisation of Higher Education: Integrating International Students into Canadian Academic Environment." *Teaching in Higher Education* 16, no. 3: 305–18.

Hahs-Vaughn, D. 2004. "The Impact of Parents' Educational Level on College Students: An Analysis Using the Beginning Post-secondary Students Longitudinal Study 1990–92/94." *Journal of College Student Development* 45, no. 5: 483–500.

Halberstam, J. 1998. *Female Masculinity*. Durham: Duke University Press.

Hall, M., D. Lasby, G. Gumulka, and C. Tryon. 2006. "Caring Canadians, Involved Canadians: Highlights from the 2004 Canada Survey of Giving, Volunteering and Participating." Statistics Canada Catalogue 71-542 XIE. http://sectorsource.ca/sites/default/files/csgvp_highlights_2004_en_0.pdf. Accessed 24 January 2016.

Hamrick, J. 1999. "Internationalizing Higher Education Institutions: Broadening the Approach to Institutional Change." Unpublished manuscript: University of Michigan.

Hanassah, S. 2006. "Diversity, International Students, and Perceived Discrimination: Implications for Educators and Counselors." *Journal of Students in International Education* 10, no. 2: 157–72.

Handel, S., and A. Herrera. 2003. "Access and Retention of Students from Educationally Disadvantaged Backgrounds: Insights from the University of California." In *Improving Completion Rates Among Disadvantaged Students*, edited by Jocey Quinn, Michael Cooper, and Liz Thomas, 33–52. Sterling: Trentham Books.

Hango, D.W., and P. De Broucker. 2007. *Postsecondary Enrolment Trends to 2031: Three Scenarios*. Statistics Canada.

Hannah, D.A. 1998. *Postsecondary Students and the Courts in Canada: Cases and Commentary from the Common-Law Provinces*. Asheville: College Administration Publications, Inc.

Hardy Cox, D., and C. Strange, eds. 2010. *Achieving Student Success: Effective Student Services in Canadian Higher Education*. Montreal: McGill-Queen's University Press.

Hardy Cox, D., and R. Walsh. 1998. "Questions to Consider in Policy Development for Post-secondary Students with Disabilities." *Journal of Post-Secondary Education and Disability* 13: 51–67.

Harpham, B. 2006. "Whatever It Is, We're Against It: Just What Are 'Know Radical Islam Week' and 'Israeli Apartheid Week' Fighting For? Zionist Group Kicks Off a Two-week Ideological Faceoff." *Varsity*. http://thevarsity.ca/articles/16058. Accessed 15 October 2010.

Harrell, P.E., and W.S. Forney. 2003. "Ready or Not, Here We Come: Retaining Hispanic and First-generation Students in Post-secondary

Education." *Community College Journal of Research and Practice* 27, no. 2: 147–56.

"Hate." (n.d.). In *Oxford English Dictionary*. http://www.oed.com. myaccess.library.utoronto.ca. 11 February 2016.

Hayes, R.L., and H.R. Lin. 1994. "Coming to America: Developing Social Support Systems for International Students." *Journal of Multicultural Counselling and Development* 22, no. 1: 7–16.

Healey, N.M. 2008. "Is Higher Education Really 'Internationalizing'?" *Higher Education* 55: 333–55.

Hemingway, F., and K. McMullen. 2004. *A Family Affair: The Impact of Paying for College or University*. Ottawa: The Canada Millennium Scholarship Foundation.

Hidalgo, H., ed. 1995. *Lesbians of Color: Social and Human Services*. New York: Haworth Press.

Hill, J. 1994. "Speaking Out: Perceptions of Students with Disabilities at Canadian Universities Regarding Institutional Policies." *Journal of Post-Secondary Education and Disability* 11: 1–15.

Himel, M. 2003. *Confrontation at Concordia* [Motion Picture]. Canada *History of Israeli Apartheid Week*. n.d. http://apartheidweek.org/about/. Accessed 10 February 2016.

Holton, S.A. 1998. *Mending the Cracks in the Ivory Tower: Strategies for Conflict Management in Higher Education*. Bolton: Anker Publishing Company, Inc.

Horn, M. 1999a. *Academic Freedom in Canada: A History*. Toronto: University of Toronto Press, Inc.

– 1999b. "Students and Academic Freedom in Canada." *Historical Studies in Education*, 11, no. 1: 1–32.

Horse, P.G. 2001. "Reflections on American Indian Identity." In *New Perspectives on Racial Identity Development: A Theoretical and Practical Anthology*, edited by C.L. Wijeyesinghe and B.W. Jackson, 91–107. New York: New York University Press.

Hossler, D. 1986. *Managing College Enrollments*. San Francisco: Jossey-Bass.

Hottinger, J.A., and C.P. Rose. 2006. "First Generation Students." In *Understanding College Student Subpopulations: A Guide for Student Affairs Professionals*, edited by Lyle A. Gohn and Ginger R. Albin, 115–35. Waldorf: NASPA.

Howard-Hamilton, M.F. 2003. *Theoretical Frameworks for African American Women: Meeting the Needs of African American Women: New Directions for Student Services* 104. San Francisco: Jossey-Bass.

Houle, F. 2010. "Les établissements : Réalités, recherches, défis." L'Université d'Ottawa. Paper presented at L'accès des francophones aux études postsecondaires en Ontario, Toronto, Ontario.

Hsiao, K.P. 1992. "First-generation College Students." ERIC Digest ED351079. http://eric.ed.gov/?id=ED351079. Accessed 24 January 2016.

Hujaleh, F., J. Iacampo, and G. Werkneh. 2009. *Lifelong Learning among Canadians Aged 18 to 64 Years: First Results from the 2008 Access and Support to Education and Training Survey*. Statistics Canada, Culture, Tourism and the Centre for Education Statistics Division.

Human Capital Strategies. 2005. *Review of Aboriginal Post-Secondary Education Programs, Services, and Strategies/Best Practices and Aboriginal Special Projects Funding (ASPF) Program*. http://www.aved.gov.bc.ca/aboriginal/docs/educator-resources/2005-Jothen-Report.pdf. Accessed 24 January 2016.

Hunt, D.E., and E.V. Sullivan. 1974. *Between Psychology and Education*. Hinsdale: Dryden Press.

Huntington, S.P. 1993. "The Clash of Civilizations?" *Foreign Affairs* 72, no. 3: 22–49.

Isaacs, W. 1999. *Dialogue and the Art of Thinking Together*. New York: Doubleday.

Ishitani, T. T. 2003. "A Longitudinal Approach to Assessing Attrition Behavior among First-Generation Students: Time-varying Effects of Pre-college Characteristics." *Research in Higher Education* 44, no. 4: 433–49.

Johnson, D.R., M. Soldner, J. Brown Leonard, P. Alarez, K. Kurotsuchi Inkelas, H. Rowan-Kenyon, and S. Longerbeam. 2007. "Examining Sense of Belonging among First-Year Undergraduates from Different Racial/Ethnic Groups." *Journal of College Student Development* 48, no. 5: 525–42.

Jones, S.R., and M.K. McEwen. 2000. "A Conceptual Model of Multiple Dimensions of Identity." *Journal of College Student Development* 41: 405–13.

Jorgensen, S., C. Fichten, A. Havel, D. Lamb, C. James, and M. Barile. 2005. "Academic Performance of College Students with and without Disabilities: An Archival Study." *Canadian Journal of Counselling* 39: 101–17.

Joy, C. 1996. "A Comparison of the Experiences of Canadian University Students of French and English Language of Origin." Master's thesis, Bowling Green State University.

Junor, S., and A. Usher. 2004. *The Price of Knowledge 2004: Access and Student Finance in Canada*. Montreal: The Canada Millennium Scholarship Foundation.

Kamazi, P.C., S. Bonin, P. Doray, A. Groleau, J. Murdoch, P. Mercier, C. Blanchard, M. Gallien, and R. Auclair. 2010. *Academic Persistence among Canadian First-Generation University Students* (Project Transitions, Research Paper 9). Montreal, Centre interuniversitaire de recherche sur la science et la technologie (CIRST)

Kane, M.A., C. Beals, E.J. Valeau, and M.J. Johnson. 2004. "Fostering Success among Traditionally Underrepresented Student Groups: Hartnell College's Approach to Implementation of the Math, Engineering, and Science Achievement (MESA) Program." *Community College Journal of Research and Practice* 28, no. 1: 17–26.

Karenga, M., and T. Karenga. 2007. "The *Nguzo Saba* and the Black Family: Principles and Practices of Well-Being and Flourishing." In *Black Families*, 4th ed., edited by Harriet Pipes McAdoo, 7–28. Thousand Oaks: Sage Publications, 2007.

Kaufman, B. 2010. "Students' Union Pulls Complaint about Anti-abortion Group." *Calgary Sun*. http://www.calgarysun.com/news/alberta/2010/06/24/14506716.html. Accessed 25 January 2016.

Kaufman, R. 2007. "Dare to Discover Logos." *University Affairs*, letter to the editor. http://search.proquest.com/docview/233305839/8C66444959B0470BPQ. Accessed 1 February 2016.

Kerr, A. 2011. *Adult Learners in Ontario Postsecondary Institutions*. Toronto: Higher Education Quality Council of Ontario.

Kidwell, C.S. 1991. "The Vanishing Native Reappears in the College Curriculum." *Change* 23, no. 2: 19–23.

Killean, E. and D. Hubka. 1999. *Working towards a Co-Ordinated National Approach to Services, Accommodations and Policies for Post-Secondary Students with Disabilities: Ensuring Access to Higher Education and Career Training*. Ottawa: National Educational Association of Disabled Students.

Kim, Y. 2010. "York Students Protest Galloway Speech." *The Brock Press*. http://www.brockpress.com/2010/11/york-students-protest-galloway-speech/. Accessed 25 January 2016.

Kim, J. 2001. "Asian American Identity Development Theory." In *New Perspectives on Racial Identity Development: A Theoretical and Practical Anthology*, edited by C.L. Wijeyesinghe and B.W. Jackson III, 67–90. New York: New York University Press.

Kirby, D. 2009. "Widening Access: Making the Transition from Mass to Universal Post-secondary Education in Canada." *Journal of Applied Research on Learning* 2, no. 3: 1–17.

Kirkness, V.J., and R. Barnhardt. 1991. "First Nations and Higher Education: The Four R's – Respect, Relevance, Reciprocity, Responsibility." *Journal of American Indian Education* 3. http://www.ankn.uaf.edu/IEW/winhec/FourRs2ndEd.html. Accessed 25 January 2016.

Kitchen, J. and C. Bellini. 2013. "Gay-straight Alliances: Making Ontario Schools Safe and Inclusive." *Teaching and Learning* 7, no. 3: 62–75.

Klak, T., and P. Martin. 2003. "Do University-Sponsored International Cultural Events Help Students to Appreciate 'Difference'?" *International Journal of Intercultural Relations* 27, no. 4: 445–65.

Knefelkamp, L., C. Widick, and C.A. Parker. 1978. *Applying New Developmental Findings: New Directions for Student Services* 4. San Francisco: Jossey-Bass.

Knight, J. 2000. *Taking the Pulse: Monitoring the Quality and Progress of Internationalization Including Tracking Measures* (Millennium Series no. 2). Ottawa: Canadian Bureau of International Education.

– 2004. "Internationalization Remodeled: Definition, Approaches, and Rationales." *Journal of Studies in International Education* 8, no. 1: 5–31.

Knighton, T., and S. Mirza. 2002. "Post-secondary Participation: The Effects of Parents' Education and Household Income." *Education Quarterly Review* 8, no. 3: 25-32.

Kodama, C.M., M. McEwen, T.H. Liang, and S. Lee. 2002. "An Asian American Perspective on Psychosocial Student Development Theory." *New Directions for Student Services* 97: 45–59. San Francisco: Jossey-Bass.

Kohlberg, L. 1969. "Stage and Sequence: The Cognitive Developmental Approach to Socialization." In *Handbook of Socialization Theory and Research*, edited by D. Goslin, 347–480. Chicago: Rand McNally.

Kraus, A. 2010. "Professional Perspective." Review of "Yes We Can Change: Disability Studies – Enabling Equality" by Michael Rembis. *Journal of Post-Secondary Education and Disability* 23, no. 1: 28. http://www.ahead.org/uploads/publications/JPED/jped_23_1/JPED%2023_1_Full%20Document.pdf. Accessed 25 January 2016.

Kroeger, S. 2010. "From the Special Issue Editor." *Journal of Post-Secondary Education and Disability* 23, no. 1: 3–4. http://www.ahead.org/uploads/publications/JPED/jped_23_1/JPED%2023_1_Full%20Document.pdf. Accessed 25 January 2016.

Kuh, G.D. 2003. "What We're Learning about Student Engagement from NSSE." *Change* 35, no. 2: 24–32.

– 2005. "Student Engagement in the First Year of College." In *Challenging and Supporting the First-Year Student: A Handbook for Improving the First College Year*, edited by M.L. Upcraft, J.N. Gardner, B.O. Barefoot, 86–107. San Francisco: Jossey-Bass.

Kuh, G.D., J. Kinzie, J. Schuh, and E. Whitt. 2005. *Student Success in College: Creating Conditions That Matter*. San Francisco: Jossey-Bass.

Kuitenbrouwer, P. 2006. "'Radical Islam Week' Sparks U of T Furor." *National Post*. http://www.canada.com/nationalpost/news/toronto/story.html?id=be4c288a-8613-45a7-95b0-9d5ee7037357. Accessed 25 January 2016.

Kunin, R., and Associates. 2012. "Impact of International Education in Canada – An Update." Ottawa: Department of Foreign Affairs and International Trade.

Labrie, N. 1995. L'Éducation franco-ontarienne. Special Commemorative Issue OISE News.

Labrie, N., and S. Lamoureux. 2010. "L'accès des francophones aux études postsecondaires en Ontario : Le choix des jeunes. " Paper presented at L'accès des francophones aux études postsecondaires en Ontario, Toronto, Ontario.

Labrie, N., S. Lamoureux, and D. Wilson. 2009. "L'accès des francophones aux études postsecondaires en Ontario : Le choix des jeunes. rapport final." Toronto: Centre de Recherches en Éducation franco-ontarienne. http://crefo.oise.utoronto.ca/UserFiles/File/rapportsprojets/rapport%20finalLabrie.pdf. Accessed 25 January 2016.

Landry, R. 2014. "Life in an Official Minority Language in Canada." Moncton: Canadian Institute for Research on Linguistic Minorities.

Landry, R., and R. Allard. 1997. "L'exogamie et le maintien de deux langues et de deux cultures: le rôle de la francité familioscolaire." *Revue des sciences de l'éducation* 23, no. 3: 561–92.

Leclerc, C. 1987. *Reception and Integration of Persons with Disabilities at the College Level*. Québec: Ministère de l'Enseignement supérieur et de la Science, Direction générale de l'Enseignement collégial.

Lederman, D. 2010. "More Legal Risk for Canada's Universities." *Inside Higher Ed*. http://www.insidehighered.com/news/2010/10/18/canada. Accessed 25 January 2016.

Lennon, M.C., H. Zhao, S. Wang, and T. Gluszynski. 2011. *Facteurs influençant l'accès des jeunes à l'éducation postsecondaire en Ontario, Toronto*. Conseil ontarien de la qualité de l'enseignement supérieur en Ontario.

Lev, A.I. 2004. *Transgender Emergence: Therapeutic Guidelines for Working with Gender-Variant People and Their Families.* New York: Haworth Clinical Practice Press.

Levinson, D.J. 1978. *The Seasons of a Man's Life.* New York: Ballantine.

Levinson, D.J., and J. Levinson. 1996. *The Seasons of a Woman's Life.* New York: Ballantine Books.

Lewis, C. 2010. "Pro-life Students at Carleton University Arrested." *National Post.* http://news.nationalpost.com/2010/10/04/pro-life-students-at-carleton-university-arrested/. Accessed 25 January 2016.

Livingstone, D.W. 2012. "Probing the Icebergs of Adult Learning: Comparative Findings and Implications of the 1998, 2004 and 2010 Canadian Surveys of Formal and Informal Learning Practices." *Canadian Journal for the Study of Adult Education* 25, no.1: 47–71.

Livingstone, D.W., and M. Raykov. 2013. *Adult Learning Trends in Canada: Basic Findings of the WALL 1998, 2004 and 2010 Surveys.* Toronto: Centre for the Study of Education and Work, Ontario Institute for Studies in Education, University of Toronto.

Loewen, G., and W. Pollard. 2010. "The Social Justice Perspective." *Journal of Post-Secondary Education and Disability* 23: 5–17.

Loewen, G., and J. Wolforth. 2005. "Universal Design." Paper presented at the annual conference of the Canadian Association of College and University Student Services, Kingston, Ontario, 21–25 June.

Lohfink, M., and M. Paulsen. 2005. "Comparing the Determinants of Persistence for First-generation and Continuing-generation Students." *Journal of College Student Development* 46, no. 4: 409–28.

Longerbeam, S.D., K. Inkelas, D. Johnson, and Z. Lee. 2007. "Lesbian, Gay, and Bisexual College Student Experiences: An Exploratory Study." *Journal of College Student Development* 48, no. 2: 215–30.

Lotkowski, V.A., S.B. Robbins, R.J. Noeth. 2004. "The Role of Academic and Non-Academic Factors in Improving College Retention: ACT Policy Report." *American College Testing (ACT) Inc.* https://www.act.org/research/policymakers/pdf/college_retention.pdf. Accessed 25 January 2016.

Lyakhovetska, R.A. 2003. "Welcome to Canada? Experiences and Views of International Graduate Students at the University of British Columbia." Master's thesis, University of British Columbia.

Maclean's. 2008. "You Can't Say That!" *Maclean's.* http://oncampus.macleans.ca/education/2008/03/04/you-cant-say-that/. Accessed 25 January 2016.

Madgett, P.J., and C. Belanger. 2008. "International Students: The Canadian Experience." *Tertiary Education and Management* 14, no. 3: 191–207.

Malatest, R.A, and Associates Ltd. 2004. "Aboriginal Peoples and
Post-secondary Education: What Educators Have Learned." www.kpu.ca/
_shared/assets/Aboriginal_Peoples_PostSecondary6358.pdf. 25 January
2016.

Marjoribanks, K. 2005. "Family Environments and Children's Outcomes."
Educational Psychology 25, no. 6: 647–57.

Martel, L., A. Bélanger, J. Berthelot, and Y. Carrière. 2005. "Healthy
Today, Healthy Tomorrow? Findings from the National Population
Health Survey." *Healthy Aging* 4, no. 1: Statistics Canada Catalogue
82-618-MWE2005004. http://www5.statcan.gc.ca/olc-cel/olc.
action?objId=82-618-M&objType=2&lang=en&limit=1. Accessed
25 January 2016.

Martell, A. 2008. "Students Rally to Abort 'Genocide' Demonstration."
Varsity. http://thevarsity.ca/2008/04/07/students-rally-to-abort-
genocide-demonstration/. Accessed 25 January 2016.

Martin, J. 2001. "Voices From the Heart of the Circle: Eight Aboriginal
Women Reflect on Their Experiences at University." PhD dissertation,
University of Alberta.

Martinello, F. 2007. "Student Transitions and Adjustments in Canadian
Post-secondary Education." Paper presented at the All in the Family:
Evidence from the YITS on PSE Access and Persistence conference
hosted by the Canada Millennium Scholarship Foundation, Montreal,
Quebec, 19 October. http://socserv.mcmaster.ca/rdc/RDCwp11.pdf.
Accessed 25 January 2016.

Mavondo, F.T., Y. Tsarenko, and M. Gabbott. 2004. "International and
Local Student Satisfaction: Resources and Capabilities Perspective."
Journal of Marketing for Higher Education 14, no. 1: 41–60.

McBride, K. 1998. "A Warm Welcome? Recruitment and Admission of
International Students to Canadian Universities: Policy, Procedures and
Capacity." Ottawa: Association of Universities and Community Colleges
of Canada.

McCormack, E., and A. Labi. 2007. "Worldwide Competition for International Students Heats Up." *Chronicle of Higher Education* 54, no. 2: 34.

McGinnis, S. 2009. "U of C Pro-life Students Charged with Trespassing
on Campus." *Calgary Herald.* http://www2.canada.com/calgaryherald/
news/city/story.html?id=1448c5bc-2ab0-414c-9445-df1e8834982f.
Accessed 2 October 2010.

Meloche-Holubowski, M. 2006. "Concordia Out for Book: Novel." http://
thelinknewspaper.ca/archive/view.php?aid=38730. 30 November 2010.

Mohr, J.J., and W. Sedlacek. 2000. "Perceived Barriers to Friendship with Lesbians and Gay Men among University Students." *Journal of College Student Development* 41: 70–9.

Moon, R. 2000. *The Constitutional Protection of Freedom of Expression.* Toronto: University of Toronto Press.

Moore, L.V., ed. 1990. *Evolving Theoretical Perspectives on Students: New Directions for Student Services* 51. San Francisco: Jossey-Bass.

Moore-Eyman, E. 1981. "The Support Service Approach to University Education for Native Students in Alberta." *Integrated Education* 19, nos 3–6: 109–12.

Moores, L., and N.E. Popadiuk. 2011. "Positive Aspects of International Student Transitions: A Qualitative Inquiry." *Journal of College Student Development* 52, no. 3: 291–306.

Morrow, A. 2010. "Former Student Leaders Sue U of T after Brush with Campus Police." *Globe and Mail.* http://www.theglobeandmail.com/news/national/toronto/former-student-leaders-sue-u-of-t-after-brush-with-campus-police/article1778732/. Accessed 26 January 2016.

Motte, A., and P. Schwartz. 2009. *Are Student Employment and Academic Success Linked?* Ottawa, Ontario: The Canadian Millennium Scholarship Foundation, Millennium Research Note #9.

Mullins, L., and M. Preyde. 2013. "The Lived Experience of Students with an Invisible Disability at a Canadian University." *Disability & Society* 28: 147–60.

Murphy, C., L. Hawkes, and J. Law. 2002. "How International Students Can Benefit from a Web-Based College Orientation for College Orientation." *New Directions for Higher Education* 117: 37–43. San Francisco: Jossey-Bass.

Nakamura, K. 1998. "Transitioning on Campus: A Case Studies Approach." In *Working with Lesbian, Gay, Bisexual and Transgender College Students: A Handbook for Faculty and Administrators*, edited by R. Sanlo, 179–88. Westport: Greenwood Press.

National Post. 2008. "Student Anti-abortion Group Fights Ban." http://www.canada.com/cityguides/toronto/info/story.html?id=003edbd7-63d3-4705-925d-bf97880c476b. Accessed 25 October 2010.

National Post. 2010. "Letter from Carleton Undergraduate Students Association to anti-abortion group about funding." http://life.nationalpost.com/2010/11/16/letter-from-carleton-undergraduate-students-association-to-anti-abortion-group-about-funding/. Accessed 25 October 2010.

Naumann, W.C., D. Bandalos, and T.B. Gutkin. 2003. "Identifying Variables that Predict College Success for First-Generation College Students." *Journal of College Admission* 181: 4–9.

Naylor, D. 2006. *Presidential Statement to Governing Council Regarding Concerns about Racist and Offensive Incidents on Campus.* http://www.president.utoronto.ca/speeches/regarding-concerns-about-racist-and-offensive-incidents-on-campus. Accessed 25 January 2016.

– 2008. "Open Letter Regarding Israel Apartheid Week." *National Post*, 7 February.

Nesmith, A.A., D.L. Burton, and T.J. Cosgrove. 1999. "Gay, Lesbian, and Bisexual Youth and Young Adults: Social Support in Their Own Words." *Journal of Homosexuality* 37, no. 1: 95–108.

Neufeldt, A. 2003. "Disability in Canada." In *In Pursuit of Equal Participation: Canada and Disability at Home and Abroad,* edited by H. Enns and A. Neufeldt, 22–83. Concord: Captus Press.

Neufeldt, A., and J. Egers. 2003. "Disability and Institutions of Higher Learning in Canada and Internationally." In *In Pursuit of Equal Participation: Canada and Disability at Home and Abroad,* edited by H. Enns and A. Neufeldt, 296–343. Concord: Captus Press.

Neugarten, B.L. 1968. "Adult Personality: Toward a Psychology of the Life Cycle." In *Middle Age and Aging,* edited by B.L. Neugarten, 137–47. Chicago: University of Chicago Press.

Office of the Vice-President and Provost. 2006. "Principles and Policies Concerning Controversial Campus Event, Activities and Issues at the University of Toronto: Discussion Paper (Consultation Draft)." Paper presented at Freedom of Expression on Campus conference, University of Toronto. 25 October 2006.

O'Hare, A. 2006. "To Print or Not to Print?" *The Strand.* http://www.safs.ca/issuescases/ohare.htm. Accessed 25 January 2016.

O'Leary, J., and Benjamin, P. 1982. *Ethnic Variations in Leisure Behavior: Studies, Theories and Directions for Future Research.* Co-operative research project. US Forest Service, North Central Forest Experiment Station. Indiana University and Purdue University.

Ontario Human Rights Commission. 2003. "The Opportunity to Succeed: Achieving Barrier-free Education for Students with Disabilities." http://www.ohrc.on.ca/en/resources/discussion_consultation/Consult EduDisablty2/pdf. Accessed 25 January 2016.

– 2004. "Guidelines on Accessible Education." http://www.ohrc.on.ca/en/guidelines-accessible-education. Accessed 25 January 2016.

Orbe, M.P. 2004. "Negotiating Multiple Identities within Multiple Frames: An Analysis of First-Generation College Students." *Communication Education* 53, no. 2: 131–49.

Outcomes Working Group and British Columbia Ministry of Advanced Education. 2006. BC *Student Outcomes: Job Destinations of Former College and Institute Students.* http://www.outcomes.bcstats.gov.bc.ca/libraries/dacso_discontinued_papers/2005_jdr_pdf. Accessed 2 August 2007.

Pace, C.R. 1984. *Measuring the Quality of College Student Experience.* Los Angeles: Higher Education Research Institute, The University of California.

Palmer, P. 1987. "Community, Conflict, and Ways of Knowing." *Change* 19, no. 5: 20–5.

Papademetriou, D.G., and M. Sumption. 2011. "The Role of Immigration in Fostering Competitiveness in the United States." *Migration Policy Institute.* http://www.migrationpolicy.org/research/role-immigration-fostering-competitiveness-united-states. Accessed 4 February 2016.

Paré, F. 1995. "Les franco-ontariens ont-ils droit au discours identitaire?" In *Identité et cultures nationales: L'amérique française en mutation,* edited by Simon Langlois, 167–78. Sainte-Foy: Les Presses de l'Université Laval. http://www12.statcan.ca/census-recensement/2006/as-sa/97-555/table/A5-eng.cfm. Accessed 25 January 2016.

Paris, P. 1993. "The Spirituality of African People." Paper presented to James Robinson Johnston Chair in Black Canadian Studies Lecture Series. Halifax, Nova Scotia, March 9.

Parker, C.A., ed. 1978. *Encouraging Development in College Students.* Minneapolis: University of Minnesota Press.

Parkin, A., and N. Baldwin. 2009. *Persistence in Post-secondary Education in Canada: The Latest Research.* Ottawa: The Canadian Millennium Scholarship Foundation, Research Note no. 8.

Parks, S.D. 2011. *Big Questions Worthy Dreams: Mentoring Emerging Adults in Their Search for Meaning, Purpose, and Faith.* San Francisco: Jossey Bass.

Pascarella, E.T., C.T. Pierson, G.C. Wolniak, and P.T. Terenzini. 2004. "First-Generation College Students: Additional Evidence on College Experiences and Outcomes." *Journal of Higher Education* 75, no. 3: 249.

Pascarella, E.T., and P.T. Terenzini. 1991. *How College Affects Students.* San Francisco: Jossey Bass.

– 2005. *How College Affects Students: A Third Decade of Research.* 2nd ed. San Francisco: Jossey Bass.

Paul, F. 2012. *Exploring the Experiences of Black International Caribbean Students at a Canadian University.* Master's thesis, University of Western Ontario.

Pearson, M. 2010. "Anti-abortion Activists Arrested for Posting Provocative Posters." *The Edmonton Journal.* http://www. edmontonjournal.com/life/Anti+abortion+activists+arrested+posting+ provocative+posters/3624642/story.html. Accessed 23 October 2010.

Pedersen, P. 1994. "International Student and International Student Advisors." In *Improving Intercultural Interactions: Modules for Cross Cultural Training Programs*, edited by R. Brislin and T. Yoshida, 148–67. Thousand Oakes: Sage Publications.

Perry, W.G. 1970. *Forms of Intellectual and Ethical Development in the College Years: A Scheme.* New York: Holt, Rinehart, and Winston.

Peter, T., C. Taylor, and L. Chamberland. 2015. "A Queer Day in Canada: Examining Canadian High School Students' Experiences with School-Based Homophobia in Two Large-Scale Studies." *Journal of Homosexuality* 62, no. 2: 186–206.

Peters, H. 2005. "Contested Discourses: Assessing the Outcomes of Learning from Experience for the Award of Credit in Higher Education." *Assessment & Evaluation in Higher Education* 30, no. 3: 273–85.

Phinney, J.S. 1990. "Ethnic Identity in Adolescents and Adults: Review of Research." *Psychological Bulletin* 108: 499–514.

Picot, G., and A. Sweetman. 2012. "Making It in Canada: Immigration Outcomes and Policies." *IRPP Study* 29: 1.

Pidgeon, M. 2001. "Looking Forward … A National Perspective on Aboriginal Student Services in Canadian Universities." Master's thesis, Memorial University of Newfoundland.

– 2005. "Weaving the Story of Aboriginal Student Services in Canadian Universities. *Communique* 5, no. 3: 27–9.

– 2008a. "It Takes More Than Good Intentions: Institutional Accountability and Responsibility to Indigenous Higher Education." PhD dissertation, University of British Columbia.

– 2008b. "Pushing against the Margins: Indigenous Theorizing of 'Success' and Retention in Higher Education." *Journal of College Student Retention: Research, Theory & Practice* 10, no. 3: 339–60.

Pidgeon, M., and D. Hardy Cox. 2005. "Perspectives of Aboriginal Student Services Professionals: Aboriginal Student Services in Canadian

Universities." *Journal of Australian & New Zealand Student Services* 25: 3–30.

Pike, G.R., and G.D. Kuh. 2005. "First- and Second-Generation College Students: A Comparison of Their Engagement and Intellectual Development." *Journal of Higher Education* 76, no. 3: 276.

Pilote, A., M. Magnan, and K. Vieux-Fort. 2010. "L'identité linguistique et le poids des langues: une étude comparative entre des jeunes en milieu scolaire francophone au Nouveau-Brunswick et anglophone au Québec." *Nouvelles perspectives en sciences sociales* 6, no. 1: 65–98.

Pintrich, P.R. 1995. *Understanding Self-Regulated Learning: New Directions for Teaching and Learning 63*. San Francisco: Jossey-Bass.

Plant, G. 2007. "Campus 2020: Thinking Ahead: The Report." BC Ministry of Advanced Education. http://www.aved.gov.bc.ca/campus2020/.

Policy on the Disruption of Meetings. 1992. University of Toronto. http://www.governingcouncil.utoronto.ca/Assets/Governing+Council+Digital+Assets/Policies/PDF/ppjan281992.pdf. Accessed 25 January 2016.

Porter, C. 2003. "York to Allow Controversial Speaker." *Toronto Star*. http://pqasb.pqarchiver.com/thestar/doc/438548865.html?FMT=ABS&FMTS=ABS:FT&type=current&date=Jan+25%2C+2003&author=Porter%2C+Catherine&pub=Toronto+Star&edition=&startpage=&desc=York+to+allow+controversial+speaker+%3B+University+overturns+ban+on+pro-Israel+academic+Some+students+say+he%27s+a+hatemonger%2C+spreading+racism. Accessed 27 January 2016.

Potter, J. 1998a. *Financial Needs of Part-Time University Students in Canada*. Fredericton: University of New Brunswick.

– 1998b. *Listening to Their Voices: What Former Part-Time Students at the University of New Brunswick Are Telling Us*. Fredericton: University of New Brunswick.

Potter, J., and T.E. Alderman. 1992. *A Profile of Adult Learners at the University of New Brunswick*. Fredericton: University of New Brunswick.

Pounds, A.W. 1989. "Black Students." In *The Freshman Year Experience: Helping Students Survive and Succeed in College*, edited by M. Lee Upcraft and John N. Gardner, 277–86. San Francisco: Jossey-Bass.

Powell, M.H. 1998. "Campus Climate and Students of Color." In *The Multicultural Campus: Strategies for Transforming Higher Education*, edited by L.A. Valverda and L.A. Castenell, 95–118. Walnut Creek: Altamira Press.

Poyrazli, S., and K.M. Grahame. 2007. "Barriers to Adjustment: Needs of International Students within a Semi-urban Campus Community." *Journal of Instructional Psychology* 34, no. 1: 28–45.

Poyrazli, S., and M.D. Lopez. 2007. "An Exploratory Study of Perceived Discrimination and Homesickness: A Comparison of International and American Students." *The Journal of Psychology* 141, no. 3: 263–80.

Pridgen v. University of Calgary (2010), 644 (Court of Queen's Bench, 2010). CanLII. http://canlii.ca/t/2cxd9. Accessed 28 November 2010.

Provincial Advisory Committee. 1990. *Report for the Provincial Advisory Committee on Post-Secondary Education for Native Learners to the Honorable Bruce Strachan, Minister of Advanced Education, Training and Technology.*

Public Safety Canada. n.d. "Currently Listed Entities." Public Safety Canada, Government of Canada. http://www.publicsafety.gc.ca/prg/ns/le/cle-eng.aspx. 25 October 2010.

Purdie-Vaughns, V., and R.P. Eibach. 2008. "Intersectional Invisibility: The Distinctive Advantages and Disadvantages of Multiple Subordinate-group Identities." *Sex Roles* 59, nos 5–6: 377–91.

Qing, G., M. Schweisfurth, and C. Day. 2010. "Learning and Growing in a Foreign Context: Intercultural Experiences of International Students." *Compare: A Journal of Comparative and International Education* 40, no. 1: 7–23.

Queen's University International Centre. 1992. "Strangers and Prodigals Educational and Cross-cultural Exchanges Between Canada and Developing Countries." Discussion paper. Kingston: Queen's University International Centre.

Rabble.ca. 2009. *Galloway Breaks the Ban and Speaks via Rabbletv.* http://www.rabble.ca/blogs/bloggers/rabble-staff/galloway-breaks-ban-and-speaks-rabbletv. Accessed 25 January 2016.

Ramsay, S., E. Jones, and M. Barker. 2007. "Relationship between Adjustment and Support Types: Young and Mature-Aged Local and International First Year University Students." *Higher Education* 54: 247–65.

Rankin, S., G. Weber, W. Blumfeld, and S. Frazer. 2010. *2010 State of Higher Education for Lesbian, Gay, Bisexual and Transgender People.* Charlotte: Campus Pride.

Ravensbergen, J. 2010. "UQAM Terrorist Blames Racism for False Arrest: Slimane Zihaf Roughed Up after Report of Suicide Bomber at Downtown Campus." *Montreal Gazette.* http://www.alameenpost.com/articles.aspx?categoryname=Canada&newsid=1948. Accessed 25 January 2016.

Ren, J., K. Bryan, Y. Min, and Y. Wei. 2007. "Language Preparation and the First Year Experience: What Administrators and Policy Makers Should Know." *Florida Journal of Educational Administration and Policy* 1, no. 1: 11–24.

Renn, K.A. 2007. "LGBT Student Leaders and Queer Activists: Identities of Lesbian, Gay, Bisexual, Transgender, and Queer Identified College Student Leaders and Activists." *Journal of College Student Development* 48, no. 3: 311–30.

– 2004. *Mixed Race Students in College: The Ecology of Race, Identity, and Community on Campus*. Albany: State University of New York Press.

Ritchie, C.A., and J. Banning. 2001. "Gay, Lesbian, Bisexual, and Transgender Campus Support Offices: A Qualitative Study of Establishment Experiences." *NASPA Journal* 38, no. 4: 482–94.

Robson, D. 2008. "York U to Ban Funding for Anti-abortion Groups." *Toronto Star*. http://www.thestar.com/News/GTA/article/435137. Accessed 26 January 2016.

Rockquemore, K.A. 2002. "Negotiating the Color Line: The Gendered Process of Racial Identity Construction among Black/White Biracial Women." *Gender and Society* 16, no. 4: 485–503.

Rodriguez, S. 2003. "What Helps Some First-Generation Students Succeed?" *About Campus* 8, no. 4: 17–22.

Rosenthal, D.A., J. Russell, and G. Thomson. 2008. "The Health and Wellbeing of International Students at an Australian University." *Higher Education* 55, no. 1: 51–67.

Rowe, W., S.K. Bennett, and D.R. Atkinson. 1994. "White Racial Identity Models: A Critique and Alternative Proposal." *The Counseling Psychologist* 22, no. 1: 129–46.

Royal Commission on Aboriginal Peoples (RCAP). 1996a. *Gathering of Strength*, Volume 3. In *Report of the Royal Commission on Aboriginal Peoples (RCAP)*. Ottawa: Minister of Supply and Services.

– 1996b. *Report of the Royal Commission on Aboriginal Peoples*. Ottawa: Minister of Supply and Services.

Russell, J., G. Thomson, and D. Rosenthal. 2008. "International Student Use of University Health and Counseling Services." *Higher Education* 56: 59–75.

Rynor, M. 2004. "Taking Pride in Sexual Diversity: U of T Pioneers Lay Foundations for an Inclusive Environment for the LGBTQQ Community." *News@UofT*. http://www.news.utoronto.ca/bin6/040618-149.asp. Accessed 15 February 2005.

Sanderson, G. 2008. "A Foundation for the Internationalization of the Academic Self." *Journal of Studies in International Education* 12, no. 3: 276–307.

Sanford, N., and J. Adelson. 1962. *The American College: A Psychological and Social Interpretation of Higher Learning.* New York: Wiley.

Sanlo, R., S. Rankin, and R. Schoenberg. 2002b. "Safe Zones and Allies Programs." In *Our Place on Campus: Lesbian, Gay, Bisexual, Transgender Services and Programs in Higher Education,* edited by R.L. Sanlo, S. Rankin, and R. Schoenberg, 95–100. Westport: Greenwood Press.

Sarna, N. 2010. *Does the Charter Apply to Universities?* http://educationlawblog.ca/tag/canadian-charter-of-rights-and-freedoms/. Accessed 28 November 2010.

Saskatchewan Human Rights Commission. 2004. "Submission to the Special Education Review Committee." http://saskatchewanhumanrights.ca/learn/publications-guidelines-resources/reports/special-education-review-committee. Accessed 25 January 2016.

Schellenberg, E.G., J. Hirt, and A. Sears. 1999. "Attitudes towards Homosexuals among Students at a Canadian University." *Sex Roles* 40, no. 1: 139–52.

Schofield, L. 2009. "Exposed: University of Toronto Suppresses Pro-Palestinian Activism." http://www.rabble.ca/news/exposed-university-toronto-suppressed-pro-palestinian-activism. Accessed 25 January 2016.

Scott, S., G. Loewen, C. Funckes, and S. Kroeger. 2003. "Implementing Universal Design in Higher Education: Moving Beyond the Built Environment." *Journal of Post-Secondary Education and Disability* 16: 78–89.

Seele, H.N. 1996. *Experiential Activities for Intercultural Learning,* Volume 1. Yarmouth: Intercultural Press.

Serebrin, J. 2010. "We Need to Stop Talking about Israel and Palestine So Much." http://oncampus.macleans.ca/education/2010/12/01/we-need-to-stop-talking-about-israel-and-palestine-so-much/. Accessed 25 January 2016.

Shapiro, J. 1993. *No Pity: People with Disabilities Forging a Civil Rights Movement.* New York: Times Books.

Shaw, S.F., S.S. Scott, and J.M. McGuire. 2001. *Teaching College Students with Learning Disabilities.* ERIC Clearinghouse on Disabilities and Gifted Education.

Siddiqui, H. 2005. "The Canadian Ripples of an Arab-Israeli dispute." *Toronto Star.* http://www.thestar.com. Accessed 28 November 2010

Simms, G. 1993. *Diasporic Experience of Blacks in Canada: A Discourse.* Paper presented at James Robinson Johnston Chair in Black Canadian Studies Lecture Series, Halifax, Nova Scotia. 15 February.

Simoni, J.M. 1996. "Pathways to Prejudice: Predicting Students' Heterosexist Attitudes with Demographics, Self-esteem and Contact with Lesbians and Gay Men." *Journal of College Student Development* 37: 68–78.

Slade, D. 2010. "Students Win Facebook Battle with U of C." *Calgary Herald*. http://www.calgaryherald.com/technology/Students+ Facebook+battle+with/3670183/story.html. 28 November 2010.

– 2010b. "U of C Files to Appeal Ruling on Facebook Criticism of Professor." *Calgary Herald*. http://www.calgaryherald.com/files+appeal +ruling+Facebook+criticism+professor/3890822/story.html. Accessed 28 November 2010.

Smith, C., and S. Gottheil. 2011. "Increasing Accessibility: Lessons Learned in Retaining Special Population Students in Canada." *College and University* 86, no. 4: 47–52.

Smith, L.T. 1999. *Decolonizing Methodologies: Research and Indigenous Peoples*. London: Zed Books Ltd.

Smith, M. 1999. *Lesbian and Gay Rights in Canada: Social Movements and Equality Seeking, 1971–1995*. Toronto: University of Toronto Press.

Smith, W.A., P.G. Altbach, and K. Lomotey. 2002. *The Racial Crisis in American Higher Education: Continuing Challenges for the Twenty-First Century*. New York: SUNY Press.

Somers, P., S. Woodhouse, and J. Cofer. 2000. "Persistence of First-Generation College Students." Paper presented at the Association for the Study of Higher Education conference, Sacramento, California.

Sovic, S. 2008. "Coping with Stress: The Perspective of International Students." *Art, Design and Communication in Higher Education* 6, no. 3: 145–58.

Spears, T. 2010. "Carleton Students' Association Kicks Out Anti-abortion Group." *Ottawa Citizen*. http://www.ottawacitizen.com/news/Carleton +students+association+kicks+anti+abortion+group/3844100/story.html. Accessed 25 October 2010.

Spencer-Rodgers, J., and A. Cortijo. 1998. "An Assessment of Career Development Needs of International Students." *Journal of College Student Development* 39, no. 5: 509–13.

Spurr, B. 2006a. "Dialogue, Animosity at IAW." *The Varsity*. http:// thevarsity.ca/2006/02/16/dialogue-animosity-at-iaw/. Accessed 25 January 2016.

– 2006b. "Preaching to the Choir." *The Varsity*. http://thevarsity.ca/ 2006/02/09/preaching-to-the-choir/. Accessed 26 January 2016.

Stamps, S., Jr, and M. Stamps. 1985. "Race, Class and Leisure Activities of Urban Residents." *Journal of Leisure Research* 17, no. 1: 40–56.

ation in Canada. www.parl.gc.ca/content/sen/committee/411/soci/
rep/rep06dec11-e.pdf. Accessed 26 January 2016.
Statistics Canada. 1999. "How Healthy Are Canadians?" Health Reports
Catalogue 82-003-XPB, 11(3). http://www.statcan.gc.ca/pub/82-003-x/
82-003-x1999003-eng.pdf. Accessed 26 January 2016.
- 2001. "A Report on Adult Education and Training in Canada:
Learning a Living" (Catalogue No. 81.586-XPE). Ottawa: Government
of Canada.
- 2006. Population by mother tongue and age groups, 2006 counts, for
Canada, provinces and territories, and census metropolitan areas and
census agglomerations – 20% sample data, Census 2006 (table).
http://www12.statcan.ca/census-recensement/2006/dp-pd/hlt/97-555/
T401-eng.cfm?Lang=E&T=401&GH=6&GF=35&SC=1&S=0&O=A.
Accessed 26 January 2016.
- 2008a. "2006 Census: Educational Portrait of Canada." In 2006
Analysis Series. Ottawa: Statistics Canada. http://www12.statcan.ca/
census-recensement/2006/as-sa/97-560/pdf/97-560-XIE2006001.pdf.
Accessed 26 January 2016.
- 2008b. "Earnings and Incomes of Canadians Over the Past Quarter
Century, 2006 Census: Findings." Statistics Canada Catalogue 97-563
XIE2006001. http://www12.statcan.ca/census-recensement/2006/
as-sa/97-563/index-eng.cfm. Accessed 26 January 2016.
- 2008c. National Graduates Survey – Class of 2005. http://www5.
statcan.gc.ca/olc-cel/olc.action?objId=81M0011X&objType=2&lang=
en&limit=0. Accessed 26 January 2016.
- 2011a. Youth in Transition Survey. http://www23.statcan.gc.ca/imdb/
p2SV.pl?Function=getSurvey&SDDS=4435&lang=en&db=imdb&adm=
8&dis=2. Accessed 26 January 2016.
- 2011b. National Household Survey. http://www12.statcan.gc.ca/
datasets/index-eng.cfm? Temporal=2013. Accessed 12 February 2016.
Sterling, S. 1995. "Quaslametko and Yetko: Two Grandmother Models for
Contemporary Native Education Pedagogy." In First Nations Education
in Canada: The Circle Unfolds, edited by M. Battiste and J. Barman,
165–74. Vancouver: UBC Press.
Stewart, C. 1988. The National Report on International Students in
Canada 1988. Ottawa: Canadian Bureau of International Education.
Strange, C. 2000. "Creating Environments of Ability." New Directions for
Student Services 91: 19–30. San Francisco: Jossey-Bass.

Strange, C., and J. Banning. 2001. *Educating by Design: Creating Campus Learning Environments That Work*. San Francisco: Jossey-Bass.

– 2015. *Designing for Learning: Creating Campus Environments for Student Success*. San Francisco: Jossey-Bass.

Strayhorn, T.L. 2006. "Factors Influencing the Academic Achievement of First-Generation College Students." *NASPA Journal* 43, no. 4: 82–111.

Sue, D.W., and D. Sue. 1990. *Counseling the Culturally Different*. 2nd ed. New York: Wiley.

Sukhai, M.A., C.E. Mohler, T. Doyle, E. Carson, C. Nieder, D. Levy-Pinto, E. Duffett, and F. Smith. 2014. "Creating an Accessible Science Laboratory Environment for Students with Disabilities." Toronto: Council of Ontario Universities. In *Accessible Campus*. http://www.accessiblecampus.ca/wp-content/uploads/2014/06/Creating-an-Accessible-Science-Laboratory-Environment-for-Students-with-Disabilities.pdf. Accessed 26 January 2016.

Sumner, L.W. 2004. *The Hateful and the Obscene: Studies in the Limits of Free Expression*. Toronto: University of Toronto Press.

Swail, W.S. 1995. "The Development of a Conceptual Framework to Increase Student Retention in Science, Engineering, and Mathematics Programs at Minority Institutions of Higher Education." PhD thesis, The George Washington University.

– 2004. *The Affordability of University Education: A Perspective from Both Sides of the 49th Parallel*. Washington: Educational Policy Institute, Inc. http://www.educationalpolicy.org/pdf/Affordability.pdf. Accessed 26 January 2016.

Sylvestre, P. 2010. "Cent ans de leadership franco-ontarien." Ottawa: Les Éditions David.

Talbot, D.M. 2003. *Multiculturalism*. In *Student Services: A Handbook for the Profession*, edited by S.R. Komives and D.B. Woodward, 423–46. San Francisco: John Wiley and Sons, Inc.

Taras, V., and J. Rowney. 2007. "Effects of Cultural Diversity on In-Class Communication and Student Project Team Dynamics: Creating Synergy in the Diverse Classroom." *International Studies in Educational Administration* 35, no. 2: 66–92.

Tardif, C., and F. McMahon. 1989. "Les francophones et les études postsecondaires." *Canadian Journal of Higher Education* 19, no. 3: 19–28.

Tate, J. 2014. "A Thin Veil of Inclusion: Sexual and Gender Minorities in Ontario Universities." PhD thesis, Ontario Institute for Studies in Education, University of Toronto.

Taylor, C., and T. Peter. 2011. "'We Are Not Aliens, We're People, and We
    Have Rights.' Canadian Human Rights Discourse and High School
    Climate for LGBTQ Students." *Canadian Review of Sociology/Revue
    canadienne de sociologie* 48, no. 3: 275–312.
Taylor, K.B. 2008. "Mapping the Intricacies of Young Adults'
    Developmental Journey from Socially Prescribed to Internally Defined
    Identities, Relationships, and Beliefs." *Journal of College Student
    Development* 49, no. 3: 215–34.
Terenzini, P.T., L. Springer, P.M. Yaeger, E.T. Pascarella, and A. Nora.
    1996. "First-Generation College Students: Characteristics, Experiences,
    and Cognitive Development." *Research in Higher Education* 37, no. 1:
    1–22.
Théberge, R. 2010. "Ressources, besoins, visions d'avenir. Division de
    l'éducation en langue française, l'éducation des autochtones et de la
    recherche." Paper presented at Symposium sur l'accès des francophones
    aux études postsecondaires en Toronto, Ontario.
Thomas Bernard, W. 1996. "Survival and Success: As Defined by Black
    Men in Sheffield England and Halifax, Canada." PhD thesis, University
    of Sheffield.
– 2004. Letter dated 10 March 2004 to the General Research Community.
Thornton, M. 2007. "Universal Design in the Disabilities Office." Pre-
    conference session at the annual conference of the Canadian Association
    of College and University Student Services, Saskatoon, Saskatchewan,
    10–13 June.
Thornton, M., and S. Downs. 2010, "Walking the Walk: Modeling Social
    Model and Universal Design in the Disabilities Office." *Journal of
    Postsecondary Education and Disability* 23, no. 1: 72–8.
Tidwell, R., and S. Hanassab. 2007. "New Challenges for Professional
    Counselors: The Higher Education International Student Population."
    Counselling Psychology Quarterly 20, no. 4: 313–24.
Tinto, V. 1993. *Leaving College: Rethinking the Causes and Cures of
    Student Attrition.* 2nd ed. Chicago: The University of Chicago Press.
– 1997. "Classrooms as Communities." *Journal of Higher Education* 68,
    no. 6: 599–623.
– 2000. "Taking Student Retention Seriously: Rethinking the First Year of
    College." *The National Academic Advising Association* 19, no. 2: 5–10.
    http://www.nacadajournal.org/doi/abs/10.12930/0271-9517-19.2.5.
    Accessed 26 January 2016.
– 2003. "Establishing Conditions for Student Success: Lessons Learned in
    the United States." In *Improving Completion Rates Among*

Disadvantaged Students, edited by Jocey Quinn, Michael Cooper, and Liz Thomas, 1–8. Sterling: Trentham Books.

– 2005. *Student Success and the Building of Involving Educational Communities. Syracuse University.* http://www.mcli.dist.maricopa.edu/ fsd/c2006/docs/promotingstudentsuccess.pdf. Accessed 27 January 2016.

Tirone, S.C., L.L. Caldwell, and C. Cutler Riddick. 1992. "Cultural Variations in Leisure: the Perspective of Immigrant Women from India." In *Abstracts from the Proceedings of the 1992 NRPA Leisure Research Symposium held in conjunction with the 1992 National Congress for Recreation and Parks,* 15–18 October 1992, Cincinnati, Ohio. National Recreation and Park Association.

Tousignant, J. 1989. "Les personnes handicapées inscrites dans les universités québécois : situation et perspectives." Québec: Ministère de l'enseignement supérieur et de la science du Québec, direction générale de l'enseignement et de la recherche universitaires.

– 1995. "La vie étudiants des personnes handicapées dans les établissements d'enseignement universitaire québécois : un bilan des années 1989–1995." Québec: ministère de l'éducation, direction générale des affaires universitaires et scientifiques.

Turcotte, M. 2011. *Intergenerational Education Mobility: University Completion in Relation to Parents' Education Level.* In *Statistics Canada.* http://www.statcan.gc.ca/pub/11-008-x/2011002/article/ 11536-eng.pdf. Accessed 26 January 2016.

University of British Columbia. 2008. *UBC Statement on Respectful Environment for Students, Faculty, and Staff.* http://www.hr.ubc.ca/ respectful environment/files/2010/09/UBC_Respectful_Environment_ Statement.pdf. Accessed 26 January 2016.

– 2012. "Place and Promise: the UBC Plan." http://strategicplan.ubc.ca. Accessed 26 January 2016.

University of Calgary. n.d. *Rights, Responsibilities, Services and Resources.* http://www.ucalgary.ca/discrimination/rightsresponsibilities. Accessed 15 October 2010.

– n.d. *Statement on Principles of Conduct.* http://www.ucalgary.ca/hr/ about_hr/policies_procedures/statement_on_principles_of_conduct. Accessed 15 October 2010.

University of Saskatchewan. 1993. "The University of Saskatchewan Mission Statement." http://policies.usask.ca/policies/general/the-university-of-saskatchewan-mission-statement.php Accessed 26 January 2016.

University of Toronto. 1992a. "Mission and Purpose." http://www. utoronto.ca/about-uoft/mission-and-purpose. Accessed 26 January 2016.

– 1992b. *Statement on Freedom of Speech.* http://www.governingcouncil. utoronto.ca/policies/frspeech.htm. Accessed 26 January 2016.

– 1992c. *Policy on the Disruption of Meetings.* http://www.governing-council.utoronto.ca/policies/disrupt.htm. Accessed 26 January 2016.

– 2016. *LGBTQ History at U of T.* http://sgdo.utoronto.ca/about-the-office/lgbtq-history-at-u-of-t/. Accessed 7 February 2016.

University of Victoria, Committee on the Status of Sexual Minorities 2000. *GLBTTQ Spoken Here: Creating a Script for a Taboo Subject.* http://web.uvic.ca/equity/antiopp/glbttq/glbttq.pdf. Accessed 21 February 2005.

Urback, R. 2009. "Charges against University of Calgary Students Dropped." *Maclean's.* Retrieved from http://oncampus.macleans.ca/ education/2009/11/03/charges-dropped-against-university-of-calgary-students/. Accessed 26 January 2016.

Usher, A. 2005. "Much Ado about a Very Small Idea: Straight Talk on Income-Contingent Loans." Educational Policy Institute. http://www. educationalpolicy.org/pdf/ICR.pdf. Accessed 26 January 2016.

Usher, A., and R. Dunn. 2009. "On the Brink: How the Recession of 2009 Will Affect Post-secondary Education." Educational Policy Institute. http://www.educationalpolicy.org/publications/pubpdf/0902_recession. pdf. Accessed 7 April 2009.

Wade, M., and C. Belkhodja. 2012. "Managing a New Diversity on a Small Campus: The Case of l'Université de Moncton (Canada)." In *Critical Perspectives on International Education,* edited by Yvonne Hébert and Ali A. Abdi, 184–96. Rotterdam: Sense Publishers.

Walton-Roberts, M.W. 2011. "Immigration, the University and the Welcoming Second Tier City." *Journal of International Migration and Integration* 12, no. 4: 453–73.

Wang, C.W., C. Singh, B. Bird, and G. Ives. 2008. "The Learning Experiences of Taiwanese Nursing Students Studying in Australia." *Journal of Transcultural Nursing* 19, no. 2: 140–50.

Warner, T. 2002. "Never Going Back: A History of Queer Activism in Canada." Toronto: University of Toronto Press.

Washburne, R. 1978. "Black Under-Participation in Wild Land Recreation: Alternative Explanations." *Leisure Sciences* 1, no. 2: 175–89.

Weber-Pillwax, C. 1999. "Indigenous Research Methodology: Exploratory Discussion of an Elusive Subject." *Journal of Educational Thought* 33, no. 1: 33–45.

Weinryb, A. 2008. "The University of Toronto – The Institution Where Israeli Apartheid Week Was Born." *Jewish Political Studies Review* 20, no. 3/4: 107–17.

Welch, P., ed. 1995. *Strategies for Teaching Universal Design*. Boston: Adaptive Environments Center.

Wesley, P. 1988. *Access for Disabled Persons to Ontario Universities*. Toronto: Ontario Council on University Affairs.

Westwood, M., and M. Barker. 1990. "Academic Achievement and Social Adaptation among International Students: A Comparison Groups Study of the Peer-Pairing Program." *International Journal of Intercultural Relations* 14: 251–63.

White, G.W., J.A. Summers, E. Zhang, and V. Renault. 2014. "Evaluating the Effects of a Self-Advocacy Training Program for Undergraduates with Disabilities." *Journal of Postsecondary Education and Disability* 27: 229–44.

White, J.P., P.S. Maxim, and D. Beavon, eds. 2004. *Aboriginal Policy Research: Setting the Agenda for Change*. 2 vols. Vol. 1. Toronto: Thompson.

Winters, J. 2002. "The Power of a System-wide Organization: The University of California LGBTQI Association." In *Our Place on Campus: Lesbian, Gay, Bisexual, Transgender Services and Programs in Higher Education*, edited by R. Sanlo, S. Rankin, and R. Schoenberg, 121–9. Westport: Greenwood Press.

Wolforth, J., and A. Harrison. 2008. "Findings from a Pan-Canadian Survey of Disability Services Providers in Postsecondary Education." Paper presented at the British Dyslexia Association, Harrogate, United Kingdom, 27–29 March.

Woolf, D., and P. Deane. 2010. "Statement on Racist Incidents on Campus." *Queen's Gazette, March 11*. http://www.queensu.ca/gazette/mc_administrator/content/statement-racist-incidents-campus. Accessed 7 February 2016

Wright, B. 1985. "Programming Success: Special Student Services and the American Indian College Student." *Journal of American Indian Education* 24, no. 1: 1–7.

Yaffe, B. 2010. "Dangerous Double Standard at Toronto's York University." *Vancouver Sun*. http://communities.canada.com/vancouversun/blogs/powerplay/archive/2010/11/20/dangerous-double-standard-at-toronto-s-york-university.aspx. Accessed 25 November 2010.

York-Anderson, D., and S.L. Bowman. 1991. "Assessing the College Knowledge of First-Generation and Second-Generation College Students." *Journal of College Student Development* 32, no. 2: 116–22.

York University. 1996. *Report from the President's Task Force on Homophobia and Heterosexism*. http://www.yorku.ca/sexgen/documents/1997_Task_Force_on_Homophobia_and_Heterosexism_Report.pdf. Accessed 26 January 2016.

– 2001. *Hate Propaganda Guidelines*. http://www.yorku.ca/univsec/
policies/document.php?document=19. Accessed 26 January 2016.

Yosso, T.J. 2005. "Whose Culture Has Capital? A Critical Race Theory
Discussion of Community Cultural Wealth." *Race Ethnicity and
Education* 8, no. 1: 69–91.

Zerbisias, A. 2003. (June 29). "Global Documentary Seems Unfair."
Toronto Star. http://pqasb.pqarchiver.com/thestar/doc/438604645.html?
FMT=ABS&FMTS=ABS:FT&type=current&date=Jun+29%2C+2003&
author=&pub=Toronto+Star&edition=&startpage=&desc=Global+
documentary+seems+unfair. Accessed 26 January 2016.

Zhao, H. 2012. "Postsecondary Education Participation of Under-
Represented Groups in Ontario: Evidence from the SLID Data." Higher
Education Quality Council of Ontario.

Zhou, Y., D. Jindal-Snape, K. Topping, and J. Todman. 2008. "Theoretical
Models of Culture Shock and Adaptation in International Students in
Higher Education." *Studies in Higher Education* 33, no. 1: 63–75.

Contributors

LISA BUCKLEY has held leadership positions in student services for more than a decade at several institutions, including the Technical University of British Columbia and the University of British Columbia. Most recently, she was director of student development at Simon Fraser University, overseeing new student orientation, student leadership, and training of student leaders and volunteers. While parenting full-time, she is currently pursuing from home her passion for promoting community involvement and volunteering. She holds a BA (Hon.) in English from Simon Fraser University and an MA in English from the University of Toronto.

JAMES DELANEY has been a higher education and student affairs professional at the University of Toronto since 1988, with a focus in policy development and interpretation, clarification of complex problems, analysis and management of intergroup and intragroup conflict, and bridging relationships with campus organizations. He also consults on campus alcohol policies as a national speaker and trainer, having served as chair of the BACCHUS Alcohol Awareness Canada/Student Life Education Company board. He is a former president of the Canadian Association of College and University Student Services (CACUSS) and recipient of the association's Award of Honour (2006) and Life Membership Award (2014). He holds a BSc in human biology from the University of Toronto and an MA in conflict analysis and management from Royal Roads University.

BARBARA HAMILTON-HINCH is an assistant professor of recreation and leisure studies in the School of Health and Human

Performance at Dalhousie University. Formerly Dalhousie's Black student advisor, a position she was instrumental in creating in the late 1980s, Barb continues her strong interest in supporting and advocating for marginalized populations, including Aboriginal people, LGBTQQI people, persons with (dis)Abilities, and people of African ancestry. She originates from the historical African Nova Scotian communities of Beechville and Cherrybrook, where her ancestors and family have lived for over four hundred years. Barb holds a BEd in secondary education from Mount St Vincent University, a BSc in recreation management, an MA in leisure studies, and an interdisciplinary PhD from Dalhousie University.

DONNA HARDY COX is dean and professor in the School of Social Work, with cross-appointments to the Faculty of Education and the Centre for Collaborative Health Professional Education at Memorial University of Newfoundland. She is also honorary research associate in the School of Graduate Studies at the University of New Brunswick. She was founding director of student development at Memorial University and the Canadian Institute in Student Affairs and Services. Donna is former president of the Canadian Association of College and University Student Services, the Atlantic Association of College and University Student Services, and the Student Affairs Division of the Student Affairs and Services Association. She holds a BSW from Memorial University, an MSW from Carleton University, and an EdD from the University of Maine.

KEITH HOTCHKISS is senior director of student services at Saint Mary's University (NS), building on a base of forty-one years of experience in student affairs. While overseeing twelve departments and responding to the challenges of a diverse campus, he has been a strong advocate for internationalization, providing leadership in the support of the university's international students and encouraging their full participation in employment and student government. Keith has led workshops on student services in Sarajevo, the Gambia, and China, and has recruited international students for the university for the past twenty years. A long-time associate of the Canadian Bureau for International Education, he has presented at both regional and national conferences, and served as a member of its board for seven years. He holds a BA in history from Saint Mary's University.

CHANTAL JOY is director, advising and student academic support at the Humber Institute of Technology and Advanced Learning. Chantal has over fifteen years of experience in Canadian higher education, developing and delivering quality programs to engage students and support their learning – while in transition to the post-secondary experience, living in residence, and pursuing opportunities for campus leadership. She holds a BA in sociology and women's studies from Victoria University of the University of Toronto and an MA in college student personnel from Bowling Green State University (OH). A native Canadian Francophone, Chantal focused her thesis research on the Francophone student experience in English post-secondary institutions in Canada.

TAMARA LEARY is associate professor/program head for the master's of arts in higher education administration and leadership at Royal Roads University (BC). Previous to this, she served as a faculty member in the master's of post-secondary education program at Memorial University of Newfoundland. Tamara has held a variety of positions with the Department of Student Services at UPEI, providing leadership for student inclusion and success in support of overall student development. She holds a BA in sociology from the University of Prince Edward Island, a BSW from the University of Victoria, an MEd in adult education from St Francis Xavier University, and an EdD in higher education administration and leadership from the University of Calgary.

LOUISE LEWIN, following twelve years as associate principal, student services at Glendon College, York University, is director of the Ontario Rhône-Alpes Student Exchange Program, offering options to students of fourteen Ontario universities and twelve Rhône-Alpes universities to study abroad in their second language, to do science internships, and to participate in summer language courses. She holds a BA in French Studies from York University, an MEd from the Ontario Institute for Studies in Education, and a PhD in education from the University of Toronto. Her research now focuses on the student experience while abroad on exchange.

SUSAN MCINTYRE has been a passionate advocate for student success in a variety of positions in student services, most recently as

associate vice-president of student services at Saskatchewan Poly-
technic. Prior to that she provided student services leadership at the
University of Northern British Columbia and Dalhousie University.
She is a 2015 recipient of the Canadian Association of Colleges and
University Student Services (CACUSS) Life Membership Award.
Susan holds a BA (Hon.) in political science and MPA in policy and
program evaluation from Dalhousie University.

MICHELLE PIDGEON, originally from Newfoundland and
Labrador, resides in the Coast Salish Territories, where she is associate professor in the Faculty of Education at Simon Fraser University.
She has published in the areas of Indigenous student experience and
success, Aboriginal student services, and Indigenous research methodologies. Her research interests focus on ways in which Indigenous
knowledges can inform student services practices and transform
post-secondary institutions in support of Indigenous student success.
She holds a BSc in psychology and an MEd in post-secondary education, student affairs and services from Memorial University of
Newfoundland, and a PhD in educational studies from the University
of British Columbia.

JUDITH POTTER is dean of continuing studies, McGill University,
where she provides institutional leadership in meeting the continuing
learning needs of individuals, communities, and organizations –
domestic as well as international. Prior to this she served as executive
director of the College of Extended Learning at the University of
New Brunswick. Judith holds a BSc in chemistry from the University
of Toronto, an MEd in adult education from Saint Francis Xavier
University, and an EdD in adult education from the University of
Toronto. Her research interests focus on policies and practices of
continuing education in Canadian universities, as well as innovative
strategies to facilitate adult learning. She has published in academic
and professional journals and has presented papers on continuing
education issues nationally and internationally.

TIM RAHILLY, associate vice-president, students, at Simon Fraser
University, has studied, taught, and worked in higher education for
more than twenty-five years. Starting his career as a student employee,
he later trained as a psychologist at McGill University. In addition
to his core duties at SFU, Tim is faculty associate in the Faculty of

Education where he teaches at the graduate level and supervises doctoral students in studying in the area of higher education. Tim has served on the board of the Canadian Association of College and University Student Services as well as the Canadian University Survey Consortium. Holds a BA (Hon.) in psychology and education from Concordia University, an MA in educational psychology and counselling, and a PhD in educational and counselling psychology from McGill University.

ALANA ROBB served as international student advisor and manager of international student services at Saint Mary's University, during a period when enrolment of international students at the university more than tripled. Prior to that, Alana was an education officer in the university's International Education Centre, where she offered international development and anti-racism education to teachers in Nova Scotia schools. She has lived and worked in Africa and China. She holds a BSc in home economics from Mount Allison University and an MA in family studies from Mount Saint Vincent University.

CARNEY STRANGE is professor emeritus of higher education and student affairs at Bowling Green State University in Ohio where, for thirty-five years, he taught graduate courses on student development and the design and impact of campus environments. An ACPA Senior Scholar and NASPA Faculty Fellow, he was the recipient of the ACPA: College Student Educators International 2010 Contribution to Knowledge Award. He has published widely in the field, serving most recently as co-editor and author of *Achieving Student Success: Effective Student Services in Canadian Higher Education* (2010, McGill-Queen's University Press) and senior author of *Designing for Learning: Creating Campus Environments for Student Success* (2015, Jossey Bass). He holds a BA in French from Saint Meinrad College, an MA in college student personnel, and a PhD in student development in post-secondary education from the University of Iowa.

AMIT TANEJA is the chief diversity officer at the College of the Holy Cross (MA), where his continuing research focuses on the intersections of race, class, gender, and sexual orientation for LGBT students of colour on historically white college campuses. Prior to that he was director of the Days-Massolo Center at Hamilton College (NY) and special assistant to the senior vice-provost for equity and inclusion and former associate director of the Lesbian, Gay, Bisexual and Transgender Resource Center at Syracuse University. He also served for five years on and co-chaired the Consortium of Higher Education LGBT Resource Professionals executive board. Amit is a consultant and speaker on a range of inclusion and diversity topics. He holds a BA in psychology from the University of British Columbia and an MA in college student personnel from Bowling Green State University (OH).

JOAN WOLFORTH served for seventeen years as director of the Office for Students with Disabilities at McGill University. Prior to that she was the founding coordinator of the equivalent service at Dawson College in Montreal. She has published widely and given many conference presentations on post-secondary students with disabilities, emphasizing the needs of students with dyslexia, the use of e-learning and adaptive technology, and the importance of universal design. She is a founding member of the Canadian Association of Disability Service Providers (CADSP), having served as its president, and has been a participant leader on a number of related association boards, including the Association on Higher Education and Disabilty (AHEAD), National Education for Assistance Dog Services (NEADS), L'Association Quebecoise Interuniversitaire Des Conseillers aux Etudiants en Situation De Handicap (AQICESH), and the Learning Disabilities Association of Quebec (LDAQ). Joan was also an active member of the Canadian Association of College and University Student Services (CACUSS) and recipient of its Award of Honour. She holds a BA (Hons) in geography from Reading University (UK), an MEd in counselling psychology from McGill University, and an EdD in applied psychology and human development from the University of Toronto.

Index